DISPUTING CITIZ

John Clarke, Kathleen Coll, Eve
Catherine Neve

First published in Great Britain in 2014 by

Policy Press
University of Bristol
6th Floor
Howard House
Queen's Avenue
Clifton
Bristol BS8 1SD
UK
Tel +44 (0)117 331 5020
Fax +44 (0)117 331 5367
e-mail pp-info@bristol.ac.uk
www.policypress.co.uk

North American office:
Policy Press
c/o The University of Chicago Press
1427 East 60th Street
Chicago, IL 60637, USA
t: +1 773 702 7700
f: +1 773-702-9756
e:sales@press.uchicago.edu
www.press.uchicago.edu

British Library Cataloguing in Publication Data
A catalogue record for this book is available from the British Library

Library of Congress Cataloging-in-Publication Data
A catalog record for this book has been requested

ISBN 978 1 44731 253 6 paperback
ISBN 978 1 44731 252 9 hardcover

Cover design by Qube Design Associates, Bristol
Front cover: image kindly supplied by Jean-Louis Aucagos
Printed and bound in Great Britain by CMP, Poole

MIX
Paper from
responsible sources
FSC
www.fsc.org
FSC® C004309

For Fu, who was there at the very beginning.

Contents

Preface

Any project like this accumulates many debts in the process of coming to completion. Ours begin with the *Fondation Maison des Sciences de l'Homme* who agreed to fund our initial collaboration as an International Programme of Advanced Studies in 2007. In particular, M. Jean Luc Racine offered warm collegial support for us and our work during our period of residence. The *Fondation* also provided accommodation for the three visiting researchers at *Maison Suger* and, via its partnership with Columbia University, arranged for a wonderful working environment at Columbia's Institute for Scholars at Reid Hall. There, we benefited from the support of three wonderful women – Danielle Haase-Dubosc, Mihaela Bacou and Naby Avcioglu. We are also grateful to the colleagues who took part in the workshop/*Journées d'études* at Maison Suger in June 2007, most of whose work subsequently appeared in a special issue of *Citizenship Studies* in 2011 on *Questions de Citoyenneté/ Questions of Citizenship*.

We are also grateful to the many people who have talked to us about this work, not least the participants at the panels of papers that we presented at the Crossroads in Cultural Studies conference in 2008 and the American Anthropological Association in 2009. We would like to thank the institutions that provided financial support for our participation in these conferences: IIAC (EHESS-CNRS); the Open University's Department of Social Policy and Criminology and Centre for Citizenship, Identities and Governance; Stanford University; and the University of Campinas. Our institutions also enabled – in diverse ways – the two periods that we were able to spend together working collaboratively on the book in Long Bay, Jamaica and Florianópolis/ Santinho, Brazil.

Evelina Dagnino would like to thank her friends and colleagues from the University of Campinas in Brazil – Ana Cláudia Chaves Teixeira, Gabriel Feltran, Luciana Tatagiba and Rachel Meneguello – for both their intellectual and loving support.

Collectively, we have many people to thank for sustaining our interest in, engagement with and enthusiasm for these issues: Etienne Balibar, Ghassan Hage, Ann Holder, Engin Isin, Janet Newman, Anu Sharma, Sophie Wahnich and, not least, the members of the Oecumene project at the Open University.

Finally, the other three authors owe a special debt to Catherine Neveu for her exceptional work in translating the original French sources that we use in the book.

Milton Keynes, San Francisco, São Paolo and Paris/Tours,
January 2013.

Introduction

We begin by posing the question addressed to us by a friend: '*Why another book on citizenship?*'. It is indeed true that, in recent years, citizenship has been the focus of a torrent of books, articles and conferences, such that adding one more to this overwhelming flow looks like a strange decision. But part of our answer to the question is that this flourishing interest in citizenship is one of the ways in which it looks important and influential, and, indeed, serves as a sort of keyword for many different scholarly interests. Indeed, even a brief survey of recent publications indicates the diversity of concerns that can be articulated through citizenship: the environment; sexuality; urban politics; welfare reform; the rise of neo-liberal politics and policies; migration and migrants' rights; questions of nation, nationality and post-nationalism; the changing forms of the state; and the rising significance of civil society. In very different ways, such focal points take up, borrow and bend well-established connections between citizenship and questions of (in)equality, giving them new life and new subjects, and engaging them in new conflicts. This suggests something of the field of possibility that can be articulated through the concept of citizenship.

The proliferation of work on citizenship is part of our answer in a second way. The amount and diversity of academic work on the topic suggests something of the profound turbulence that swirls around the idea of citizenship. It is certainly not merely an academic concept. It circulates widely, is claimed and much sought after, and is the subject of never-ending attempts to revive, reform or reinvent it. It certainly does not lead a quiet life and this sense of turbulence is a key part of what draws us to the word. It acts as an urgent political and intellectual point of connection. Let us take this point about connection a little further. Citizenship is conventionally understood as a form of relation, most often as a relation between the citizen and the state, but also as a relation of membership (of a society or political community). But citizenship acts as a point of connection – indeed, a point of mobilisation – for many individuals and groups who identify themselves as citizens when they act, name themselves as people who would be citizens in demanding citizenship, or demand that citizenship be enlarged, enhanced or transformed to engage with other issues, identities and desires. Citizenship is thus a potent keyword in social, cultural and political terms, naming actual or imagined possible relationships.

Citizenship is, for us, a connective word in a more specific sense: it connects and draws together the four authors of this book from their very diverse locations. We occupy different places in the world – Europe and North and South America; occupy different academic locations in disciplinary and institutional terms; and have arrived at this collaboration from different entry points to the issue of citizenship. This makes for a rather odd sort of book, not least in the sense that it is a cross-national collaboration that is not structured as a comparative text. Although we draw on disputes over citizenship from our different national and regional contexts, this is not an attempt to compare citizenship between Brazil, France, the US and the UK. As will become clear, we make use of these different national and regional formations, histories and trajectories to dispute citizenship, making these differences rub up against one another to illuminate different aspects, issues and problems of citizenship. In short, we think our differences animate the study of citizenship, rather than merely exemplifying it.

So, what difference does this collaboration make to the study of citizenship? What makes us think that the world needs not just another book on citizenship, but this book in particular? Like many others, we are committed to unlocking citizenship from conceptions of it that focus on it as a legal/juridical and political status, expressed as a series of rights and responsibilities (*droits et devoirs*, in French discussions). Like many others, too, we are committed to viewing citizenship as being constituted in practices, processes and relationships. And, like many others, we are committed to viewing citizenship in terms of political contestation: the sense that citizenship has been, and remains, a keyword because it is mobilised by very different political programmes and projects. Nevertheless, we think that we approach citizenship somewhat differently. Our approach tries to liberate the study of citizenship from a number of restrictive covenants that shape both orthodox and some critical approaches.

First, we attempt to challenge the recurrent claims of disciplinary ownership of the concept of citizenship, most evidently, those of political science and political philosophy. Our own approach to citizenship is relatively undisciplined. We certainly draw on and make use of our own different disciplinary inheritances, but we view them as resources to be drawn into our own disputes about citizenships, rather than establishing a priori claims to the terrain of citizenship. We are located in specific intellectual disciplines: anthropology, politics, social policy and cultural studies among them. But what has brought us together is a shared interest in citizenship as a disputed terrain, as a keyword that is valued and as a powerful mobilising image for social and political action. As we will show during the book, the entanglements between citizenship, culture, politics and power are the organising themes of our own conversations. While many other scholars would share some, if not many, of those terms as a basis for critical work on citizenship, we intend to make them matter precisely in their interlocking specificity. What is at stake in this book is the problem of how citizenship is formed out of contextually located and animated entanglements of culture, politics and power – and never culture in general, politics in general or power in general. Our shared orientation brings us to conversations across disciplinary boundaries – with ourselves and with others who work at the margins, or even beyond, such disciplined spaces.

Our collaboration has also required us to address the different national formations of citizenship that provide the starting points for our individual work. It is difficult to 'de-normalise' such formations, and to see their peculiarities through the critical eyes of others. This is particularly so for Clarke and Neveu, whose national formations have, in different ways, been turned into 'models' of citizenship: the Marshallian model on the one hand; the Republican model on the other. Distinguishing specific histories, formations and trajectories is a demanding process, but we have also found it important to separate out those national formations from their conversion into more generalised models, conceptions or types of citizenship. At the same time, we do not underestimate the challenges of addressing the turbulent and contested history of citizenship in Brazil, nor the struggles over rights, identities and forms of sovereignty that have shaped citizenship in the US. In our collaborative work, we have tried to use these national differences to illuminate, or to throw into relief, the distinctive features of each formation of citizenship as a way of undermining the temptation to abstract, generalise, reify or even universalise citizenship as a status, as an identity and as a concept.

We are also conscious of the ways in which disciplinary formations also have a national character, such that approaches to citizenship in French and North American anthropology may have a different character and set of organising concerns. So, too, may the formations of political science dominant in the UK and Brazil, respectively. We have discovered ourselves stumbling over such differences when we have tried to understand how citizenship is framed in political science, and then having to backtrack to ask how French political science grasps citizenship as a national, state-centred, republican model of participation in a political community as the uneasy coincidence of national trajectory and the disciplined structure of academic thinking.

Our collaboration has tried to use these differences – in dynamic tension with our shared orientations towards culture, politics and power – to engage in the process of *disputing citizenship*. Such disputes are intended to parallel, refract and act upon the other disputes about citizenship that engage us: the mobilisations, articulations and reinventions of citizenship in different places and in the hands of widely diverging political projects. Dispute, in that sense, is an organising idea for thinking about citizenship and a description of our way of working together. Our collaboration has been a long drawn-out and sometimes geographically very strained conversation. We came together to work in Paris in a three-month International Programme of Advanced Studies (IPAS) project, supported by the *Fondation Maison des Sciences de l'Homme* and the Columbia University Institute in Paris, to discuss and reflect upon the problem of 'Comparing Scales of Citizenship'. The collaboration was invented by Catherine Neveu, who drew the others into this conversation – and conversation here is more than a polite term for working together. Our collaboration has been conversational in its basic practice: we have talked, and talked and still carry on talking, even now. Our differences, our shared orientations and our conversational mode all have their impact on the form, substance and style of the book. We try to make it clear how specific differences have animated our understanding of citizenship (and its entanglements); we have tried to make visible the sorts of examples in which we have found puzzles, problems and illumination; we have tried to allow readers to see the focal points of continuing disagreements (rather than pretending we have resolved everything into a bland consensus); and we have not tried to dissolve our different voices and writing styles into a unified mode of expression. We are not sure whether such unfinished business is a betrayal of academic convention, but in our analysis of citizenship and in our mode of working, we think that the 'unfinished' (*imparfait*, in French) character of social, political and intellectual projects is of considerable significance.

We have several times described citizenship as a keyword. Here, we want to pause a moment and talk about citizenship as a *keyword*, in the sense articulated by the British literary and cultural analyst Raymond Williams (1983 [1976]). Williams' approach to keywords has been a recurrent unifying theme for our work together: in his exploration of a 'vocabulary of culture and society', Williams offered a profound reflection of the significance of words and a model of how to attend to their shifting and contested meanings. Williams did not himself write an entry on citizenship in his *Keywords* in the 1970s, although its presence in a volume called *New Keywords* (Bennett et al, 2005) suggests that the turbulence of struggles over citizenship in recent decades had brought it a new visibility. Despite citizenship's absence from his book, we have continued to find Williams' way of thinking about words and meaning an inspiration, not least because he too is engaged by the relationships between culture, politics and power.

Williams' work begins by rejecting the search for the 'proper meaning' of words: those meanings that might be discovered by consulting authoritative dictionaries. He does, of course, acknowledge that the 'proper' or 'correct' meaning is itself a focus of historical contestation, noting that while '[n]o single group is "wrong" by any linguistic criterion … a temporarily dominant group may try to enforce its own uses as "correct"' (1983 [1976]: 12) But, says Williams:

> when we go beyond these to the historical dictionaries, and to essays in historical semantics, we are quite beyond the range of 'proper meaning'. We find a history and complexity of meanings; conscious changes, or consciously different uses; innovations, obsolescence, specialization, extension, overlap, transfer; or changes which are masked by a nominal continuity so that words which seem to have been there for centuries, with continuous general meanings, have come in fact to express radically different or radically variable, yet sometimes hardly noticed, meanings and implications of meanings. (1983 [1976]: 17)

We think this represents a compelling place to start to think about citizenship. His radical rejection of the desire for a 'proper meaning' remains a scandalous challenge to the orthodoxies of much academic work, on citizenship and beyond. Where much scholarly work would like to fix the meaning of citizenship, to specify its elements and their fixed configuration, Williams invites us to a different investigation: the 'history and complexity of meanings' by which keywords are marked. Challenging the 'sacral attitude' that seeks the proper, strict or correct definition (and scorns 'vulgar' use or misuse), Williams pursues instead the practical and political making of meanings:

> The emphasis of my own analysis is deliberately social and historical … it is necessary to insist that the most active problems of meaning are always primarily embedded in actual social relationships, and that both the meanings and the relationships are typically diverse and variable, within the structures of particular social orders and the processes of social and historical change. (1983 [1976]: 21–2)

This might be enough to get us started, but Williams, as always, demands that we should go further. Rather than seeing words and their meanings as merely reflecting the social and historical circumstances of their time, Williams prefigures many later discussions about the constitutive, productive and performative force of language (or discourse) by insisting that the changes, challenges and contestations that concern him take place 'within language':

> This does not mean that the language simply reflects the processes of society and history. On the contrary, it is a central aim of the book to show that some important social and historical processes occur *within* language, in ways which indicate how integral the problems of meanings and of relationships really are. New kinds of relationship, but also new ways of seeing existing relationships, appear in language in a variety of ways.... But ... such changes are not always either simple or final. Earlier and later senses coexist, or become actual alternatives in which problems of contemporary belief and affiliation are contested. (1983 [1976]: 22)

We remain compelled by Williams' view of keywords. It both fits and sustains our own sense of citizenship as invested with meanings that are always being reworked, refashioned and realigned. It carries 'historical weight' (just think of all those references to Athenian democracy, or Roman citizenship: *civis Romanus sum* was the first Latin phrase that JC learned at school). It is mobilised by very different groups, forces and projects, in part because it carries such historical echoes, but also because it provides a lens through which new relationships might be imagined and, possibly, brought into being. However, our collaboration has introduced an extra dynamic to the idea of keywords – the question of multiple languages and translation. For two of us, English is our first language, such that citizenship is the obvious term of reference. We began from the assumption that even if the political, social and cultural contexts were different, the concept would translate as *cidadania*, *citoyenneté* or *ciudadanía* in our three other working languages. Not surprisingly, we discovered that much is concealed by that apparent simplicity, culminating in the terrible moment when CN proclaimed "but I don't believe that citizenship is the same as *citoyenneté*". The different struggles to make meaning inflect these terms in their specific places makes working in a single ('international') language – English – a problematic process for working cross-nationally and cross-culturally.

In one sense, such problems cannot be overcome; rather, they require a *Keywords* sensibility to variation and the differences that apparent continuity might create (Morris, 2006: ch 7). We have not written a multilingual *Keywords* about citizenship, but have tried to keep questions of culture, politics and language visible to our readers (and ourselves). But it is also true that (as Williams also recognised) words circulate transnationally, sometimes in their original language, sometimes in translation. Citizenship's accumulated weight of meaning makes it a significant, attractive and enabling keyword that makes it move across time and place. While attending to differences of culture, language and politics, our aim is not to be trapped into national 'containers' as though ideas, politics, policies and people do not flow across their borders.

The structure of the book

The book has both an idiosyncratic approach and an idiosyncratic structure, being organised into three very large chapters, each with a number of subsections. The three chapters reflect our processes of trying to think about citizenship. Our work began with rather more chapters, each centred on the word 'and', as a way of linking citizenship with other keywords: citizenship and states; citizenship and culture; citizenship and politics; citizenship and scale. Although each of these terms remains central to our analysis and argument, we abandoned this way of structuring our presentation as not adequately capturing our emerging way of thinking about citizenship. Instead, the three chapters/parts of the book are organised around processes: recentering citizenship; decentering citizenship; and imagining the communities of citizenship (astute readers will note that, although English is our *lingua franca*, we nevertheless move between British English and American English ...).

In the first chapter, we argue for the need to recentre citizenship, stressing its necessary connection to culture and politics. In particular, this involves loosening the hold of universalising conceptions of citizenship that seek to establish its general, proper or correct meaning. In other words, contextualisation is explored not as an exercise in exposing the empirical diversity of citizenship regimes and forms, but as a necessary and required move in theorising citizenship. In the second chapter, we argue for the importance of decentring citizenship, disentangling its taken-for-granted connections with states, while also taking into account both a wider variety of actors and the changing configuration of governance bodies and agents, and the contested politics of scale associated with them. The third chapter builds on the decentring work to argue for the heterogeneity of citizenship's sites, settings, spaces and scales. In all these ways, we are inspired by Etienne Balibar's metaphor of citizenship as always '*imparfaite*' (unfinished), as an object of social and political desire that is always 'under construction' (*en travaux*). The briefer conclusion tries to pull these analyses and arguments together into not a Theory of Citizenship, but a set of principles or guidelines for thinking about citizenship. This conclusion ends where we began – conversationally, exploring our own 'unfinished' project and our unresolved disputes.

CHAPTER ONE

Recentering citizenship

Introduction

What is at stake when we speak of citizenship? For some, it is the relationship between the political subject and the state. Others treat it as the ground of a critical distinction between citizens and aliens. Some view citizenship as the focal point for struggles over equality and inequalities. Still others emphasise its foundational character in Hannah Arendt's much-cited phrase 'the right to have rights', or define it as 'being political' (Isin, 2002). As studies of citizenship proliferate, so, too, do the definitions and characterisations of its core features. Indeed, this multiplicity of definitions can be seen as a tribute to the polysemic quality of citizenship: like so many other keywords, its meaning is historically and socially variable (Williams, 1983 [1976]). *Recentring* the analysis of citizenship thus requires 'thick contextualisation', insisting on the significance of contexts as active and animating forces that make some forms of citizenship imaginable, possible and achievable. Citizenship always takes specific forms that are the outcomes of sets of processes, and are related to specific political projects, particular social contexts and distinctive cultural configurations. Its constitutive *versatility* has to be stressed so as to move it away from universalised, abstracted or culturally neutralised theorisations.

Such a contextualist view remains a major point of division in the social sciences (Pollitt, forthcoming). For some, it represents the scandalous abandonment of claims to be scientific or surrender to mindless and apolitical relativism. By contrast, others view it as a necessary condition for the production of meaningful knowledge by insisting on the specificity of social, cultural and political formations. In particular, such a contextualist orientation implies placing limits on the Olympian or imperial standpoint of the Observer and insisting that – in the case of citizenship – its heterogeneous forms are more than mere variations on a theme. Although there is growing recognition of the polysemic character of citizenship (Dagnino, 1994, 2005a; Menéndez-Carrión, 2002/03; Wappenstein, 2004), it remains important for us to take a fundamental step in affirming that citizenship does not have an essence that is immutable across time and space. As Beyers states, we need to:

> move beyond the fallacy of presuming that the problems of defining citizenship can be resolved theoretically or normatively, whether under the guise of communitarianism or liberalism.... As a phenomena that exists vis-à-vis dynamic social relations and political struggle, citizenship can only be adequately understood through a context specific analysis. (Beyers, 2008: 362)

Similarly, Leca has argued that citizenship is not 'an ideal category born out of the thought of "great authors", it is also an element of specified social configurations' (1991: 171) that can be reduced neither to normative injunctions to civicism, to the modern liberal conception of citizenship, nor to its connection with 'nation-building'.

Conventional understandings of citizenship have typically connected it to the state, articulating the relationship between the state and the individual subject in classical liberal terms. Such understandings generally include several elements, such as the rights and duties of both the state and the citizen, but they are articulated under the broader and basic idea of membership or belonging to a specific political community, equally conventionally understood as the nation. The conflation between state and nation, both materially and symbolically, has crucial implications for prevailing understandings of citizenship. One of them is the strengthening of a unique view of citizenship as membership that naturalises both the centrality of the state to citizenship and of nationality to the state. However, as the idea of citizenship becomes increasingly important and visible in a growing number of different contexts, including the university, the diversity of views of citizenship leads to the explosion of any analytical frame structured around that essentialised set of connections. Indeed, we would go so far as to argue that the proliferation of forms and sites of citizenship has enabled a much richer and more complex set of analyses of citizenship that are more attentive to its social and historical variation (see, eg, Isin's [2002] work on the historical-political formations of citizenship; see also www.oecumene.eu).

Such work forms part of the scholarly landscape that we inhabit. However, rather than trace out specific lines of difference and disagreement at this point, it may be more important to establish more clearly our own orientation. In this chapter – and, indeed, in the book as a whole – we aim to find a course that avoids making abstractly universal statements of citizenship's 'essence' and merely accumulating instances of its diversity. On the one hand, we reject the possibility of an act of theoretical purification that announces a new and better definition of citizenship. On the other hand, cataloguing as many instances of citizenship as we can find is not an attractive prospect for intellectual work and always leaves open the possibility of the undiscovered to disrupt the catalogue (and its pretensions to completeness). That is to say, if citizenship is now increasingly recognised as a contested idea, this diversity not only involves a multiplicity of views, but also entails disputes between distinct, divergent or even antagonistic meanings. Specific contexts typically contain such conflicting conceptions of citizenship – and the associated attempts to install them as the recognised, legitimated and institutionalised form. Such conflicts continue even after one conception of citizenship has been institutionalised; it remains the focus of further efforts to challenge, inflect or translate it.

If this is true about citizenship in practice, it is equally true for its analysis. For us, working on citizenship means that we must always talk about:

> imperfect (*imparfaite*) citizenship … [this] is not only suggesting that citizenship is a defective, rectifiable, improvable institution, it is above all suggesting that citizenship is rather a *practice* and a *process* than a stable form. It is always 'in the making'. (Balibar, 2001: 211; emphasis in original)

We have found ourselves returning time and again to this idea of Balibar's: thinking of citizenship as always, everywhere, unfinished/ imperfect is a powerful way of keeping the location of citizenship in practices and processes visible. This understanding of 'imperfect/ *imparfaite*' is, we think, rather different from T.H. Marshall's (1950: 29) conception of citizenship as an ideal: 'an image of an ideal citizenship against which achievements can be measured and towards which aspirations can be directed'. There, citizenship is the normative pole, and progress towards it can be measured along a linear scale. The proliferation of focal points of citizenship struggles – for example, cultural citizenship (Rosaldo, 1999), sexual citizenship (Richardson, 2000), intimate citizenship (Plummer, 2003), genetic citizenship (Heath et al., 2004) or environmental citizenship (Dobson, 2003) – is precisely evidence of the 'imperfection' of citizenship. What these adjectival qualifications reveal is the multiplication of places, people, sites and forms of struggle, and sets of relationships that are at stake in citizenship or that consider 'citizenship' as a powerful enough keyword for it to be used to try and make claims. They also indicate the continuing potential of citizenship to act as a focal point – a symbolic marker – through which social and political demands can be voiced and around which social and political movements can be mobilised. This proliferation of qualifications also reminds us how normative views make it difficult to recognise, much less accommodate, how certain issues come to be at stake. These emergent issues are often silenced or omitted in the naturalising tendencies of dominant representations.

Nonetheless, the second element of Marshall's comment leads in a rather different direction: the view of citizenship as an 'ideal ... towards which aspirations can be directed'. Here, the capacity of citizenship to act as a mobilising imaginary can be seen – and we will return to the significance of citizenship as an ideal, aspiration and symbol recurrently in this book. However, that capacity takes us directly back to questions of contexts, practices and processes – since references to that ideal are always mobilised in particular ways, and given particular meanings, through specific projects. In this chapter, we explore this diverse and processual character of citizenship by making visible two relatively obscured dimensions of citizenship's dynamics: the constitutive connection between citizenship and political projects and cultural formations. We then pursue a discussion of the possibilities and problems that arise in addressing cultural dimensions of citizenship processes. In the last section, we argue for the 'centrality of the margins' in ways that enlarge the processes to be considered when analysing citizenship processes. Throughout the chapter, we stress the need to include academic theorisations alongside the political-cultural projects of citizenship in the 'thick contextualisation' that we propose. Such theorisations contribute to the repertoire of images and ideas through which citizenship is imagined and pursued.

Contextualising citizenship

Citizenship's specific forms are constituted in and through distinct political projects and cultural formations. By exploring some instances of how forms of citizenship are situated in historical contexts, political projects and cultural formations, we want to give substance to the assertion that citizenship is a 'contested concept' involving the 'fluid and changing character of its meanings' (Menéndez-Carrión, 2002/03: 205); but we also want to emphasise the (specific) conflicts and antagonisms that are at stake in the contestations that surround it in both theory and practice. Our aim here is not only to elaborate the diverse forms and contents of citizenship, but also to underline the dynamic, contentious and mutually constitutive relationship between narratives of citizenship. In order to trace the varieties of citizenship while avoiding the re-inscription of essential meanings, we have found Raymond Williams' notion of *Keywords* an invaluable resource. As we observed in the Introduction, Williams expressed strong reservations about any positive effect to be gained from defining the meaning of these 'difficult words'. We share his conviction that 'nobody can "purify" the dialect of the tribe', and above all the idea that 'variations and confusions of meanings are not simply defaults of the system, or feedback errors, or deficiencies in education', but their very historical and contemporary substance. Such variations and confusions 'incarnate experiences and readings of such experiences, diversified and this will continue to be true, in relations and active conflicts, despite and beyond clarification exercises by academics and committees' (Williams, 1983 [1976]: 24). This underpins our resistance to any search for the proper, correct or real definition of citizenship. Instead, the idea of keywords directs us to *meanings-in-use* – the meanings that are used, invented and contested in specific settings. Williams' refusal to seek out the 'correct' meaning did not, of course, blind him to just how important the legitimation of some meanings as 'correct' is. Indeed, much of his work (not just in *Keywords*) is devoted to rich explorations of the ways in which 'a temporarily dominant group may try to enforce its own uses as 'correct' (1983 [1976]: 11). And it is this capacity to attend to the specific, multiple and contested uses while recognising that language, culture and power are intimately connected that we hope to borrow from Williams and put to work here.

Conceptions of citizenship convey views of power, of the state, of citizens, of society and of what life in it should be. Such views – such images of desired possibility – may be articulated by individuals; they may be expressed by representatives of state agencies or members of social movements. They both demarcate, and are demarcated by, a broader set of orientations that are always present in political action: *political projects.* Indeed, underlining the need to contextualise citizenship does not mean flatly observing how its forms and contestations vary from place to place and across time; it means understanding citizenship as socially and politically constructed, as located within cultural formations and inscribed in the conception and contestation of political projects. How are the notions of political projects and cultural formations to be understood here and how do they contribute to the analysis of citizenship?

Careful attention to the specific historical and cultural constitution of forms of citizenship highlights the divergent views of citizenship, voiced by differently situated subjects, in particular contexts. This enables us to stress the importance of understanding the (variable) meanings of citizenship in its different contexts: social, political, cultural, spatial and temporal. These forms of citizenship emerge from particular contexts that animate meanings and the desire to make them come true (or create the capacities to resist or contest other meanings). They carry specific sets of cultural meanings, including powerful imaginings of how life might be lived. These are also temporally specific contexts in which ideas of citizenship connect challenges to past ways of life and to imagined possible futures. They are contexts in which specific conceptions of citizenship both mobilise and are mobilised by political projects: the collective actions that seek to make or remake citizenship.

At this point, it is also important to stress a further issue: these contexts are certainly specific, but they are never entirely closed or self-contained. Indeed, all contexts are also the product of profound transnational and trans-local relationships, connections and flows (most obviously, but not only, in colonial forms). These are not just the flows of people, capital or material objects. Ideas, images and meanings also travel (Appadurai, 1996; Czarniawska and Sévon, 2005), though they may come to mean different things as they arrive in their new homes. Citizenship is one such travelling idea: it has been exported, sometimes through colonial missions of governing and improving colonial subjects. Mamdani notes the conditionality of such colonial transfers in the African context:

> Citizenship would be a privilege of the civilized; the uncivilized would be subject to an all-round tutelage. They may have a modicum of civil rights, but not political rights, for a propertied franchise separated the civilized from the uncivilized. The resulting vision was summed up in Cecil Rhodes's famous phrase, 'Equal rights for all civilized men'.
> (Mamdani, 1996: 17; see also Chatterjee, 2004)

But citizenship has also been imported – borrowed, appropriated and translated into new alignments, whether by slaves in revolt against colonial rule or by the excluded, marginalised or subordinated for whom citizenship offered an ideal and an expansive and egalitarian imaginary around which political mobilisation was possible (for the French context, see Larcher, 2011; for Brazil, see Chalhoub, 1990). We will return to this set of issues, but it is important to stress that contextualising citizenship practices and regimes cannot be accomplished while maintaining a conventional 'national' frame of comparison. On the contrary, we will argue throughout the book that the conventional equation of citizenship and nationality must be problematised so that its own contextual – historical and geographical – specificity is made visible. Indeed, such national formations have to be themselves (re)inscribed in wider contexts, where, for instance, both the colonial metropole and its colonies are analysed in the same move (see Hall, 2002; Wemyss, 2009).

As with other words or notions that are saturating political or public discourses today (sustainability or participation, to mention just two), it could be argued that the success of citizenship is precisely due to its very flexibility, to its 'blurred' character. Since it can mean so many different things, it can be appropriated and put to work by a large diversity of agents and projects. It enables potentially interesting encounters between different political projects, as well as perverse confluences between different projects through apparently shared meanings. We use the notion of *political project* here to designate the specific combinations of beliefs, aspirations, desires, interests, conceptions of the world and representations of what life in society should be that guide the political action of different subjects (Dagnino, 2002, 2004, 2006). This definition of 'political project' is not restricted to broad and systematised formulations, such as, for example, political party projects, but covers a wide spectrum of forms in which representations, beliefs and interests are translated into political actions with varying degrees of explicitness and coherence. The most visible examples of such political projects are those that succeed in installing themselves in states as ways of governing populations and producing (particular types of) citizens. However, as contestation and dispute over the meanings and contents of citizenship are always there, even if in less visible forms, so are there 'struggles for citizenship' trying to enact or install other political projects. Following Arditi, it is important to stress that while many such 'political projects' do not reach state power, they may nevertheless bring about very powerful social and political changes, in particular, challenging the taken-for-granted or given organisation of the social order. Arditi responds to accusations that insurgent movements lack a grand plan by arguing that:

> Insurgencies from the North of Africa to New York endeavor to perform a similar re-partitioning of the given. They *are* the plan in the sense that their occurrence is significant in itself regardless of what they propose. Demands, manifestos, programs and other things we associate with content are

figured out on the go because insurgencies are more about opening up possibilities. They do so by challenging our political imaginaries and cognitive maps rather than by designing the new order. To put it slightly differently, and perhaps more strongly given that it involves something in excess of programs: policies and policymaking are not the higher moment of insurgencies – markers of their passage from revolts to revolution – but signs that insurgent activism has been taken over by mainstream politics. There is nothing wrong with this, but it is certainly different from what rebels do. (Arditi, 2011: 4)

Throughout this book, we will work with examples taken from very different contexts, both in terms of time and location, as a means of exploring the different conceptions of citizenship that are mobilised by political projects – and how some of them come to be installed as the official, authoritative or dominant conception. We use this approach – the constant return to examples – as a way of achieving two sorts of objectives. The first is the constant problematisation of those conceptions of citizenship that have become dominant, institutionalised or taken for granted as the norm. Our examples aim to demonstrate that such conceptions are neither normal nor universal, but emerge from particular contexts, are driven by particular projects and typically require the subordination, displacement or incorporation of alternative conceptions. The second objective for this working through examples is to make the book resemble our own mode of working together: we brought our own different examples to our conversations as a way of testing propositions about citizenship. These enabled us to challenge our own assumptions, as well as those of arguments and analyses that we read and confronted in our working together. We hope it proves as productive for readers as it did for our collaborations.

We begin where this collaboration began – in France or, more accurately, with French conceptions of citizenship (*citoyenneté*). Certain dominant conceptions of citizenship in France provide a valuable starting point, not least because the French context represents a configuration that is part and parcel of much of the mental schemes through which we are used to think: it is often considered as the basis for conceptions of *republican* citizenship, and one in which nationality and citizenship are closely intertwined. Lochak's analysis of this configuration is inspiring because it insists on the need to contextualise it, to locate it within a specific history:

in the French tradition, which on that issue has largely faded in other countries, only the national is a citizen … access to nationality is a compulsory entry point to gain citizenship. There is thus a necessary link between nationality and citizenship, *the origins of which and implications thereof, both need to be reconstituted.* (1988: 81, emphasis added)

According to Lochak, this 'necessary link' finds its origins in the period of the French Revolution, when:

the word 'citizen' gains a radically new meaning: the citizen is not any more simply the inhabitant, it is the member of the nation – *also a new concept* that designates the collective entity formed by all the citizens and sole depositary of sovereignty within the State. The word citizen thus from now on condenses in itself two distinct but inseparable conceptual meanings: it designates the national of the country and the bearer of civic rights as if (*en tant que*) they are one and the same person; French citizenship is French nationality in so far as the latter confers the prerogatives attached to the quality of citizen.… By transferring sovereignty from the head of the king to the nation, by making each citizen, as a member of the nation, the bearer of a share of national sovereignty, the Revolution created the conditions for the development of democracy; but it has simultaneously locked the Nation-state and instituted a tighter than ever border between the national-citizen and the non-citizen alien by reserving to nationals access to and exercise of civic rights. (1988: 81, emphasis added)

Lochak underlines that such an 'origin' is only true if one takes into account two reservations: the first one being that it took a long time (a century and a half) for the national = citizen equation to be fully translated into the law. The second one is in our eyes even more important: the transformation of the national idea into an exclusion mechanism against aliens was not there from the beginning. Indeed, French citizenship was largely granted to aliens, of whom some, like Thomas Paine, even became part of the Convention. During the Revolution, 'The "fatherland" to be defended was indeed fidelity to principles more than a territory limited by borders; it was, very simply, the country where one was a citizen' (Lochak, 1988: 82). Thus, the 1793 Constitution stated that:

> Any alien aged above 21 who, having had his residence in
> France for more than a year, lives here from his work, or buys
> a property, or marries a French woman, or adopts a child, or
> supports an old person, or lastly any alien whom the legislative
> body judges to be well-deserving of humane treatment, is
> admitted to exercise the rights of a French citizen.

The shift has thus been from a 'universalist conception of the nation to
one that is both territorial and "nationalist", the latter being understood
with the meaning this term is endowed with today' (Lochak, 1988:
82; for a stimulating analysis of 'the foreigner' during the French
Revolution, see Wahnich, 1997).

This inheritance, and the distinctive 'isomorphism' that was
progressively constructed between nationality and citizenship, is clearly
expressed during the current ceremonies organised to 'welcome' newly
naturalised persons into the national community of France. During one
such ceremony, and after an introduction underlining that 'reaching
the quality of French *citizen* … is a unique event in [your] life', new
French nationals are reminded by the Préfet (head of the central state's
local embodiment) of the 'invaluable dimension of French *nationality*'
and that 'French people have a demanding conception of citizenship',
defined as 'a way of thinking, a way of debating, a way of acting, indeed
rules of the game that are common to all of us' (Fassin and Mazouz,
2007: 741). The following quotation from an official report on the
reform of the French Nationality Act also highlights such a confusion:
'*Nationality* understood as *citizenship*, i.e. adhesion to a *nation*, as a *citizen*,
that gives the rights and duties of a citizen and makes one accept the
value system' (Long, 1998: 615).

Such elements of a specific national configuration, even briefly
introduced, make visible some of our concerns and orientations. This
example reminds us that while historical and political processes can
have produced, through time, a conception in which citizenship and
nationality are entwined, they are not necessarily equivalent: the forms
of their connection have varied from place to place and from time
to time (Farhmeir, 2007; Bosniak, 2009). Indeed, the revolutionary
moment in France saw the (re)construction of both terms – the national
and the citizen – and their weaving together. But this example also
makes visible the contingent nature of other relationships in which
citizenship is enmeshed. When Lochak points to the earliest republican
formulations of citizenship as attachment to, and membership of, a
political community, we must be careful to hear the political, rather
than territorial, specification of this community and the citizen's

membership of it. What made citizens in this moment was their affiliation to the principles of the republic, not their birth, or even permanent residence, in the territory of France. The territorialisation of the political community occurred later.

The nation, the political community (the republic) and the state were crafted simultaneously in this historical moment, enabling a series of equivalences to be constructed between the people, the republic, the nation and the state. Such dominant narratives of citizenship and the uses to which they are put, tend to obscure the conditions of their own construction as they become naturalised and normalised. But they are rarely without contestation. For example, in 1983, young people organised the March for Equality and against Racism. Its aim was to denounce racist crimes, to claim a 10-year residence permit for all migrants and to fight for equality. This movement gathered several thousands of participants at its arrival in Paris in December 1983 and marked the emergence in the political and public sphere of a new generation of citizens. It was within this movement that a debate on a 'new citizenship' was launched; the French 'model' of citizenship was questioned from the experience of these youths as unadapted to the situation of contemporary French society and unable to provide for equality. Among the proposals made were the necessity to disconnect more clearly nationality and citizenship, to consider citizenship as a set of practices and not a status, and to develop a notion of citizenship that would be less state-centred and not limited to participating in elections. Some groups thus suggested replacing the national identity card with a 'citizen card' bearing on its cover the words 'justice, culture, equality' and 'Republic of France' (instead of French Republic) (see Texture, 1987; Im'Média, 1993).

What these first examples demonstrate is the extent to which in different political projects, different ways to perceive, define and connect citizenship to other notions are proposed and debated. Indeed, the literature on citizenship, even when it does not grasp them as 'political projects' in the sense we are using the notion, is largely made of such renditions of citizenship as a powerful dimension and device for different political projects (eg in France at different historical periods, see, for instance, Godineau, 1988; Luhtakiallo, 2012). In France, again, the analysis of the conflict provoked in 1882 by the creation of free and compulsory 'godless schools' allows Déloye (1994) to highlight how Republican moralists of the early 20th century aimed at producing an individual-citizen who would accept to be governed while being able to discipline his/her own acts and passions ('to favour both self-government and voluntary submission to a government henceforth elected by universal suffrage (*suffrage universel*)'; Déloye, 1994: 27). Following Foucault, Déloye considers this as a 'governmentality strategy': 'the aim of the Republic's pedagogues was to create a type of rationality that would be intrinsic to the art of democratic government: citizens' self-discipline' (1994: 27). We might draw out several points about this approach to citizen-making. First, it views pedagogy as the proper site of citizen-making (and many practices of citizen education follow in its wake; see Bénéï, 2005; see also the special issue of *Citizenship Studies* on the 'pedagogic state' edited by Pykett [2010]). Second, this particular conception of citizenship was struggled for against other political projects and forces, not least the claims of religious organisations to be educators. Third, we might note that the strategy was so successful that it shaped Foucault's own obsession with the character of liberal governmentality as the production of exactly this form of subject – the responsibilised and self-disciplining self (see Burchell, 1993).

Ong's analysis of 'citizenship regimes' in Asian 'Tiger states' provides for a different example of such political projects. According to her:

> more than in the West, the liberal Asian state plays a
> pedagogical role in educating the public as to the ethico-
> political meaning of *citizenship*. Expertise in the social and
> human sciences is deployed to provide 'a certain style of
> reasoning' [among citizens]. (Ong, 1999a: 58, emphasis in
> the original)

This emerges from the political projects of these states since 'the post-developmental strategy of middle-range Asian economies seeks to produce technically proficient and socially unified citizens attractive for capital' (Ong, 1999a: 65). So, paralleling 19th-century French Republican moralists engaged in 'a State enterprise of promoting an encompassing civic and national identity' (Déloye, 1994), the conception of citizenship promoted by Asian Tiger states' governments is to be understood within the framework of a political project aiming at attracting capital in the contemporary global economy.

In recent decades, what some have called 'market citizenship' has become a significant theme, not least among those that seek a closer alignment with the principles and powers of the market in the provision of public services (see, *inter alia*, Root, 2007; Somers, 2008; on 'consumer citizenship' in India, see Lukose, 2009). In the UK (one of the leading sites for these innovations), Tony Blair, then Prime Minister, enrolled ideas of citizens, consumers and choice into a characteristic argument that:

> In reality, I believe people do want choice, in public services as in other services. But anyway, choice isn't an end in itself. It is one important mechanism to ensure that citizens can indeed secure good schools and health services in their communities. Choice puts the levers in the hands of parents and patients so that they as citizens and consumers can be a driving force for improvement in their public services. We are proposing to put an entirely different dynamic in place to drive our public services; one where the service will be driven not by the government or by the manager but by the user – the patient, the parent, the pupil and the law-abiding citizen. (Blair, 2004)

The attempt to transform citizens into consumers represented a means to install markets and market-mimicking devices into what had previously been public or state-based practices and relationships. It drew more generally on the images of freedom – and especially the right to choose how to spend one's own money – promoted by Anglo-American neo-liberals in the late 20th and early 21st centuries (on market populism, see Frank, 2007).

Such narratives are always contested, disputed and, at times, resisted: dominant and/or state political projects do not simply impose themselves on passive agents (Clarke et al, 2007a). As Bénéï underlines: 'Indeed if citizenship comprises the modern nation-state's range of attempts to define and produce "ideal, loyal and dutiful citizens", no less does it also comprehend social actors' negotiated responses to these' (Bénéï, 2005: 8). Nevertheless, looking for political projects of citizenship only by examining those that become installed as state or governmental policy and practice would reduce the significance of our concern with political projects. It is important to take a wider view of the political than this. Indeed, the flexibility of the concept of political projects allows us to take into account the multiplicity and diversity of the political subjects that are involved in the process of defining and redefining citizenships, including the 'non-citizen' sectors excluded from dominant definitions, who struggle against them and formulate through these struggles new discourses of citizenship. It also allows us to take into account those movements and insurgencies that are 'vanishing mediators' (Arditi, 2011), ushering in a different order or modifying parcels of that order, without 'succeeding' in a conventional sense:

> This is the core of emancipatory politics. It is about
> opening up new possibilities and not designing the new
> order. Insurgencies are symptoms of our becoming other.
> Like rabbit-holes of the *Alice in Wonderland* variety, they are
> portals or passageways that connect the present with the
> possibility of something other to come. (Arditi, 2011: 9)

We will come back in the last part of this chapter to the issue of the
agents who contribute to citizenship projects, but need now to discuss
further the reasons that underlie our use of this notion of political
projects. This implies making visible their different forms of political
action that, although a constitutive part of the process of citizenship
making, are too often ignored in its analysis.

Citizenship: political projects and cultural formations

We have used the idea of 'political projects' quite often in the preceding
pages as a way of approaching the question of citizenship. In this section,
we address a little more fully how we see the analysis of citizenship
requiring a conceptual repertoire that both addresses and combines
politics, culture and power. As Sassen argues: 'Citizenship results in part
from the practices of those who are excluded from it' (Sassen, 2006:
65) – a view echoed by Balibar's claim that 'The practical confrontation
with different modes of exclusion … always constitutes the founding
moment of citizenship, and consequently its periodical litmus test'
(Balibar, 2001: 125). Placing an emphasis on citizenship as articulating
political projects allows us to recognise the sites of struggles around and
about citizenship, wherever they are, as *sites of politics*. If we consider that
political projects orient political action and that citizenship aspirations
reflect or translate specific political projects, this converts sites where
action towards citizenship takes place into sites of politics, whether or
not they are conventionally understood as such (see, eg, Rajaram, 2009;
Isin, 2012). This goes against arguments and analyses that either locate
citizenship in specific sites (for instance, at the national level, but not the
local) or, even more problematically, confine the definition of politics
itself to a set of predetermined locations or forms of practice, rather
than treating politics as always emergent and often insurgent. Knowing
what counts as 'political' in advance – knowing where it takes place,
or who the actors are, or what the stakes of politics can be – seems at
least inappropriate to us (Neveu, 2013a). We are committed to a view
of politics as a field of possibilities in which mobilisations, contests and

conflicts take place in unpredictable, as well as predictable, forms (a set of issues we will come back to in Chapter Two).

This concept of political projects allows us to emphasise intentionality as a component of political action, affirming the role of the subject (individual and collective) and of human agency as fundamental dimensions of politics. Such an emphasis counterbalances determinist conceptions of politics that naturalise social and political processes, thereby obscuring the fact that they result from political action, and giving them an inexorable appearance that occludes the existence of other possible political choices. Part of the history of citizenship and its institutionalised forms is the drive to make its political conditions disappear, whether these are the naturalising claims of biology (around gender, race and other conditions of exclusion); the presumption of stable links between people and place (indexed in lines of descent or blood and its measurement); or the more recent presumptions that citizens are naturally independent, active and self-regarding agents. The notion of political projects thus enables us to conceive of politics as a terrain that is in part structured by choices expressed through the actions of subjects and guided by sets of representations, values, beliefs and interests.

Hence, we do not treat intentionality as pure rationality, which would transform political action into a pure exercise of rational choice and individualised calculation (although many approaches to politics take precisely this view). As E.P. Thompson underlined in his analysis, collective political action is a process in which subjective desires, needs and aspirations are *articulated* – both in the sense of being expressed/finding a voice and performing the work of connection and mobilisation. Criticising objectivist and utilitarian conceptions of 'interests', Thompson defined interest as 'everything that interests people; including that which is nearest to their heart' (Thompson, 1978: 92). We share this sense that political action can be, and is, oriented by desires, needs and aspirations as much as by objective interests or shared locations in social relations. This is particularly relevant when one thinks about emerging projects of citizenship in which subjectivities play a crucial connective role. Such shared desires, needs and aspirations are one basis for the articulation of mutual recognition, solidarities and action.

This emphasis on agency, however, should not obscure the crucial importance of context. Agency is always contextualised: contexts produce the conditions through which meanings of citizenship are elaborated; they establish both the fields of possibility and the capacities of potential action to transform meanings. It is important to stress this generative or animating quality of contexts because they are more often thought of as constraining. Certainly, they do constrain, limiting the possibilities for both thought and action. But they also create conditions of possibility and make spaces for imagination and inventiveness. As Terray suggests:

> The inventory of the constraints historical agents face …
> and that of the values to which they adhere delimit the space
> where they will deploy their imagination, their intelligence
> and their capacity of initiative; and what interests me is
> precisely this dialectic of necessity and freedom. (Terray,
> 1986: 246)

Such a dialectic is generated in the multi-contextuality of people's existences – in which the multiple contexts they inhabit produce juxtapositions, disjunctions, antagonisms, contradictions, paradoxes and the glimpses of possibilities that can fuel imaginations. Contexts thus need to be grasped as both productive and constraining. Although they articulate subjective desires, anxieties and aspirations, political projects are collective practices that can be characterised by their societal dimension, in the sense that they articulate visions of what social life should be like.

Thus, the concern of Brazilian social movements with the need to affirm 'a right to have rights' was clearly related not only to extreme levels of poverty and exclusion, but also to the pervasive *social authoritarianism* that presided over the unequal and hierarchical organisation of social relations as a whole in Brazil. Class, race and gender differences constituted the main bases for a form of social classification that has historically pervaded Latin American societies, establishing different categories of people hierarchically disposed in their respective 'places' in society. Thus, for excluded sectors, the political relevance of cultural meanings embedded in social practices is obvious in their daily life. As part of the authoritarian, hierarchical social ordering of these societies, to be poor meant not only economic, material deprivation, but also to be submitted to cultural rules that conveyed a complete lack of recognition of poor people as subjects or bearers of rights. In what Telles (1994) called the incivility embedded in that tradition, poverty signifies inferiority, a way of being in which individuals become unable to exercise their rights. This cultural deprivation imposed by the absolute absence of rights – which ultimately expresses itself as a suppression of human dignity – becomes then constitutive of material deprivation and political exclusion.

The perception of this social authoritarianism as a dimension of exclusion in addition to economic inequality and political subordination constituted a significant element in the struggles to redefine citizenship. First, it made clear that the struggle for rights, for the right to have rights, had to be a political struggle against a pervasive culture of social authoritarianism, thus setting the grounds for the urban popular movements to establish a connection between culture and politics, which became embedded in their collective action (see, eg, Dagnino's [1995] analysis of a dwellers' [*favelado*] movement in the city of Campinas). Such a connection has been a fundamental element in establishing a common ground for articulation with other social movements – such as ethnic, women, gay, ecology and human rights movements – in the search for more egalitarian relations at all levels, helping to demarcate a distinctive, enlarged view of democracy. The reference to rights and citizenship grew to constitute the core of a common ethical-political field where a large part of those movements and other sectors of society were able to share their struggles and mutually reinforce them. For instance, the emergence of the '*Sindicato Cidadão*' (Citizen Trade Unions) in the early 1990s indicates the recognition of that reference even within the Brazilian labour movement, traditionally more inclined to stricter class-based orientations (Rodrigues, 1997).

That perception also underlay a broadening of the scope of citizenship, the meaning of which became far from restricted to the formal-legal acquisition of a set of rights limited to the political-judicial system. The struggle for citizenship was thus presented as a project for a new sociability: a more egalitarian format for social relations at all levels, new rules for living together in society (negotiation of conflicts, new sense of a public order and of public responsibility, a new social contract) and not only for the incorporation into the political system in the strict sense. This struggle marks an important distinction – that between the conventional 'vertical' conception of citizenship as a relationship between the state and the citizen and a 'horizontal' conception of a relationship between people. This second view raises questions of how people may recognise one another as citizens and as social and/ or political equals. A more egalitarian format for social relations at all levels implies the recognition of the other as a subject-bearer of valid interests and of legitimate rights. It also implies the constitution of a public dimension of society where rights can be consolidated as public parameters for the interlocution, the debate and the negotiation of conflicts, making possible the reconfiguration of an ethical dimension of social life. Such a project unsettles not only social authoritarianism as the basic mode of social ordering in Latin American societies, but also more recent neo-liberal discourses that erect private interest as a measure for everything, hence obstructing the possibilities for an ethical dimension of social life (Telles, 1994).

In yet another context – the US – the importance and productivity of such horizontal dimensions of citizenship practices are also visible. While some narrative accounts of US history focus on difference as impeding a vernacular politics of solidarity, the persistence of efforts at horizontal citizenship starting in the inter-racial colony of 17th-century Jamestown, Virginia, and continuing through the so-called Third World liberation movements of internationalist wings of African-American, Chicano/Latino, Asian-American and Native American activists in the 1960s and 1970s provides for a different history. The simultaneous hyperconsciousness and denial of certain categories of difference as particularly salient to US citizenship led Kimberlé Crenshaw to posit 'intersectionality' as a mode of critique that recognises how race and gender interact with class to produce not only modes of oppression and exclusion, but also opportunities for elaborating counter-politics, especially when led by women of colour activists and analysts (Crenshaw, 1991).

For instance, despite a long history of segregation and significant barriers of language and culture between Asian and Latino immigrants in the US, Coll documents one such local coalition between immigrant Chinese and Latinas in the wake of immigration and welfare reforms at the end of the 20th century (Coll, 2010). Through an analysis developed in dialogue over individual experiences with an eye to collective political mobilisation, women came to identify their commonalities in terms of the needs and problems they seemed to share as immigrant women, mothers and workers. The ideal of meeting citizens' needs resonated deeply with the women's stories about making demands on individuals and institutions on their own behalf, but also for their children and others as well. They defined shared needs and interests as including quality education, health care and housing, but also dignity at work and respect for their cultures, particularly, freedom from racism and discrimination in US society. This reformulation of needs and problems as matters of collective well-being, and of citizenship as the right to have these issues addressed by the state and community, was forged transnationally. It drew often quite directly on the needs-based agendas of non-governmental organisations (NGOs), community-based organisations and feminist advocacy in Latin America (Díaz-Barriga, 1996; Gutmann, 1997). The concept of basic needs and rights and the interrelated responsibilities of states and citizens are implicit in an emerging pan-American discourse of universal human rights that immigrant women used to describe their expectations, frustrations and strategies for claiming their rightful place in US society. In such processes, the terms of belonging and entitlement in the US are reconfigured in dialogue with other national traditions through immigrant actors.

In a similar spirit, David Taylor has also called for a 'liberatory … internationalist and anti-nationalist' concept of citizenship in which the 'right to satisfy need becomes dynamic, political, and comes into a confrontation with power' (1989: 143). As low-income, sometimes undocumented and often non-English-speaking women of colour, these Chinese and Latina women occupy multiple positions and offer diverse perspectives usually excluded from normal definitions of US citizenship. New collective alliances, such as this one formed by immigrant women of colour in one US city, demand not only recognition of their differences, but also the legitimacy of their needs, the significance of their problems; it offers important avenues for understanding how new social and political values are forged in dialogue, collective struggle and dispute in a dynamic polity. This situation underlines several of our arguments: that the 'ideal' of citizenship is a travelling keyword that may be appropriated for new uses in new contexts; that contexts are always multiple and form the ground for new connections and articulations; and that political projects typically both borrow existing cultural resources and rework them into new configurations. 'Citizenship', 'needs' and 'problems' are terms with long political and policy histories, but here they have been translated into new connections and alignments, not least those of new solidarities.

Another instance of political projects around citizenship draws on work by Dagnino, which developed this concept. When people began to organise themselves in social movements, they soon learnt that their first task was to affirm their right to have rights. Dona Marlene was a *favelada* leader of *Assembléia do Povo* (People's Assembly), a social movement that, during the authoritarian regime that had suppressed human rights, brought together 60 *favelas* in Campinas, S. Paulo, Brazil in the late 1970s and early 1980s. She expressed that task very clearly: 'We began to struggle for the right to the land. We didn't have this right to struggle for the right to the land. Because they thought we were taking land which wasn't ours, it belonged to the City Government.' She goes on, explaining it very carefully and spelling out a view of the state that is crucial to the conception of a new citizenship:

You have to look closely at the City Government: it owns nothing. Nothing. Neither the Mayor nor anybody there owns anything; when they enter there they do not become owners, they become employees of the people. Everybody has the right to claim what they want and they have the duty to answer if it is right, if it is wrong, but they must answer.... Because they [people in City Hall] didn't have anything. The strength they had came from the people, it was not theirs. You never saw a bird flying without its feathers; it needs the feathers to fly. And the feathers they have are not theirs. If they are up in those heights, who put them there? So I began to see this and then I began to lose any fear I had. (Dagnino, 1995: 48)

A conception of citizenship as the struggle for rights is also clear in the statement of a member of a radical Brazilian NGO, created during the dictatorship in defence of human rights, interviewed in 1998:

Human rights are there, entire chapters. For the first time our Constitution [the 1988 Brazilian Constitution, known as the 'Citizen Constitution'] has a whole chapter.... Now, [the task] it is to demand that that is put in practice.... That is why I think it is a citizenship growth: people are not begging for rights anymore. They begin to claim.

And he quotes a conservative Mayor of S. Paulo (1979–83) as telling him: 'What is happening with this people? They always came here to ask for; now they come with the petulance of claiming!' (Dagnino, 2008a: 43). A project of citizenship that emphasised the constitution of citizens as active subjects confronted the hierarchical and authoritarian Brazilian social order, well expressed in the motto 'In Brazil, either you order or you beg' (Sales, 1994: 27).

However, members of other Brazilian NGOs interviewed in the same period, deeply influenced by the neo-liberal project implemented in Brazil from 1989 onwards, offered a strikingly different vision of citizenship:

We work deeply with citizenship. But not with that concept [that emphasises rights], which is a little simplistic. The question of human rights is also OK, but I think that what is needed is to provide the individual with conditions to

assume his or her role in society as a responsible element,
not only a claiming role – 'I want all my rights'.

A member of another associated NGO adds to this definition of
citizenship:'Our concern is with the insertion within the labor market,
having conditions of developing themselves as citizens.... Bringing
awareness of each one's potential. But without any political direction.
This is our concern: global development as a human being' (Dagnino,
2008a: 42–3).The contrast between these divergent views of citizenship
reflects the dispute between a democratic participatory project that
emerged in Brazil as part of the struggle against the military regime
and that was able to include the extension of rights and the principle
of direct participation in the Constitution of 1988, and the neo-liberal
project introduced around 1989, following the global move, and
consolidated by the eight years of President Cardoso's government
(1995–2002).These later views of citizenship express the attempt to
redirect its meaning towards an individually oriented conception, where
emphasis is put on participating in the market and social responsibility,
as well as on refusing conflict and political participation.

Such struggles over the form and character of citizenship inform
our understanding of the interrelations between citizenship and
political projects in a number of ways. First, they reveal both the
potency and the plasticity of citizenship – as a mobilising idea that is
valued because of the weight of political meaning that it carries and
its capacity to be rearticulated to new contexts, new meanings and
new projects; the recent 'Arab revolutions' are another clear example
of this mobilising power of citizenship. Second, this comment about
potency and plasticity applies both to its place in democratising popular
movements and to its neo-liberal remaking. Both take up the idea
of citizenship and articulate it to very different imaginaries, societal
conceptions and institutionalisations. Third, it underlines the point
that conceptions of citizenship rarely exist alone and uncontested.
Brazilian social movements had to contest actually-existing forms
of citizenship, institutionalised in authoritarian social relations and
state apparatuses and practices; and the same goes for the 1983 youth
movement in France. Equally, this expansive conception of citizenship
was itself contested by an alternative political project – that of neo-
liberalisation – which sought to reinvent or re-inflect citizenship into
new configurations of individualised relations between self-reliant
citizens, the state, the market and civil society (Dagnino, 2005a, 2008a,
2011); the 'citizen-as-consumer' led by 'choice' is yet another figure
of citizenship inscribed in yet another political project. Fourth, what

the preceding examples underline is also the importance to take into account the 'horizontal dimensions' of citizenship processes and political projects, that is, the fact that such political projects of citizenship always include not only the conventional 'vertical' conception of citizenship as a relationship between the state and the citizen, but also a set of 'horizontal' relationships between people (see Dagnino, 1994, 2005b; Telles, 1994; Kabeer, 2005; Neveu, 2005); indeed, rights are not only a set of predefined formal rights, but an aspect of social relatedness (Holston and Appadurai, 1996). Thus, in many contexts, notions of citizenship include expectations of seeing rights operating as parameters of social relations as a whole, from ordinary daily exchanges to economic and political ones. This expresses a claim for new, more egalitarian forms of sociability and cultural matrixes to replace authoritarian and excluding ones. In important respects, this takes citizenship beyond Arendt's much-cited idea of the 'right to have rights' (Arendt, 1968 [1951]: 177). Arendt locates the right to have rights within the framework of the nation-state system – and membership of an organised political community – which can be understood as the vertical articulation of citizenship (the citizen and the state). But the quest for egalitarian social relationships of a 'horizontal' kind – in which social action is conducted through principles of mutuality and recognition – brings another dynamic of citizenship to the fore.

Hence, taking into account such horizontal dimensions is all the more important as political projects cannot be reduced to strategies of political action in a strict sense; not least because they express, convey and produce meanings that are a part of wider cultural matrixes. This intimate relationship between political projects and cultural formations is connected to the wider field of the relations between culture and politics. We know that working at the intersection of these two terms gives rise to a variety of difficulties and troubles, some of which we explore later. In particular, culture has been one of those terms that has attracted considerable acrimony – in anthropology (eg Kuper, 1999), in sociology (where C. Wright Mills once described it as a 'soggy concept') and in the form of cultural studies, where it has been accused of everything from undermining realism and materialism to creating the conditions for neo-liberalism. Despite such challenges, we continue to find the concept of culture valuable in overcoming certain disciplinary narrowness and making visible the interwoven formations of power, meaning and politics. The constitutive nature of this relationship needs to be defended against conceptions that neglect or ignore it. It also needs to be championed against those that offer narrower or stricter approaches to both culture and politics, such as anthropological notions that resist the idea of recognising that culture is always pervaded by power relations (as in Durham, 1984) or political science's strangely persistent category of political culture, which defines only a part of the culture as being 'political'. Consistent with the disciplinary predominance of a notion of power that is restricted to the system of political institutions and often seen as 'condensed' in the state, political culture conveys a very limited relationship between culture and politics.

Gramsci's inestimable contribution to the understanding of those relationships shows how the basis of a truly hegemonic exercise of power – the construction of active consent – is built upon a conception of the world, a politico-cultural project, without which power is reduced to simple domination. Along the same lines, he asserts the pervasiveness of power with the notion of an 'enlarged state' that includes both the state and civil society as its terrain. Fundamentally concerned with social transformation and the construction of a new society, Gramsci does not reduce power to domination, but conceives of a transforming power, whose constitution requires not 'taking over an apparatus', but 'transforming social relations as a whole' (Portantiero, 1977: 24) to achieve a 'social, moral and intellectual reform'. In a sort of pre-Foucauldian way, he emphasises the multiple 'trenches' throughout society where power has to be fought and transformed, thus transcending a single 'vertical' view of power. In what follows, we take up this sense of the heterogeneous sites and forms of power. Like many others, we find ourselves working with a somewhat unfinished hybrid of Gramscian and Foucauldian views of power. While recognising the importance of Foucault's relational understanding of power, we nevertheless resist the abstract view that it is always active, everywhere. More accurately, we think it may be unevenly dispersed, with particular fields of intensity or concentration in specific societies at particular times. Tracing the contours of struggles over citizenship makes visible both existing formations and the desire to challenge, transform or reassert them. It is this messy understanding of power that informs our view of its persistent entangling with culture and politics.

The notion of cultural politics, in its several versions, has become increasingly significant as an analytical instrument to reflect on that relationship:

> Our working definition of cultural politics is enactive and relational. We take cultural politics to be the process enacted when sets of social actors shaped by, and embodying, different cultural meanings and practices come into conflict

> with each other. This definition of cultural politics assumes
> that meanings and practices – particularly those theorized
> as marginal, oppositional, minority, residual, emergent,
> alternative, dissident, and the like, all of them conceived
> in relation to a given dominant cultural order – can be
> the source of processes that must be accepted as political.
> (Alvarez et al, 1998: 7)

Not by chance, the entry point to this reflection has been the practices of social movements and their not-so-often-recognised capacity to re-signify existing meanings and formulate new ones through their political action. This capacity is crucial in struggles for citizenship, whose formulations have been predominantly seen, until recently, as situated strictly within the domain of dominant forces. Although this capacity is more easily recognised in social movements perceived as of a 'more cultural' character, such as those articulated around gender, sexuality and race/ethnicity, for example, it is important to assert that it is very much embedded in all social movements. Culture is political because meanings are constitutive of processes that, implicitly or explicitly, seek to redefine social power and the domain of politics itself. That is, when movements deploy alternative conceptions of citizenship – or of democracy, development, equality and more – that unsettle dominant cultural meanings, they enact a cultural politics:

> As a *simultaneous production of meanings and power relations*,
> culture finds its mirror in politics, in which the production
> and confrontation of power relations always implies cultural
> meanings. Thus, symbolic production is not only a crucial
> element in politics, particularly when we think about who
> has and who has not the power to attribute meanings, but it
> is often the main instrument (or weapon) in political action.
> (Dagnino, 2008b: 17; emphasis in original)

The main challenge faced by this conceptual emphasis lies in finding relational and non-reductive ways of conceiving culture and politics. There is an indispensable need to clarify the specificities and different modes of this basic relationship between culture and politics. That is to say, we need to recognise that both power relations and cultural signifying practices and their relationships do operate differently in different spaces and with respect to different subjects involved. Hence, if we examine how these relationships work with respect to political projects, we find that they are, at the same time, anchored in existing cultural configurations, and elaborate and introduce new elements into them, creating tensions in and transforming society's cultural repertoires. In this orientation to the entangled relationships of politics and culture, we draw on long-standing theoretical resources associated with cultural studies – the work of Raymond Williams already mentioned; the distinctive approach to the making of social classes developed by E.P. Thompson (1963); and, perhaps most importantly, the uses made of Gramsci's work in developing cultural studies (see, eg, Hall, 1996; Hall et al, 2013 [1978]). All of us have been shaped by these ways of thinking – and, despite their apparent age, we have found that they retain their productive value in wrestling with questions of citizenship.

This relationship between culture and political projects is characterised by a *constitutive ambiguity* that is particularly crucial from the point of view of citizenship processes. On the one hand, projects – especially those that are not conservative – are formulated precisely to confront and modify elements present within the histories and contexts to which they belong. On the other hand, and for the same reasons, these projects, and the practices they give birth to, are not immune to the very traits they attempt to criticise and hold at bay. This is one of the reasons why it cannot be assumed that projects of citizenship, either in their concrete implementation or in their discursive practices, are exempt from contradictions or endowed with a high level of internal coherence (Dagnino et al, 2006). In different degrees, they will be ambiguous, contradictory, combinations of and negotiations between 'old' and 'new', established and contested, dominant and insurgent, elements (Holston, 2008) that may be articulated in 'hybrid' citizenship narratives (the concept of articulation is another central term that we borrow from Stuart Hall's work in cultural studies; see, eg, Morley and Chen, 1996).

The case of the British 'New Labour' discourse about public service reform mentioned earlier provides a revealing example of such 'hybridity', especially in the uses it made of the figure of the consumer in the reworking of ideas of the citizen. These usages did not mark a wholesale dismantling or disappearance of more collective terms: notions of the public, communities, service users and so on continued to appear. So, too, did more service-specific terms, such as patients, passengers, pupils and parents, when health, public transport and education were being discussed. Nevertheless, these other identities were increasingly subordinated to – or articulated around – the idea of the consumer. It was this interlocking net of themes and identities that enabled the consumer to play such a central and organising role in New Labour discourse of public service reform in the UK. But how de we understand this process in which multiple identities (and the social relations they imply) were brought together in this uneasily hyphenated assemblage: *citizen-consumers*? Some writers have used the idea of hybridity to analyse both New Labour and neo-liberalism. For example, Hesmondhalgh argues that:

> it is important to see the British Labour Party as having invented its own distinctive governmental project; one which undoubtedly involves neo-liberal elements, but on different terms from the neo-liberalism of the New Right of the Reagan and Thatcher governments of the 1980s. Labour represents a new hybrid. Such hybridity on the part of Labour governments is not new, but this does not mean that the Labour government is simply accommodating itself to capitalism in the same way as previous Labour governments … there is a strong neo-liberal element to this hybrid governmental formation that takes for granted marketisation and the erosion of the public domain. (2005: 99)

Like the preceding examples, this case draws attention to the contradictoriness and instability of political projects. They are combinations or assemblages of political discourses that are articulated *unities-in-difference*. They are forged in the face of paradoxes, tensions, incompatibilities and contradictions, rather than being coherent implementations of a unified discourse or plan (Clarke, 2004). This suggests two important issues about this hyphenated citizen-consumer. The first is that the hyphen denotes the focus of political work: the effort to give the 'citizen' new meanings through its articulation with the image of the consumer. The second is that neo-liberalism itself comes to take on a particular local/national character precisely through its necessary encounters with other political discourses, oppositions and projects (see, inter alia, Kingfisher, 2002; Ong, 2006; Clarke, 2008a; Peck, 2010). Political projects are, then, always complex combinations rather than 'pure' articulations of singular positions or ideologies.

Citizenship, politics and the adventures of culture

We have argued that addressing the complex connections between political projects and cultural formations is essential in order to recentre citizenship(s) and its analysis; but other issues connected to the wider theme of 'culture' have to be considered. Indeed, in the many theoretical discussions around the notion of citizenship, which most of the time take place in what Lister (2005: 114) describes as 'an empirical void', its connections with cultural dimensions are simultaneously much debated and much ignored. On the one hand, there are substantial arguments around the idea of cultural citizenship, to which we will soon come back. On the other, many theorisations of citizenship present a universalised, abstracted and culturally neutralised version of it. From the abstraction of the 'right to have rights' to the extension of Marshall's trinity of legal, political and social rights, particular formations and specific formulations become abstracted and generalised as if they provided a culture-free conception.

Although it is mostly perceived and used, in academic literature, as a universally valid 'model', Marshall's work on citizenship traced a sociological history of the development of citizenship in the UK that captured the outcomes of particular struggles, conflicts and negotiations between social forces (Marshall, 1950). In a recent essay, Turner thus argues that Marshall's theory of citizenship as social rights is so well established that 'there is no need to describe the theory in detail' (2009: 67), but he summarises it as follows:

> It is sufficient to say that he divided citizenship into three parts, namely, civil, political and social rights. The civil component embraced the achievement of individual freedoms and included such elements as freedom of speech, the right to own property and the right to justice. The rights to participate in the exercise of political power, in particular the rights to free elections and a secret ballot constituted the political component. Finally, the social component is the right to 'a modicum of economic welfare and security to the right to share to the full in the social heritage and to live the life of a civilized being' (Marshall, 1950, p 69). Borrowing overtly from Maitland's *The constitutional history of England* (1908, p 105), Marshall claimed that these three aspects had evolved from the seventeenth to the twentieth century, becoming firmly established through various institutions that had evolved to articulate these rights.... *Because Marshall was primarily interested in social rights*, the core of the theory is in fact an account of the emergence of welfare services as an amelioration of the condition of the working class. (2009: 68, emphasis added)

This is a familiar account of Marshall's view of citizenship, which has indeed been profoundly influential. But Marshall's analysis is often used as a universal or contextually neutral model or theory; this is troubling for several reasons. First, there are continuing arguments about the adequacy and accuracy of Marshall's own account of British and/or English history of citizenship's development (see, eg, the discussion in Lewis, 1998). Second, there are competing analyses of the development of welfare states, for example, Marxist, Foucauldian and feminist, which place other political projects at their centre (eg Wilson, 1977; Offe, 1984; Petersen et al, 1999; Guy, 2009). These differ in many respects from Marshall's stress on social rights as a means of ameliorating class inequalities. But more importantly, Marshall's account is based on an analysis of a set of political cultural developments emerging from particular contexts in which a specific series of rights were institutionalised in a specific historical sequence. The set of rights he identified may not be the same elsewhere; neither may their substantive content (formed in different constitutions, in different legal codes and in different welfare systems). Equally, rights may arise in a different sequence or may be focused on other issues and relationships. For instance, in Brazil, they developed in a sequence that is profoundly different from that mapped by Marshall (Carvalho, 2001). Francoist Spain provides yet another example of such a different sequence; according to Garcia:

> the paths [to citizenship] used by Southern European societies are not simply a slower and more chaotic version of a similar process, but a completely different version. The British classical model brilliantly exposed by Marshall is only partially relevant to understand citizenship in Spain. (Garcia, 1994: 263)

This is not as much an argument against Marshall (although there are many worth making) as against forms of theoretical generalisation that conflate the political-cultural-historical specificity of forms of citizenship with the conceptualisation of citizenship through inappropriate abstraction.

In other words, citizenship *theories* should also be 'contextualised'. They are produced in specific contexts, and aim at 'crystallising', however temporarily, specific configurations (see Chapter Two). Indeed, in the intense circulation and transformation of meanings around and about citizenship that seem to us best grasped if read as embedded in political projects, such theorisations might also require some 'thick contextualisation'. Recentring citizenship, then, implies critically connecting such theorisations to political projects, thus modifying how we understand the centre. Our contention here is not that theorisations are only and always formulated so as to serve political projects (even if it may happen). It is to insist on the fact that academics' theorisations are also embedded in this complex field, and that reflexivity is important here if we want to critically question abstracted and universalised versions of citizenship.

One dimension of such a reflexive move would be to clarify whom 'we' as academics are arguing with when discussing citizenship. Thus, for instance, it is important to locate Aihwa Ong's interest in an analysis of Asian citizenship regimes. At the beginning of her chapter entitled 'Clash of civilization or Asian liberalism? An anthropology of the state and citizenship', she states very clearly that her analysis is inscribed within the context of the 'clash of civilisations' debate that contrasts Western civilisation based on the Enlightenment and individualism with non-Western societies based on 'communitarian values' (Ong, 1999a: 48). According to Western political theorists, Asian democracies, where the market economy flourishes without a parallel development of 'civil society', constitute a paradox that can only be explained by the role played by 'Asian values' that would found a collectivist ethos according to which it is the state, and not citizens, that determines what the 'public good' is. However, far from flowing from some 'cultural essence', Ong argues that this symbiosis between economic liberalism and political conservatism is better understood as a different form of liberalism. In her analysis, Ong addresses a series of academic and political issues; she strongly suggests that anthropologists should 'avoid using culture as the starting point of any investigation of social phenomena' and argues that a more fruitful approach would aim at investigating the 'varying kinds of conditions under which different, but all equally modern citizens are formed in a range of societies' (1999a: 66). But if her analysis rightly brings back political and social dimensions in what has been framed as a 'purely' cultural issue and thus gets closer to our view of culture and politics as necessarily intertwined, it falls in the rut of another oversimplification: that of reducing 'Western citizenship' to its liberal version, with its insistence on individual rights and freedoms. The contrast between her approach to the 'educative state' and Déloye's one in the French 19th-century context discussed earlier clearly demonstrates that political projects on citizenship other than the modern liberal one have been, and still are, powerful ones, even in Western societies. So Ong's contribution to the analysis of citizenship(s) needs both to be located (as a contestation of the 'clash of civilisation' framework and of its deterministic use of cultural dimensions) and critically engaged with (for the resulting oversimplification about 'the' Western citizenship regime being reduced to its liberal version).

So 'thick contextualisation' is also required when considering citizenship *theorisations* as much as for the forms and practices of citizenship itself. In saying that, we are not arguing for a relativistic or empiricist conception that would deny any attempt at conceptualising citizenship. Rather, we are pushing a step further our contention that citizenship has no essence that is immutable through time and space, and arguing for a more reflexive position in citizenship studies. Our working together, during the three-month-long IPAS project in Paris and our meetings to produce this book, has always returned to this problem of properly contextualising concepts and theories. Living and working in Brazil, the UK, the US or France, having been trained as political scientists, anthropologists or in cultural studies, being differently engaged, as academics and as citizens, with debates and struggles in our society, all these differences made for both strong shared views (all the stronger because we share them coming from such different backgrounds) and relevant differences, and our conviction is that they provide us with more assets than obstacles. Locating ourselves is what allows us to discuss across our different views and approaches, and to use them to further our critical views, as underlined by Shore and Wright when discussing the task of an anthropology of the present as unsettling and dislodging the certainties and orthodoxies that govern it: 'it involves detaching and repositioning oneself sufficiently far enough from the norms and categories of thought that give security and meaning to the moral universe of one's society' (Shore and Wright, 1997: 17). This challenge is both more pressing and more difficult when 'one' has more than one society.

Thus, if there are no universally valid and contextually neutral theories of citizenship, it is necessary to analyse how citizenship (and its theories) takes its meanings and characteristics from the conditions in which it is produced and manufactured, from the political projects such formulations, contestations and discussions are part of. As has just been discussed earlier, most theories of citizenship either tend to mistake a particular brand of it (liberal, republican, etc) for a generally valid and culturally neutral one, or reduce its variety to only a few easily opposed regimes. Even Leca's attempt to define those 'fundamental cultural traits without which the concept [of citizenship] itself disappears' (1991: 164; for more details on these traits, see Leca, 1991: 165–78) seems to be an exercise that aims at 'purifying' citizenship of 'the cultural codes' that colour it differently in different societies, an exercise most of this book tends to show is not only impossible, but also counterproductive, since citizenship cannot be grasped outside of its uses or meanings-in-use and because such 'cultural codes' are not just 'obstacles' to get rid of. When compared to other theorisations of citizenship, Leca's nevertheless allows for a connection between vertical and horizontal dimensions of citizenship, even if these last dimensions seem to be more conceived of as a necessary support to a political relation that, while connected to them, remains outside their direct reach. His attempt is also interesting in that his effort at elaborating a 'culture-blind' concept of citizenship not only addresses what is usually understood as 'cultural' (ethnic and national identities), but also tries to include in this process of 'neutralisation' the various philosophical traditions that underpin many theories of citizenship. But, in the end, we suspect that Leca's view of making citizenship 'culture-blind' conceals a remarkably French/political science understanding of the core of citizenship, especially around the issues of participation and his insistence on a disconnection between citizenship and other domains of social life. It tends to favour a conception of citizenship as participation and consent in a state-centred view (rather than emphasising the constitutive place of struggles, projects and conflicts) and largely underplays issues of equality. In the process, what Leca neutralises is a very narrow conception of culture (as particular national/ethnic value systems, or ways of life), rather than the wider conception of culture as the site of contested meanings and their entanglement with power.

An attempt such as Leca's raises the very possibility of a disconnection between citizenship and other spheres of social life, and presents a specific view of the very processes through which the realm of citizenship is built, as if it must and could be 'protected' from 'external' influences and processes. Indeed, not only is the public, civic sphere of citizenship not immune to cultural dimensions, but its very constitution relies on 'cultural politics'. So, instead of being a separate sphere of social and political life, citizenship, including in its 'specific', civic sphere, is permeated by cultural formations and their political effects. What is at stake is a discussion of how such dimensions weigh in citizenship processes, and why they are important to be grasped and problematised; as Rancière rightly reminds us:

> The political community is not defined by the gathering of all those having the same belonging. It is defined by all the disputes on belonging. It is the community based on sharing such disputes … the political community is made of this: not of added belongings (appartenances), not of a

wide belonging that denies all the others, but of conflicts on belonging. (Rancière, 2000: 65)

In other words, the issue is not to render citizenship 'purer' by disconnecting it from cultural dimensions, but to examine the ways in which culture and politics are *necessarily* entangled. That implies addressing both those cultural dimensions conventionally described or analysed as 'ethnic' or 'national', and the wider cultural formations in play, including in academic theorisations: what we earlier described as 'cultural politics'. But we need to be attentive to the ways in which conceptions of culture have been deployed in relation to citizenship, not least in arguments presenting culture as a distinct and separate social domain, as well as in debates around the notion of cultural citizenship. As Balibar stresses, against theorists of the social compact, it is:

> impossible to imagine that the constitution of [the public sphere] can be obtained through a whether *forced* ..., *fictitious* ... or historically *acquired* 'clean sweep' of 'collective identities' and belongings.... Since *everybody*, including the 'autochtones', have to at least symbolically stake again their acquired, inherited from the past, civic identity, and *rebuild it in the present* with all the others. This does not mean the past does not exist anymore or that it is of no use; but it means it is not an inheritance, that it confers no birthright. That there are no 'first occupiers' of the civic territory. (Balibar, 2001: 211–12, emphasis in original)

Like other concepts, 'culture' has no single, correct or uncontested meaning, so our own use of it as a key term demands that we pay attention to the other ways in which it circulates around questions of citizenship (Clarke, 2009).

The instabilities of citizenship in recent decades (as its forms and taken-for-granted connection to both nations and states have become destabilised or unbundled) have created a fertile terrain for arguments about the possible relationships between culture and citizenship. Debates about the national, ethnic and other cultural conditions and character of citizenship continue to rage, both practically (especially in debates about nationality, national identity and citizenship) and in academic arguments. For instance, in her criticism of the notion of 'post-national citizenship', Schnapper insists on the importance of attending to 'not only the ethnic realities of any concrete society, but above all the necessity to integrate these ethnic realities in the concrete political organization, even the one calling on the principle of citizenship' (1997: 219). She then argues that 'the Nation' is not just a civic project based on the abstraction of citizenship:

> participation in a national society is concretely founded on all kinds of elements that can be called ethnic: usage of a common language ... a common culture and particular historical memory shared by all nationals; participation in the same institutions.... (Schnapper, 1997: 214)

Here, a characteristic set of equivalences between culture, ethnicity and the nation is being constructed that insists upon the unifying effect of, and the need for, a common national culture.

This echoes the efforts of many governments, especially those of the global North, to discover and re-establish the national culture in the face of its proclaimed or declared erosion or dilution. For example, British governments have tried to identify the shared values, traits and traditions of Britishness:

> 184. ... Our relative stability as a nation is reflected in a relative lack of precision about what we mean to be British.
>
> 185. However, there is common ground between British citizens, and many cultural traits and traditions that we can all recognise as distinctively British. The Government believes that a clearer definition of citizenship would give people a better sense of their British identity in a globalised world. British citizenship – and the rights and responsibilities that accompany it – needs to be valued and meaningful, not only for recent arrivals looking to become British but also for young British people themselves.
>
> 186. The Government believes that everyone in the UK should be offered an easily understood set of rights and responsibilities when they receive citizenship. This might serve to make citizenship more attractive but also to make it clearer to potential citizens what it is to be a member of Britain's democratic society. There might also be a case for extending this to those who have the right to permanent residence in the UK.... The Government has already improved a considerable range of measures aimed at raising the profile and meaning of citizenship, introducing

language and Knowledge of Life tests for new applicants and starting the highly successful citizenship ceremonies which are organised in Town Halls across the country. But more could be done to create a simpler, fairer and more meaningful system, ensuring that the benefits and rights of citizenship are valued and offered to those prepared to make a contribution to the UK's future. (Secretary of State for Justice and the Lord Chancellor, 2007: 54)

These governmental concerns overlap and intersect with academic debates, investigations and speculations about national identity. As Déloye argues, the political stake of citizenship in these projects would be 'to homogenize the culture of the citizens of a Nation-State ... and thus to delimit the space of the civic and national identity' (Déloye, 1994: 23). The equivalences constructed between culture, ethnicity and nation thus tend to have a political character that shapes a particular dynamics of inclusion and exclusion, most obviously around actual or perceived 'foreign' populations and migrant groups. The attempt to reinvent the national (cultural) identity excludes those who are deemed not to share in it ('they are not *really* British/French etc') and demands of them a form of cultural assimilation ('they must learn to become more like us'). Such overdetermined notions of 'culture as a thing' in and of itself create the illusion that culture is a difference-producing machine and renders some people unable to 'participate' in the political community, defined as the nation. Yet, as Rancière very relevantly reminds us when discussing the contemporary development of new forms of racism:

Against the current of consensual wisdom, one has to remember that it was precisely the dissensual forms of political subjectification that yesterday operated those integrations today declared impossible. It is not through the sole principle of republican universality that migrants of yesterday's France, the families of Polish, Italian or Spanish workers, were integrated to French citizenship at the beginning of the century. Nor by the sole mediation of their own culture. It is through the very forms of class conflict that they were included in this working class subjectivity. (Rancière, 2000: 68)

In other words, it was because they became political subjects through working-class mobilisations, because they acted as citizens through conflicts, that they integrated in the society they lived in.

One version of this view of culture stresses its capacity to possess subjects, to bind them inescapably to narrow and traditional ways of thinking. Rather than being 'cultured' (the civilised, cosmopolitan subject), modernity's Others are viewed as being trapped by culture. Both Mamdani and Brown have described this as the 'culturalisation of politics':

> The culturalization of politics analytically vanquishes political economy, states, history, and international and transnational relations. It eliminates colonialism, capital, caste, or class stratification, and external political domination from accounts of political conflict or instability. In their stead, 'culture' is summoned to explain the motives and aspirations leading to certain conflicts....
>
> Importantly, however, this reduction bears a profound asymmetry. The culturalization of politics is not evenly distributed across the globe. Rather culture is understood to drive Them politically and to lead them to attack our culture, which We are not driven by, but which we do cherish and defend. As Mamdani puts it, 'The moderns make culture and are its masters; the pre-moderns are said to be but its conduits.' (2004: 18). (Brown, 2006: 20)

The 'culturalisation of politics' precisely inverts our interest in tracing citizenship's construction in the interplay of cultural formations and political projects. It rests on a static and totalising conception of culture as a closed and immobilising system of habits. To a certain extent, a number of contemporary processes within European societies seem to share common traits with such 'culturalisation'. Thus, according to the dominant French model, the citizen must first and above all be an abstract individual, able to 'detach' him/herself from all attachment to corporate communities, be they local, social, professional, religious or ethnic. In order to express him/herself in the public sphere as a citizen, he/she must demonstrate such capacities for abstraction and rise in generality (*montée en généralité*). The 'integration' within the (national) community of migrant (descending) populations has thus long been seen as the result of their relative individual capacity to adopt the French ideal model, according to which cultural specificities are to be maintained in the private domain, while a common 'civic culture' is supposed to be shared in the public domain (one has to remember here Clermont-Tonnerre's statement: 'Jews should be refused everything as a nation, and granted everything as individuals' (Discourse at the National Assembly, 22–23 December 1789)). A series of social movements, and much social research work, have strongly questioned both the reality and the validity of such a representation (for examples on issues of political participation, see contributions in Carrel et al, 2009; see also Rosaldo, 1999). Indeed, this ideal suffers some distortions and gives way to much more 'messy' representations when one observes actual social and political processes. Thus, in research with youth of Algerian descent, Neveu (2003) underlined the 'paradoxical injunction' they were confronted with, being 'on the one hand constantly suspected of "ethnic drifting", their attitudes and positioning systematically read through the filter of their origins; and on the other hand constantly summoned to "integrate" and to hide, or even deny such origins' (Neveu, 2001b: 225). Indeed, while the dominant discourse on the need to 'integrate' summoned them to act as pure, detached individuals in the public sphere, they were at the very same time systematically suspected of acting along 'ethnic lines' (because they were perceived as the 'conduits' of their 'culture'), and confronted with a series of discriminations in several domains of life.

Anthropology occupies a particularly troubled position in this field given the significance of culture as a concept, and how highly contested it has become (eg Kuper, 1999). One anthropological route to connecting citizenship and culture is that proposed by Nic Craith:

> From an anthropological perspective, I believe that citizenship is an inherently cultural process. The issue is not whether we can separate citizenship from culture, but which culture does the process of citizenship reflect and how should we define that culture without essentialising it. (2004: 296)

This view certainly relativises the issue of culture and resists its essentialisation, but it treats the relation as a relatively passive and external one (citizenship reflecting a culture), rather than our concern with the ways in which meanings, power and politics are entwined in the making and remaking of citizenship (for an answer to Nic Craith's argument, see, for instance, Ouroussoff and Toren, 2005). Culture is mobilised in citizenship struggles in many ways, not the least of which is public performance and discourse about membership, belonging and entitlement. These represent cultural imaginaries of citizenship and are manifest in vernaculars (Rosaldo, 1994) and semantics (Abélès, 1999) of political life (see also Clarke, 2009). Talking about citizenship in this way requires thinking harder about culture and how nations, states and people talk about 'culture'.

Culture, politics and cultural citizenship

Indeed, 'culture' can also be seen in terms of a creative resource for claims making. It is a way of making visible the invisible – both the normative/normalised/naturalised dominant and the subordinated other. Recognising the cultural dimensions of the ways that citizenship is conceived and practised opens new avenues for investigation and recognition of counter-hegemonic politics. Culture provides the framing lens – a means of making citizenship visible in forms not always recognised in theory or in political life.

Debates over the notion of 'cultural citizenship' have complicated relationships in our project to elaborate and analyse the relationships between culture, politics and citizenship. Cultural citizenship marks one terrain of what we have called the cultural politics of citizenship and it is a terrain that is characterised by the mobilisation of the idea of culture as a political resource (Ross, 1998; Clarke, 2009). Culture has, of course, always been a keyword, articulated in a wide range of political projects – to protect privilege, to educate or improve subordinate social groups, to contest exclusion, and to confirm exclusion or marginalisation, especially of those groups 'trapped' by their culture and unable to achieve republican or cosmopolitan transcendence (Brown, 2006). Cultural citizenship is one particular locus of political projects of contestation and of academic debates about the meaning and role of 'culture' in (the analysis of) citizenship practices.

Debates among and between anthropologists around the issue share some commonalities in terms of highlighting how differing political projects often underlie these apparently theoretical differences. Renato Rosaldo's notion of cultural citizenship involves both an epistemological dimension (elevating subordinated subjects to a position as analysts and practitioners of citizenship, and thereby demanding attention to the vernaculars of citizenship) and an empirical engagement with the political practices of claiming 'cultural citizenship' as articulating rights and difference (1994). He shares this view of cultural citizenship with an interdisciplinary group of Latino/a scholars in the US with an explicitly liberatory vision of the political agency of citizen-subjects like Latinos, who may be either relatively subordinated due to racism or formally excluded by legal bars to their full participation in American society

(Flores and Benmayor, 1997). His definition of cultural citizenship is clear here:

> Cultural citizenship refers to the right to be different (in terms of race, ethnicity, or native language) with respect to the norms of the dominant national community, without compromising one's right to belong, in the sense of participating in the nation-state's democratic processes. (Rosaldo, 1994: 58)

He located this project at the precise and unstable intersection of nation and culture, revealing the cultural particularity of national 'universalism' and the role of culture as a way of naming both the condition of exclusion and the basis of the demand to be included.

In contrast, Aihwa Ong's use of the same 'cultural citizenship' phrase differs in terms of epistemology and empirical engagement with subordinated citizen-subjects as political and analytical agents. Ong's principal concern is with understanding the power of governmentality to shape, indeed to produce, citizen-subjects and thereby citizens. In a vision of all-encompassing governmentality in which all positions and categorisations already exist, cultural citizenship for Ong is less about an engagement with dissenting subjects and the role of culture, identity, race or class in their agency, than it is about a process of disciplining subjects:

> This notion of citizenship as dialectically determined by the state and its subjects is quite different from that employed by Renato Rosaldo [1994], who views cultural citizenship as the demand of disadvantaged subjects for full citizenship in spite of their cultural difference from mainstream society ... his concept attends to only one side of a set of unequal relationships.... In contrast, I used 'cultural citizenship' to refer to the cultural practices and beliefs produced out of negotiating the often ambivalent and contested relations with the state and its hegemonic forms that establish the criteria of belonging within a national population and territory. Cultural citizenship is a dual process of self-making and being-made within webs of power linked to the nation-state and civil society. Becoming a citizen depends on how one is constituted as a subject who exercises or submits to power relations; one must develop what Foucault (cited by Rabinow 1984: 49) calls 'the modern attitude,' an attitude

of self-making in shifting fields of power that include the
nation-state and the wider world. (Ong, 1996: 738)

Ong certainly stresses the cultural conditions and character of
(implicitly) all forms of citizenship, recognising that they are suffused
with cultural meaning and enmeshed in the practices of producing
subjects. We think, however, that her comments underestimate the
significance of Rosaldo's recognition that culture itself is the site of
struggles over and for citizenship. The contrast between these two
views of cultural citizenship poses the question of how one mobilises
a more dynamic and complex notion of culture in which the dynamics
of power, inequality and dissent are necessarily, but contingently,
intertwined with culture. As noted earlier, Alvarez et al (1998) use the
notion of 'cultural politics' to analyse social movements seeking to
challenge, unsettle and destabilise the dominant political and cultural
groups and unequal relations of power. While in the US, such issues can
easily become conflated with identity politics, these scholars of Latin
America point to the ways in which culture, more broadly defined,
mobilises multiple and shifting identities, allegiances, coalitions and
visions of political change, in which power, culture and politics are
entangled.

Rosaldo's understanding of cultural citizenship clearly includes a
more general understanding of 'culture', close to the one we share.
Indeed, his discussion of it in his 1994 paper does not just define 'culture'
as a potential resource in struggles for equality, it also calls readers to
take into account the variety of representations about what it means
to be a 'full/first-class' citizen. Rosaldo's 'cultural citizenship' is mainly
about empirically understanding how each individual/group defines
what is full citizenship, with a diversity of criteria from well-being and
dignity to wages and services. The important point here is that Rosaldo
does not just consider 'cultural diversity' as a resource, but also calls
our attention to the fact that what we have to consider is how people
themselves define full citizenship, what qualities, values, attitudes, rights
and obligations they consider as constitutive of their subject position
as citizens. Luhtakiallo's analysis of vernaculars of citizenship among
French and Finnish activists is a revealing example of the benefits to
be gained from such an approach. Analysing their representations of
citizenship, she shows that in Lyon (France), 'Citizenship made the
activists think of state institutions, borders, the political system, and
national emblems, like the Marseillaise, that they often whole-heartedly
scoffed at. Citizenship was not "their" concept, it was "colonized" by

other forces' (Luhtakiallo, 2012: 71; for a similar analysis, see also Neveu, 2009); as for the Finnish activists:

> acting as a citizen, which consisted of, for example, participating in local social movements, was a duty, a service to the nation and of the common good, 'doing one's bit'.... In sum, they gave a strong impression that citizenship was a concept they 'owned' and felt comfortable with. Citizenship was no trouble at all for them. (Luhtakiallo, 2012: 77)

It is only by understanding such vernaculars, and their connections with both 'national political culture' and local history, that these activists' 'subject positions' can be understood and grasped.

Citizenship's relations with the notion of 'culture' are thus troubled and troubling, all the more so since the latter is used differently by differently positioned speakers (social movements, governments, but also social scientists) and within different political projects. Since the 'culturalisation of politics' discussed earlier can be located in governmental projects, social movements and academic literature, it seems to us a vital issue to stress again, on the one hand, the need to resist such attempts to consider certain groups as 'the conduits of their culture' (and including majority/dominant groups in such a position will not be a solution either) and, on the other, the deep entanglement and mutually constitutive relationships between culture, politics and power, what we referred to as 'cultural politics'. In other words, the challenge is both to critically analyse the many uses 'culture' is put to when connected to political projects of citizenship, and to maintain an analytical frame in which it cannot be disconnected from politics and power relations: 'Citizenship is not simply opposed to identity, as universalism is to particularism, but rather bears historically specific relationships with processes of group *identification*' (Beyers, 2008: 362, emphasis in original). This requires us to be attentive to the different uses of culture – recognising it as a practical concept within contemporary conflicts over modernity, diversity and citizenship, and having it available as an analytic perspective that consistently denaturalises and de-normalises dominant discourses, languages, ideologies and rhetorics – the ways in which meaning and power are being combined.

Conclusion: recentering citizenship – views from the margins

Considering citizenship processes as the processes through which citizens are formed, envisioned and transformed, implies distancing oneself from conventional understanding of them as mainly, if not exclusively, connected to the state. While the critical analysis of such state-centred approaches, and of their effects on representations of citizenship, will be developed in Chapter Two, we want here to discuss how and why such recentring might be at its most fruitful by adopting a view 'from the margins', which implies, on the one hand, fully taking into account processes usually not considered in citizenship studies and, on the other, including theorisations of citizenship in the mode of thick contextualisation called for at the beginning of the chapter. However, displacing the viewpoints also requires us to critically engage with the very localisations of both 'the margins' and the 'centre'.

A first argument in favour of a recentring of citizenship around spaces, sites and practices that are often described as its 'margins' is rather classical; according to many analysts, citizenship is largely about inclusion and exclusion, a question we will come back to soon, and its evolutions and transformations are the results of claims and/or accommodations so as to include more people. Citizenship would thus be transformed in most cases by/from its very margins, margins that henceforth tend to be central to these processes. Judith Shklar thus notes that:

> [o]ne way to undertake a historically rich inquiry into American citizenship is to investigate what citizenship has meant to those women and men who have been denied all or some of its attributes, and who ardently wanted to be full citizens. (1991: 15)

Citizenship is both exclusionary and aspirational, the object of desire and the product of dispute, as well as a dispute in itself. In this sense, citizenship is defined at its margins, by those claiming their rights, demanding their inclusion and the right to participate in the very definition of such rights and of this citizenry one can be included in. As Rancière suggests, citizenship indeed involves the development of 'a capacity to expose a dispute and to reformulate issues of right and non-right' (Rancière, 2000: 63). Coll argues that in the midst of xenophobic and anti-immigrant legislation and politicking in the 1990s, low-income immigrant women who did not speak English and, in many cases, were undocumented and non-citizens were at the centre of the 'remaking' of American citizenship (Coll, 2010). Through a dual process of individual transformation and collective civic action, these women came to think of themselves, as well as other relatively subordinated groups such as lesbians and gays, low-income African-Americans, and Asian immigrants, as legitimate, rights-bearing members of US society.

Reframing the subject of citizenship studies from a decentred/recentring perspective such as a focus on immigrant Latinas is thus not exceptionalism. It is not a view from the 'margins' of citizenship, but rather a challenge founded on the co-construction of political margins and centre that continues to exclude groups from citizenship based on gender, class, race or language. If the citizenship of excluded, marginalised or subordinated persons can be better appreciated, the polity-in-formation as these communities are incorporated (not necessarily assimilated) into the body politic can be better understood. This leads to another critique of 'central' conceptualisations of citizenship: their specific reading of the issue of inclusion and exclusion. As mentioned earlier, many writers, and Marshall can be read along such lines, consider citizenship as mainly about the need to include members of the 'subordinate classes' within the polity. But such 'inclusion' can be conceived of in two different ways: as a process through which the very definition of this polity and of its constitutive dimensions is collectively redefined; or as inclusion in an already defined polity, the fundamental elements of which are not to be challenged. This second conception became historically (as well as academically) dominant, reinforcing the view of citizenship as a status to which the excluded might be granted access. However, this was access to a model of citizenship in which the norms, qualities, attributes and conduct of the citizen were already established. The excluded were thus expected to resemble existing citizens following their inclusion. This same conception also reinforced the idea of citizenship as a set of pre-existing rights and the understanding of it as a vertical, state-centred relationship. If such a dominant view has become increasingly contested – in both theory and practice – it remains difficult to challenge it when maintaining a state- or status-centred analysis of citizenship processes. A last dimension of this inclusion–exclusion dimension is the need to qualify more precisely such inclusion and exclusion; indeed, and the abundant literature on citizenship clearly shows it, different criteria and bases have been used to organise and legitimate such inclusion or exclusion, and these have been differently organised. As Balibar rightly underlines, the Ancient city was excluding by locking up in the domestic sphere (women, children, slaves); modern democratic citizenship excluded by denaturalising those it deemed incapable of autonomous judgement; while the national-social state excludes by the disaffiliation of those who used to be included in social citizenship (Balibar, 2001).

Related arguments about the centrality of margins have been advanced by Das and Poole (2004) in their anthropological explorations of the 'margins of the state'. They suggest that, in a number of ways, the margins form a fruitful ground for anthropological investigations and, as a result, illuminate the state in ways very different from the traditions of European political philosophy. They suggest that the studies collected in their volume address:

> the precariousness of lives on the margins, but they are equally concerned with showing how forms of economic and political action, and ideas of gift and sacrifice that have been relegated to the margins, may, in some moments, also reconfigure the state as a margin to the citizen-body. (Das and Poole, 2004: 32)

Das and Poole argue against naturalised or naturalising understandings of the margins, in which 'marginal people' are imagined as people out of time and/or place (the residues of traditional ways; excluded from the centre or the mainstream; or people who do not belong). Instead, they see margins as constructed and produced through the work of regimes of power that organise the relations between people, places and practices. Margins, as a result, provide a distinctive standpoint from which to look into the workings of politics and power, as well as being the site of everyday practices of livelihood making, survival strategies and forms of refusal, recalcitrance and resistance to the normalising effects of power.

In this respect, the concern with margins links to other challenges to 'centre'-focused thinking. Some of these stress the importance of views from the margins or 'from below' within national settings or state systems (eg Steinert and Pilgram, 2006). Others derive from developments in standpoint theories, deriving from feminism or postcolonialism (on the 'politics of the governed', see, eg, Chatterjee, 2004). Larger questions about the view 'from the margins' have been raised with respect to the relation between European thought (and its colonial character) and the 'epistemologies of the Global South' (Santos, 2008; Santos and Meneses, 2009). In a similar vein, Walter Mignolo (2005) has argued for a decentring of conventional European (and European colonial) conceptions of modernity, in favour of other modernities constructed in 'the margins' of colonised Latin America. In such hands, the turn to the 'margins' – the other places and people of European colonialism – is never just an inversion. Understanding the North and South, and colonial metropole and periphery, as mutually constitutive, something is added by looking from the 'margins', since both the core and the margins are revealed in new ways – and in their interrelatedness (see Cooper and Stoler, 1997; Wemyss, 2009). The practice of recentring citizenship to look for its forms, sites and practices beyond its usual 'centres' is a critical feature of our approach, and one that may reveal the mutually constitutive relations of the multiple centres and margins of citizenship.

Thus, recentring citizenship, and critically analysing the mutual constitutions of margins and centres in specific contexts and periods, also implies a significant move in terms of the sites and types of practices and discourses that demand attention. Less visible daily practices demand attention, instead of taking only into account those practices that are either 'heroic acts' or the matters and practices that citizenship is often reduced to, such as voting. It also requires us, as has been argued before, to fully take into account those struggles led by groups excluded from formal or official definitions of citizenship.

So, the process of recentring citizenship makes the margins both more visible and more significant. It also has the effect of displacing the state from its assumed centrality as the sole producer and guarantor of citizenship by including other sources, sites and actors in its processes. Instead, we think it important to emphasise how citizenship both engages and exceeds the state. But even as we make the margins more visible, we think that it is also important to challenge and problematise the notion of margins – and the conceptual couplet of the centre and margins. Holding onto the polarising distinction between the centre and margins risks leaving the 'centre' in place (and the state as its natural occupant). Instead, we suggest that it is important to think about the articulation of the centre and margins relationally. This reorientation towards the margins also means connecting, in the same move, processes of governmentality and processes of subjectivation, where the latter term means both taking subjectivities into account and considering how people become political subjects. Foucault's concept of governmentality has been a profound influence across a wide range of fields and disciplines that are implicated in the study of citizenship. In the process, it has illuminated how subjects are framed and formed as citizens (eg Isin, 2002; Ong, 1999b) and we think this opens up spaces, processes and practices not normally at the centre of citizenship studies (especially those undertaken in political science).

While such innovations are welcome, we are left a little uneasy by their view of the subjects who are produced by governmental projects and strategies. Indeed, too many studies assume the success or effectiveness of governmental strategies: taking the view that their subjects come as and when summoned (Clarke et al, 2007a). On the contrary, subjects may prove to be more troublesome than that, acting within, between and across governmental and other discourses to: plot courses of action (and inaction); accept, bend and refuse the subject identifications on offer; and knit together other possibilities of identification, action and mobilisation (from the impure resources of political and cultural lives). Indeed, such relations, processes and practices are inescapable conditions for thinking about both the contextualisation of specific forms of citizenship and its unfinished (*imparfaite*) character (Chapter Three of this book will explore them in more detail).

Finally, such a recentring of citizenship also implies fully taking into account its horizontal dimensions (Neveu, 2005), considering that 'the relationship *between* citizens is as least as important as the more traditional "vertical" view of citizenship as the relationship between the state and the individual' (Kabeer, 2005: 23). As Dagnino (1994, 2005b) puts it, this is one point where social movements' re-signification of citizenship contested the classical liberal view centred on the relationship between state and citizen. An important issue within these horizontal dimensions of citizenship is that of the relationship between individual and collective dimensions: analysing young people's social movements, Mische (2001) points to the process of synthesis of individual and collective identities that is necessarily constitutive of the elaboration of projects or 'projective narratives' and is based on the claim that 'people incorporate the various groups to which they belong just as groups incorporate their individual members' (Mische, 2001: 141). Women's and homosexual movements are clear examples of these dynamics: what started as a single collective identity ('women' and 'homosexual') has progressively given place, not without conflicts, to the diversity of the individual identities of the members of the movements. New collective identities able to recognise and incorporate this diversity have then emerged: thus, in many countries, the 'homosexual' movement of the 1970s is now the GLBTTS, bringing together 'gays, lesbians, bisexuals, transvestites and transgenders'. There are multiple examples of these dynamics in other social movements; the Housing Movement in S. Paulo had to negotiate between their members claiming alternatively for 'the right to own a house' and 'the right to have a place to live in' (Coelho de Souza, 1997; Teixeira and Tatagiba, 2010). The contemporary international disability rights movement mobilised an originally Hungarian formulation of democratic self-governance – 'Nothing about us, without us' – as a claim for full political, social and cultural inclusion for people who may have one or more of a plethora of physical and intellectual differences considered 'disabilities' in their societies (Charlton, 2000). Political projects and their formulations of citizenship obviously follow these internal dynamics and negotiate the incorporation of such diversity.

Ethnography, with its attention to personal narrative and the contextualisation of particular experiences, offers a strategic point of entry into understanding how experiences of transformation of political subjectivity along with processes of collective struggle constitute the meanings of citizenship for individuals and groups. The assertion that citizenship is a dynamic, intersubjective and contentious process is both a rationale for, and an artefact of, an ethnographic approach that foregrounds the analyses of contemporary people as social agents. Studies that took localised community, kinship, occupational and ritual worlds as their objects of study, however, tended to separate public political and private family life into discrete, gendered domains while also privileging cultural or ethnic differences over structural analyses of race and class in migrants' experiences. Such approaches also left aside the question of what citizenship might mean for those without legal or official citizenship status. More recent social theory has suggested the importance of looking at themes, issues and experiences that span cultural domains previously deemed autonomous, or forcing the juxtaposition of domains in the analysis to advance theory (Coll, 2010).

A recentred approach to citizenship requires the taking into account of the very fabric of social relations, of processes that take place without or besides the state, thus locating 'citizenship … in the social arena and in social relationships' (Taylor and Wilson, 2004: 157). The same authors argue that:

> ordinary people often engage with the powerful in scenarios that, at first sight, seem to have little to do with the stuff of citizenship (funeral dances, religious sects, marching competitions, school gardens) yet in politicised context these activities have a great deal to do with the nitty-gritty negotiations of power, reckoning up of political deals, exercise of political agency, declaration and redefinition of 'belonging' and, therefore, the very fabric of citizenship. (2004: 157)

In his work on 'insurgent citizenship' in Brazil, Holston also emphasises the importance of such 'everyday citizenship', when he observes, for instance, apropos interactions in a queue at a bank counter, that:

> trafficking in public space is a realm of modern society in which city residents most frequently and predictably experience the state of their citizenship. The quality of such mundane interaction may in fact be more significant to people's sense of themselves in society than the occasional heroic experiences of citizenship like soldiering and demonstrating or the emblematic ones like voting and jury duty. (Holston, 2008: 15)

In this chapter, we have begun the work of recentring citizenship to provide a foundation for the following two chapters. For us, this recentring has two important and related dimensions. First, it involves opening the concept of citizenship up to dispute in analytical terms by approaching its shifting meanings and uses as constitutive, rather than mere variations on a central theme. It is the combination of plasticity and potency that marks citizenship as a keyword, and which makes it so central to the efforts of such diverse political projects. This combination also means that citizenship takes shape – in both practice and theory – in specific contexts. Second, we have stressed the ways in which citizenship is always entangled with culture, politics and power within particular contexts. Like citizenship, none of these words are particularly stable or definitive concepts – each of them always requires some effort to make it meaningful and productive. We have chosen an approach that stresses the importance of treating them as interconnected: culture without politics and power tends to revert to a catalogue of relatively static systems of meaning that may be differentiated, hierarchised or ordered in various ways. We would rather stress the way cultures come alive in processes of conflict and dispute – that is, when meanings are entangled with politics and power. The same applies to the other two terms: both politics and power come alive – and animate struggles over citizenship – through their entanglements with culture in the struggle over meaning. Finally, our approach to recentring citizenship has involved us working through two important spatial images. For the first, we have tried to contrast the desire for horizontal relationships of mutuality, solidarity and respect as modes of being citizens with the more conventional view of citizenship as organised in vertical relationships between the citizen and the state. In the second, we have tried to suggest what might be gained in looking at disputes over citizenship from the 'margins' rather than from the 'centre'. Both of these changing viewpoints underpin our explorations of citizenship in the following chapters.

CHAPTER TWO

Decentering citizenship

In Chapter One, we argued for the importance of recentring conceptions of citizenship. This need to 'recentre' citizenship so as to highlight its deep embeddedness in political projects and cultural formations implies a parallel move to 'decentre' it from its generally agreed-upon connections, in particular, to the formations of state, nation and law in which citizenship is typically understood as a status, and as necessarily and culturally 'national'. In this chapter, we will develop this decentring by making the contingent connections between citizenship and states visible as a critical analytical issue, and not merely an empirical observation. We will then discuss how a processual view of citizenship that makes visible what happens at what is usually thought of as the margins requires modifying the way the state is considered in most academic literature, particularly by stressing its deep heterogeneity. Finally, we will explore some possibilities of thinking about citizenship 'beyond the state'.

Our aim is to decentre the relationship between citizenship and the state as a means of unlocking some of the dominant assumptions about what is at stake in the idea of citizenship. In so doing, our intention is not to make the state disappear or consider it as irrelevant to citizenship processes; indeed, we see it as a crucial feature of citizenship in many respects. But its assumed centrality needs to be challenged in the process of revisiting how states and forms of citizenship are entwined, or relatively disjointed, in practice.

Citizenship has conventionally been viewed as embedded in, or articulated through, three key sets of institutional formations: the state (citizenship as a political status), the nation (citizenship as membership of a community) and the law (citizenship as a juridical status). It seems necessary to loosen these connections, treating them not as the foundational elements or 'natural state' of citizenship, but as contingent historical, political and cultural constructions, inscribed in and flowing from different political projects. Citizenship's ties to the state, to the nation and to the law are produced through what Sassen (2005) has called 'bundlings', sets of connections whose contingency has been concealed in the processes of institutionalisation that reified and naturalised them. As various authors have remarked, recent decades have been marked by processes of 'destabilisation' or 'unbundling' in which these connections have been made more visible and more contestable:

> The theoretical ground from which I address the issue is that of the historicity and the embeddedness of both categories, citizenship and the national state, rather than their purely formal features. Each of these has been constructed in elaborate and formal ways. And each has evolved historically as a tightly packaged bundle of what were in fact often rather diverse elements. The dynamics at work today are destabilizing these particular bundlings and bringing to the fore the fact itself of that bundling and its particularity. Through their destabilizing effects, these dynamics are producing operational and rhetorical openings for the emergence of new types of political subjects and new spatialities for politics. (Sassen, 2005: 80)

This is, as Sassen recognises, both an empirical and a theoretical issue. The forces, dynamics, pressures and challenges acting on the institutionalised formations of nation–state–citizenship make their contingency and particularity more available to investigation. But it is also a theoretical issue, inviting approaches to studying these issues that are more historically and spatially specific (What forms of citizenship have been bundled with what state formations and nation-building or -maintaining projects?). Such approaches are also more likely to look for 'bundles' rather than seeing blocks (such as 'the state' in all its monolithic glory). Sassen's conception of bundles echoes other recent formulations that stress the contingently constructed character of what appear to be stable structures or integrated institutions. This interest in construction coincides with developments elsewhere in the social sciences, particularly, but not only, in approaches to the state. 'Bundling' has echoes of 'assemblages' (Latour, 2005), 'ensembles' (Sharma and Gupta, 2006), 'constellations' (Leibfried and Zürn, 2005) and 'articulated formations' (Clarke, 2004). Each of these terms speaks to a sense of construction and combination – the building of elements into a *temporary* unity (see the discussion in Clarke, 2008b). This view of the varied connections between citizenship and states as contingent bundlings aligns with Chapter One's emphasis on the need to recentre forms of citizenship by locating and contextualising them in political projects and cultural formations. Such a view, then, implies analysing the diversity of state formations and forms of citizenship, not least because of how the different 'bundlings' of citizenship, nationality and national identity are often seen as politically or logically necessary, and particularly consequential.

But a second move is required: that of problematising 'the state' itself. Just as 'citizenship' tends to be built, discussed and conceived as a universal, abstract and unproblematic notion, so too is 'the state'. We will thus discuss such conceptions of the state and try to introduce a more complex, differentiated understanding of it, of its forms, roles and workings, in place of over-coherent, over-unified and excessively institutionalist conceptions. In our view, decentring the state does not imply removing it from our vision, but considering the multiple ways in which states are also located and embedded in social practices, and how they are shaped by contradictory political projects that leave traces in representations, practices and institutional arrangements. This attention to the heterogeneity of states thus points in two directions: on the one hand, to their empirical variation across place and time; on the other, towards their internal complexity of apparatuses, agencies, sites and scales.

This engagement with the heterogeneity of states and their changing locations in contemporary sets of 'governance' practices will subsequently lead us to discuss the many connections, circulations and confluences between it and other agents, like social movements or non-governmental organisations (NGOs), questioning in the same move the apparently foundational distinction between 'state' and 'civil society'. Attending to these issues will bring into view the variety of imaginaries called upon, contested and elaborated when different agents use references to 'citizenship' to make sense of their membership or ground their claims. This will be another way to shed a critical light on the classical discussion of citizenship as a way to organise inclusion and exclusion, by raising questions about the imagined nature of communities and collectivities thus created, addressed or mobilised. This issue will command our attention in Chapter Three. In the process of moving beyond the binary of inclusion and exclusion, the conditionalities and modes of such inclusion and exclusion have to be further discussed and problematised. Balibar identifies at least two issues that should be examined: the level at which the exclusion principle is located; and the very types of exclusion themselves, the logics of which are central to the characterisation of any social and political formation (Balibar, 2001: 114–16). Similarly, Lewis (1998: 65) argues for recognising the subordinated and marginalised modes of inclusion that complicate the apparently clear-cut distinction between inclusion and exclusion. Decentring citizenship(s) thus requires not only to disentangle it from state(s) or the nation-state, but also to discuss its membership dimensions: membership of the legally defined 'community of citizens', membership of a 'political community', the intermingling of memberships through which one might imagine oneself as a citizen, and how these diverse belongings are hierarchised, contested and enacted.

Unsettling citizenship

Citizenship and the state, or, more usually, the nation-state, appear to be always intertwined, even if not in a necessary connection. Although earlier forms of state (eg the city-state) are recognised as sites of citizenship, the historical articulation of the nation-state and the interstate/international system made the nation-state appear as the normal form of state in relation to citizenship (Isin, 2002). In most cases, states are the agents that inscribe, guarantee and police citizenship as a status and it is predominantly through states that rights can be legally inscribed and implemented, although 'new' institutional sites, such as the European Union (EU), tend to be endowed with similar prerogatives, an issue we will come back to in this chapter. As a consequence, legal apparatuses are sites where citizenship(s) can be grasped as a political, juridical and administrative, but also cultural and social, category that distinguishes different types of subject (citizens and non-citizens, nationals and aliens, etc) and distributes rights and responsibilities (voting, protection under the law, social or welfare entitlements, etc), without necessarily a neat correspondence between types of subjects and rights or responsibilities (ie the latter might be accessible to different types of subjects at different times and in different places). Citizenship – as we have argued – is never finished/completed, it is always '*imparfaite*'. Specific political projects and cultural formations produce different 'crystallisations' of citizenship both in terms of legal and juridical status and in terms of representation and conceptions of what being a citizen is about (conducts, competencies, attitudes, etc).

For example, the Marshallian view of citizenship is built on a juridical conception of the rights of citizens – the combination of legal, political and social rights. Nevertheless, these three fields (legal, political and social) produce very different sets of citizens in the UK context, even after the struggles to generalise such citizenship rights beyond their male, propertied and able-bodied origins (the model of the self-possessed and self-possessing subject of citizenship). Legal rights have shaped a different structure of inclusion and exclusion from political rights (most evidently in the distinction between who is entitled to exercise legal rights and who may be denied political rights: convicted criminals, those deemed mentally incompetent, etc). Social rights have been even more complicatedly conditional, both in principle and practice. Conditions of residence, of 'earned' benefit entitlement, of nationality, of age and so on produced a complex field of entitlements that are never simply 'universal'. Nevertheless, the significance of Marshall here is about the national reference – a particular historical-political-cultural assemblage of citizenship in the UK – and his partial vision of his own national formation, in which some forms of social divisions are normalised and naturalised, in favour of attention to the field of class inequalities that might be mediated by citizenship (see also Lewis, 2000; Balibar, 2001: 105–7). According to Turner:

> Historically, citizenship has been closely associated with the involvement of individuals (typically men) in the formal labour market and therefore work was a fundamental basis of citizenship and the welfare state as described in Beveridge's *Full employment in a free society* (1944) and *Voluntary action* (1948)…. Second, service to the state for example through military service has historically generated a range of entitlements for the citizen. War-time service has typically resulted in special pension rights, health provisions, and housing for returning service men and their families…. Third, people achieve entitlements through the formation of households and families that become the reproductive mechanisms of society through the birth, maintenance and education of children. These social contributions increasingly include care for the ageing and elderly as generational obligations continue to be satisfied through the private sphere. These services to the society through the family provide entitlements to both men and women as fertile adults who are replenishing the nation. (Turner, 2009: 70)

Such categorical conditions of the relationship between contribution and entitlement were, as Turner suggests, profoundly implicated in a conception of society, its normal social relations and its reproduction (through work, war and family). Citizenship is a site for producing and/ or reproducing patterns of social relationship (and the inequalities they contain), even as it formalises relations of equality. Not surprisingly perhaps, the 'normal' images of social relationships embedded in citizenship became the focus for subsequent political struggles to extend and transform the meanings of equality (eg over gendered divisions of labour and their inequalities; over hetero-normative models of intimate relationships; over the status and rights of minors; and over the troubled colonial/post-colonial relationship between racialised identities, nationality and citizenship). In the French context, Lochak's (1988) study of the legal formulations of citizenship demonstrates what she calls '*un concept flou*' ('a blurred concept'), in which particular specifications of citizenship as a rights-bearing status do not fit tidily or coherently together. We think it is important to attend to the extreme malleability of the figure of the citizen between, and even within, the different fields in which these rights are implemented. As we noted earlier, civil (legal) rights are not necessarily carried by the same people who are entitled to vote (even minors have civil rights, but cannot vote; or criminals have rights before the law even though their right to vote may be taken from them); social (or 'welfare') rights are often conditional in terms of who can claim them. As European citizens, European nationals have a right to vote in local and European elections wherever they live within the EU, whereas third-state nationals do not, even if their residence duration has been much longer. As Lochak underlines, in the French case there is no:

> true (*véritable*) definition of citizenship. Should those nationals deprived of voting rights (women until 1945, convicts who lost their civic rights, minors …) be considered as citizens?… There is no precise constitutional answer to such question, so much so that recent Constitutions make no reference to citizens. 'Voters are those French nationals of both sexes enjoying their civil and political rights', very prosaically states the 1958 Constitution. (Lochak, 1988: 82–3)

Zhang concurs with such an analysis when he states that as:

> Holston and Appadurai (1996: 4) have pointed out, 'formal membership in the nation-state is increasingly neither a necessary nor a sufficient condition for substantive citizenship.' One can no longer take formal membership as a promise for social entitlement; it is imperative to reexamine the complex relationship between formal membership and substantive rights in culturally specific contexts.… *Hukou* [household registration system erected in 1958 according to which individuals were required to register at birth as legal residents of a particular place] should thus be seen not

simply as a system of population management and material redistribution but rather as a badge of citizenship with profound social, cultural, and political implications for the lives of Chinese people – a regime of uneven citizenship under socialism that was set firmly in place through the late 1970s. (Zhang, 2001: 315–16)

Such sets of relations, and the representations they embody, indeed take different forms in different situations. In Brazil, the most important proof of citizenship is the '*carteira de trabalho*' (workers' card); this is what the police ask for from people they stop in the streets, especially if they are black and not very well dressed. The national regular ID card, the '*carteira de identidade*', is not enough: decent and honest citizens are the ones who have a formal job. This results from the emphasis of the Brazilian state, since the 1940s, on defining citizenship through the category of 'work' and the social rights attached to it, as distinct from an emphasis on a more universal criterion that would, for instance, include everybody living in the country. In spite of the fact that the original criterion has expanded quite significantly towards a more universalising one, the category of citizen remains symbolically very much linked to the 'worker'. Social rights in Brazil were granted in 1943 through the *Consolidação das Leis do Trabalho* (Consolidation of Labour Laws) to workers in professions acknowledged and regulated by the state, which meant those organised by labour unions formed according to state rules. In a complex operation of inclusion/exclusion, this version of citizenship was the first in Brazilian history to grant a significant set of formal social rights, coupled with the state's recognition of labour unions as political interlocutors. At the same time, such a version excluded not only non-workers, but also workers in non-regulated professions and rural workers. Political recognition of workers' organisations was restricted to those unions that complied with state regulations about their format. Voting rights had been granted to women in 1932, after decades of struggle by the suffragist movement; illiterate citizens, as well as minors, remained excluded until the 1988 Constitution.

In the US, it is not so much work as suffrage that has been a centrally important site for contesting inequalities in citizenship and political rights. There, the vote stands for more than a formal type of political empowerment or agency; it confers what Judith Shklar calls 'a minimum social dignity' (Shklar, 1991: 2). From the abolition movement to the women's suffrage movements of the 19th century and the civil rights movement to end segregation in the 20th century, the right to vote has meant so much to excluded classes of citizens that they were jailed, staged hunger strikes and, in some cases, faced lynching in order to secure this legal right. A specific set of norms and ideals about how voting and electoral democracy should occur are understood to embody 'democracy'. Paradoxically, these have also underpinned the forceful export of 'US-style democracy' abroad through imperial military projects and today's 'democracy-building' practices in places like Afghanistan or former Soviet republics (see Petric, 2008).

Citizenship and the right to vote have always been in a relation of tense contradiction in the US. In the colonial-era US, a voter had to be at least 21, white, male and with property, but not necessarily a US citizen. Non-citizens exercised the right to vote at various levels of government, and, in some cases, even held office, in as many as 40 US states between the 1770s and the end of World War I (see Raskin, 1993; Harper-Ho, 2000; Hayduk, 2006). For most of this period, non-citizen voting was seen as a means to train newcomer white men to be good citizens and prepare them to participate in national elections after naturalisation. In frontier states, it was also a way to lure new European immigrants to colonise Native lands as homesteaders, while diffusing pressure from women and African-Americans seeking the franchise. In doing so, it reinforced the link between race, masculinity and property that dated back to the first US Naturalization Act of 1790 and defined women, people of colour and the landless as ineligible to join the citizenry. The legacy of this particular form of white settler colonisation is fundamental to understanding US citizenship in all its permutations and historical articulations. While the history of exclusions of new immigrant groups, the annexation of Spanish and French colonial territories, and the persistent crime of human slavery claim more attention in this citizenship story, the position of colonised indigenous peoples calls into question the legitimacy of an occupying colonial power. While the formal recognition of many native nations and tribal governments allowed the US to argue for the legality of its territorial treaty claims, the fact that Native Americans were excluded from US citizenship by law until 1924 reveals the fear the federal government had about the potential power and rights claims of Native American peoples.

The rescinding of the right to vote for non-citizens happened slowly over time but corresponded to the rise of anti-immigrant sentiment and legislation that ultimately succeeded in naturalising the conflation of alienage in US public discourses with not only legitimate disenfranchisement, but inherent illegality. With the consolidation of US control over the West in the late 1800s, the exclusion of Asian immigrants, beginning with the Chinese in 1882, and the increase in immigration from South and Eastern Europe between the 1880s and the end of World War I, states one by one redefined their voting laws to require federal citizenship for voting at the state and local level. Historian Mai Ngai (2004) demonstrates how the 1924 Johnson–Reed Act and related State Department administrative rules not only ended most immigration by Asians and descendants of African slaves, but severely restricted immigration from Southern and Eastern Europe and Africa, and were ultimately responsible for the racialised regime of the 'illegal alien' (and the illegality of Mexicans in particular) as a naturalised social category in US society. After 1924, Arkansas was the last state to retain the alien franchise; that state subsequently rescinded it in 1926, ending non-citizen voting in the US after 150 years of the practice.

It is in this context that we need to both appreciate the naturalisation of the link between citizenship and the vote for Americans and understand the significant challenge that current non-citizen voting rights demands offer to deeply held American convictions about race, nationality and citizenship; today, non-citizen voting has effectively disappeared from national memory. This also helps us understand why the public narration of the history of non-citizen voting and its restriction became a central strategy for immigrant voting rights advocates in Massachusetts (Coll, 2011).

A huge variety of state-based institutionalised formations in which citizenship has been 'bundled' can thus be observed throughout the world and through time (see, for instance, Farhmeir's [2007] tracing of the elements of formal, political, economic and social citizenship in the US, Britain, Germany and France). In communist China, the *hukou* system:

> divides national space into two hierarchically ordered parts: the city and the countryside. I use the term *urban citizenship* to refer specifically to the package of rights and entitlements associated with legal residency in the city, including access to state-subsidized housing, grain, medical care, and virtually free education for one's children. Under the regime of citizenship that currently prevails in China, social equality is often sought within either of two spatially demarcated realms, not between them. Such a regime, characterized by explicit spatial and social hierarchies between rural and urban areas, presents a sharp contrast to the Western liberal ideal of a citizenship that bestows equal entitlements across the board for all members of a given political community.

> Consequently, the struggle over citizenship in socialist China often takes place between those who are officially classified as 'urban residents' and those designated as 'rural residents'.
> (Zhang, 2002: 313)

While such bundlings are usually considered as a set of rights inscribed in a juridical structure, connected to particular conditionalities, it has to be emphasised that such bundlings are never 'only' juridical and legal ones. There are three reasons for not taking the 'legal' as a superordinate terrain for the study of citizenship. First, legal arrangements are inscribed in, and emerge from, specific social and political contexts and cultural matrixes. Laws themselves are social products, shaped by social forces, interests and beliefs, or might be treated as the institutionalised outcomes of political projects (see, for instance, Rouland, 1988; Ewick and Silbey, 1998; Edelman, 2007). Whether institutionalising the rights of private property, embedding particular gender orders or attempting to manage the difficult interpersonal relations of slavery, the law does not exist outside prevailing social relationships and their associated conflicts. Even when, or perhaps especially when, it is claimed that the law stands above, and beyond, society, sociological realism can demonstrate how intimately bound together they are, and, indeed, how the very claim to be transcendent is itself socially located and socially performative (see Feenan, 2013). The law is better understood as a specific domain of the society, culture and practice in which it is made and in which, as Edelman (2007) insists, the lawyers 'invent reality'.

Second, the resulting juridical discourses on such rights and legal arrangements produce effects: their meanings, their relative importance and their practical activation in courts, tribunals and administration. They are also put to work in promoting or transforming representations about life in society, about citizenship or about the legitimacy of certain claims or groups. Third, such juridical conceptions are also the focus of contestation, to reform, re-inscribe and retrench the prevailing system of rights as different social forces and political projects contend to shape the state and forms of citizenship. While there is no doubt that 'The Law' has a particular discursive quality (especially in its representation as both transcending and promising to resolve social conflicts of different kinds), it is also never above or beyond social and political contestation (Clarke, 2013).

Such 'blurred' boundaries between and within sets or sources of rights, and the people concerned by them, while not new (as many colonial subjects/citizens would know; see, for instance, Larcher, 2011), have been brought back to full light in recent decades with the development of the set of transformations usually described under the signs of 'globalisation' or the emergence of the 'post-national', and by the migratory circulations that have unsettled the assumed superposition of the state's territory, citizenry and (national) identity; a set of issues important enough for us to explore them more fully in Chapter Three. But it is also a series of deep transformations in modes of ruling and governing that makes a more critical analysis of the relations between states and forms of citizenship necessary. Appadurai (2001) is among those who argue that we are witnessing a global process of radical transformation of the state's role, in which 'civil societies', NGOs and international agencies all play significant parts, giving birth to new configurations in terms of power and access to resources that often question established forms of citizenship or promote new ones (see Atlani-Duault, 2005a; Petric, 2008). A variety of processes have contributed to these transformations, which have been variously identified as globalisation, neo-liberalisation and privatisation – which coincide in complex and unstable ways with pressures 'from below' to transform power, inequalities and – not least – the power of the state. The resulting realignments have dragged established institutions, agencies and organisations into new arrangements – transforming both the organisations and their interrelationships (Newman and Clarke, 2009).

It is not just the sets and sources of rights that are being modified by these intersections of globalisation and governance, but also the very arrangements or bundlings of different sources of power, authority and legitimacy. In other words, we refer to these dynamics of governance and globalisation because they modify sources of rights and because they create new bundlings or power, through which citizenship, as rights and as practices, is deeply changed, challenged and so on. Recent literature on 'urban citizenship' provides an interesting example of such transformations; indeed, this notion is not mainly used as signifying a return to an 'urban' historical 'nature' of citizenship, but in order to make sense of contemporary practices and the new bundlings they give birth to. In the context of economic globalisation, many scholars of urban citizenship argue that both institutional arrangements and social and political mobilisations in 'global cities' contribute to the emergence of such new bundlings, in which cities, rather than central states, become the focus point, including in terms of entitlements and legal rights (see, inter alia, Painter, 1995; Bauböck, 2003; Varsanyi, 2006; Isin, 2009). Governance processes are increasingly engaged with multinational processes and relationships – in terms of dealing with multiple and overlapping national sovereignties, with cross-border spaces, and with transnational processes taking place both between and within particular national spaces (eg flows of objects, money and people). The increasing significance of such transnational processes, relations and organisations has given many aspects of governance a distinctively multinational character. This may merely imply that governance arrangements link several national spaces in networks, webs or partnerships. But multinational governance may require forms of cross-border working or the creation of partnerships that 'transcend' national identification – for example, the economic or social development of 'regions' that cross borders cannot be allocated to a singular national sovereignty claim; indeed, the region being brought into being may acquire its own powers and capacities beyond singular national sovereignty claims (the EU, Mercosur and other 'economic' regions embodied in governance entities). As a result, governance arrangements both negotiate and modulate the sovereignty associated with nations as bounded spaces, even as – in some cases – the 'nations' themselves are in the process of being invented, redefined or recreated. This applies equally to the reconfigurations of the countries of the former republic of Yugoslavia as it does to the countries of the increasingly disunited UK (involving differentiated forms of 'national/regional' devolution). Former Soviet republics in Central Asia are a particularly relevant site where such reorganisations can be observed. As stressed by Petric:

> It seems that, well beyond these revolutions of colour what is at stake is indeed a redefinition of the role of the state, of sovereignty in these political spaces. These societies are confronted by important external constraints. Super powers, like the USA on the one hand and China and Russia on the other, but also Muslim countries through their charitable foundations, also intend to convey their techniques of influence so as to modify social relations. States nevertheless don't have the monopoly of influence and certain institutions (NGOs, foundations) or international organisations play a dominating role. (Petric, 2008: 19)

The emerging forms of governance both within and between countries tend to be multi-agency: both in the narrow sense of engaging multiple agencies in some common project or concern and in the wider sense of drawing upon different sorts of agents (individuals, groups, organisations) to engage in the business of governing. The emerging architecture of governance requires multiple agents because specific projects or objectives are not the sole property of a single entity (government or a government department), but the shared concern of different agents and interests. These 'other agents' may be of very different kinds: they may be private corporations, to whom the 'business of the state' is outsourced or subcontracted; they may be voluntary organisations or NGOs, who are recruited to help deliver the 'social agenda' of the government or counter its supposedly negative influence; they may be communities (of interest or place), who are invited to 'govern themselves' in the pursuit of their particular interests; and they are sometimes individuals and families, who are increasingly required to be 'responsible' for their own welfare or well-being (often construed by governments as 'hard-working, responsible families').

This understanding of the multi-agentic character of governance links very different theoretical perspectives: the governance narrative of UK scholars; the dynamic systems view of governance as co-steering; and even post-Foucauldian conceptions of governing at a distance (Kooiman, 1993; Rhodes, 1997; Rose, 1999). The retreat, withdrawal or reorganisation of the state in these new governance arrangements has been the focus of considerable debate – with analyses linking it to: globalisation (and the collapse of the nation-state); neo-liberalism (and the subordination of the political and social domains to the economic); and the increasingly 'ungovernable' complexity of economic and social processes.

The interest in governance has moved analytic attention beyond the state – opening up questions of its disaggregation (Slaughter, 2004), its decentring (McDonald and Marston, 2006) or its dispersal (Clarke and Newman, 1997). These terms are rather different from some of the epochal claims about the disappearance or even death of the state, insisting that the state persists, albeit in new formations, relationships and assemblages. For example, Sharma and Gupta have argued that:

> Neoliberal governmentality is characterized by a competitive market logic and a focus on smaller government that operates from a distance. Neoliberalism works by multiplying sites for regulation and domination through the creation of autonomous entities of government that are not part of the formal state apparatus and are guided by enterprise logic. This government-at-a-distance involves social institutions such as nongovernmental organizations, schools, communities, and even individuals that are not part of any centralized state apparatus and are made responsible for activities formerly carried out by state agencies. Neoliberalism thus represents a shift in the rationality of

government and in the shape and nature of states. (Sharma and Gupta, 2006: 277)

So, rather than governance narratives that talk up the decline or disappearance of the state, our own analysis leads to a concern with the shifting forms that states take and the shifting fields of relationships in which they are enmeshed and engaged (see also Baumann, 1999):

> The conditions through which new political systems are installed, that refer themselves to democracy, bring one to wonder about politics in a context where international presence (EU, UN but also NGOs) redefines the sites of power. International and transnational actors participate in the local power game and contribute to the building and unbuilding of a political space's legitimacy. Where does power lie in these societies? Isn't it the case we have witnessed important displacements in its exercise? Can the body politic be reduced to the sole citizens and political personnel, and what is the status to be given to the various experts that influence the political reality of these countries? Isn't it the case there is a set of actors that implies a re-evaluation of the classical borders of politics? (Petric, 2008: 17–18)

Our aim here is not to pursue the debates around governance in their own terms, but to consider their implications for the changing relationships between states and forms of citizenship. If states are no longer what they were, how do the emerging forms of power and authority create new forms and conditions of, or possibilities for, citizenship? What difference does it make if national borders are policed by subcontracted private agencies? How are the social rights of citizenship affected by being 'delivered' by corporations or charities? What new demands are made of citizens when they are required to be 'active', 'empowered' or 'responsible' in the midst of these changing configurations? However, we think it is important to be wary of treating these changes as marking the death or end of the state. States were never the sole authoritative institution, nor the only site and space of politics. Rather than being faced with the binary choice of the end of the state or the continuity of the state, we need to think of the shifting forms of states and their articulation with other sites and spaces of politics and power (Tambini, 2001). We explore these issues further in the following section.

Pluralising the state

If the relationships between forms of citizenship and states are not universally the same, and if the state-based 'substance' of citizenship is empirically variable, then so too is the form of the state itself. The French state is not the same as the Brazilian state, either in its history, its current institutional formation or its symbolic and political meanings. Similarly, and despite their historic entanglements, the British state is not the state of the US. However, our aim here is not to catalogue difference, either in the forms of citizenship or the patterns of state formation. Rather, we want to insist that the variation of both terms (citizenship and state) demands that simplifying theoretical formulations be avoided. Pluralising the field of relationships between forms of state and forms of citizenship demands attention to historical and geopolitical variation, rather than assuming normative models from which empirically observed deviations or divergences could be measured and evaluated.

Two points should be stressed again here. The first is that our own collective discussion worked, and indeed is still working, through these diversities of forms, projects and enactments. And instead of pretending that their sheer juxtaposition was enough to make sense, we have been struggling with what it means to think comparatively. As noted in the Introduction, the different experiences and knowledges that we bring to bear in our collaboration make it impossible to proceed as if we are dealing with a single and stable object of inquiry: 'citizenship'. But nor can we adopt a conventional view of comparison between states, not least because the state, the national and the nation–state are inherently constructed and unstable formations. What has been called 'methodological nationalism' (Wimmer and Glick-Schiller, 2003) is, then, not a real possibility for organising our work (Clarke, 2005). Instead, we are trying to grasp contexts, conditions and consequences of different state formations as historically specific constructions, recognising that these conditions are also *transnational*. We also place a strong emphasis on the different *trajectories* of these state/national formations as a way of escaping the temptation to reify particular types of state. Such specific formations are always in motion, albeit at different tempos; they are pressed by different sorts of social forces (within and beyond the state's territory); and they are increasingly invited to compare themselves with one another, engage in processes of policy transfer or accommodate the expectations of mobile interests. This emphasis on the transnational combined with attention to trajectories has enabled us to illuminate processes of the contested production of citizenships, rather than to produce a typology or classificatory schema. Let us be clear, though, our discussion of such issues does not aim at addressing all of the dynamics of state formation; here, we are interested in those dimensions and consequences that have effects for how citizenship is thought of, fought for and struggled over.

Too often, states become identified as belonging to a particular type (from a range of typologies: pre-modern/modern/late-modern; democratic/authoritarian; liberal/corporatist/social democratic and so on); or they become treated as the direct and pure embodiment of a specific political project – the conception of 'neo-liberal' states being the most recent. While we appreciate the attraction of typing states in such ways, we think it tends to obscure the diverse political forces that have shaped particular states, leaving their marks and traces on them. Pierre Bourdieu once observed that states are a focus of political conflicts and are marked by those histories, noting that 'The state, in every country, is to some extent the trace in social reality of social conquests' (1998: 33). Those traces make states somewhat fractured and fractious entities, as new political projects not only have to overcome their current opposition, but also have to work to erase or translate those earlier traces. Sharma and Gupta argue that states should be thought of as ensembles – assemblages of ideas (imaginaries of states and state-ness), policies, practices, people and objects (in which state-ness is embodied):

> The state has to be imagined no less than the nation, and for many of the same reasons. The state system is a congeries of functions, bureaus, and levels spread across different sites. Given this institutional and geographical dispersion, an enormous amount of culture work has to be undertaken to construct 'the state' as a singular object.... In the same way, Abrams (1988) asks us to suspend belief in the state as an ontological reality that stands behind what he calls the 'state system' (the institutional apparatus and its practices) and the 'state idea' (the concept that endows 'the state' with its coherence, singularity and legitimacy) and direct our attention to how the state system and the state idea combine to legitimize rule and domination. What becomes central here is how the idea of the state is mobilized in different contexts and how it is imbricated in state institutions and practices. (Gupta and Sharma, 2006: 278–9)

States might be viewed as constituted by layers of institutions that have been formed in different political cycles or periods, containing the traces of earlier projects, struggles and their resolutions. To the extent that the transformation of these institutions is unequal and not completed, the coexistence of institutions founded on the basis of distinct organising principles characterises one version of state heterogeneity (Dagnino et al, 2006). Many – but not all – of these institutionalisations bring questions of citizenship into dispute. At this point, we are moving between the two senses in which we seek to 'pluralise the state'. The first is the insistence that there are different states (rather than 'the state') that are formed in specific historical and geopolitical settings. The second insists that each particular state is itself a composite formation, made up of diverse – and sometimes ill-fitting – elements. Citizenship may be contested, institutionalised and enacted in and by many different parts of these states.

In other words, to avoid gross generalisations and thus missing the specificities of each political project and state project when analysing states and state formations, it is necessary to better distinguish between 'epochal analysis' and 'authentic historical analysis', a distinction articulated by Raymond Williams in order to better locate dominant, residual and emergent cultural forms. 'Epochal analysis' concentrated only on a 'selected and abstracted dominant system', while in doing 'authentic historical analysis', it was 'necessary at every point to recognize the complex interrelations between movements and tendencies both within and beyond a specific and effective dominance' (Williams, 1977: 121). He went on to suggest that in a specific historical moment, it might be useful to organise the multiple – or heterogeneous – movements and tendencies in play by distinguishing between the dominant (itself *containing* different movements and tendencies), the 'residual' (older ideas and institutionalisations that have resisted transformation and persist as active forces in the present) and the 'emergent' (new movements, forces and ways of thinking). The political-cultural work of the dominant tendency involves: trying to maintain its own internal coherence; trying to displace the 'residual' elements (undermining their persistence or apparent relevance to the present); and trying to incorporate elements of the emergent and residual ('transforming' them into apparently supporting the dominant). In this way, the dominant forces can represent themselves as the path to the future that is simultaneously coherent, necessary and inevitable. Indeed, our attention to multiple projects and contestations of citizenship implies that the dominance of specific political projects – and their articulating principles or logics – is always conditional: it is provisional and needs political work to be maintained.

An example of such a moment in which the contested coexistence of dominant and residual political projects of citizenship can be traced can be taken from recent British political history. There, the reconstruction of the citizen as a consumer of public services has been typically treated as an example of anglophone neo-liberalism: the installation of marketised and/or privatised relationships in place of public and collective ones (see the fuller discussion in Clarke et al, 2007b). In such arguments, the citizen is juxtaposed with the consumer as embodying two very divergent types of political figure:

Table 2.1: Citizens or consumers?

CITIZEN	CONSUMER
State	Market
Public	Private
Political	Economic
Collective	Individual
Decommodification	Commodification
Rights	Exchange

Source: Taken from Clarke et al (2007b: 3).

This binary distinction tends to treat each figure as a coherent entity and as excessively 'heroic', standing for a set of political, philosophical principles (ignoring the problems in the practice of each as a mode of relationship to the world). It also fails to address the rather strange figure that was assembled in New Labour politics, a compound or hybrid identification that Clarke et al call the 'citizen-consumer'. Their study draws attention to the political, cultural and discursive work needed to establish this identification in both public and policy terms. That is, rather than simply announcing the neo-liberalisation of the citizen, political-cultural work was needed to make the figure of the citizen-consumer look imaginable, plausible, necessary and inevitable. This is, at least, a question about what sorts of political work are needed to 'clear the landscape', removing or marginalising other orientations, other understandings and other imaginaries so that neo-liberalism can flourish. But it is also a question of how political alliances and political blocs are constructed and how key sections of the public may be mobilised into a voting bloc. Such a bloc needs to be at least compliant with the dominant project's sense of purpose and direction.

We can trace such political work and successive translations of citizenships and political projects in Brazil, where previous dominant conceptions of citizenship have been qualified as '*cidadania regulada*' ('regulated citizenship') (Dos Santos, 1979), and '*cidadania concedida*' ('citizenship by concession') (Sales, 1995). Emerging in different historical contexts, these two versions of citizenship are deeply rooted in Brazilian culture and are still very much alive in the socio-political imaginary. Thus, the struggle of social movements to redefine citizenship and the particular directions it assumed have to be understood within a historical context, as a struggle to break up and confront dominant conceptions and the practices they guide. Dos Santos (1979) coined the expression '*cidadania regulada*' ('regulated citizenship') to designate what has been the first relatively wide and systematic recognition of social rights by the state in Brazilian history, through the Consolidation of Labor Laws in 1943. However, such recognition did not have a universal character, but was restricted to workers, and only those workers in professions recognised and regulated by the state were entitled to social rights. Most importantly, only workers belonging to unions recognised and regulated (that is to say, controlled) by the state were entitled to social rights. Such a version of citizenship ingeniously intertwined the recognition of both social rights and the political existence of workers and their organisations with state political control over unions and workers. Thanks to this ambiguity, it constituted one of the pillars of the populist arrangement that presided over Brazilian politics until 1964. In addition, it promoted an exclusionary view of citizenship as a condition strictly related to labour that, as mentioned earlier, is still very much alive in Brazilian society. In spite of all this, this version of citizenship and the notion of rights became deeply rooted in Brazilian culture. '*Buscar os meus direitos*' ('Go look for my rights') is a common expression in popular vocabulary and this awareness was surely important when social movements, in the 1980s, relied on citizenship and rights as a central element in their political projects and began to formulate new versions of them.

Although one can see signs of it in what was just described, the conception of citizenship as a concession ('*cidadania concedida*') is found by Sales (1995) to have its roots in a more remote past. Seen as emerging from the rule of large landowners (*latifundiários*), whose private power within their rural domains was converted into political power in the Brazilian state and society after the Republican advent at the end of the 19th century, this view of citizenship is an attempt to account for what would be, in fact, an absence of citizenship. It relied on a conception of rights as mediated by power relations characterised by rule and submission, transferred from the private to the public (civil) domain. In this conception, rights are conceived of as favours, as 'gifts' from the powerful, in what Sales calls 'a culture of gift' ('*cultura da dádiva'*). The maxim, as put by Sales, 'In Brazil either you give orders or you beg' (*'No Brasil ou bem se manda ou bem se pede'*) expresses an authoritarian oligarchic conception of politics, characterised by favouritism, clientelism and tutelage mechanisms. In it, the lack of distinction between the private and public realms obstructs the emergence of a notion of rights as rights and stimulates a conception of rights as favours. It is in this sense that *'cidadania concedida'* can be seen as, in fact, a peculiar 'absence' of citizenship. This peculiarity relies on the fact that rights would be present but they are not recognised as such, but rather as gifts, favours from those who have the power to concede them. The rooting of this view in Brazilian culture expresses the resilience of social authoritarianism and still obstructs the political organisation of the excluded (on this issue, see also Holston, 2008) and enlarges the political autonomy of the elites. Sales' recognition of how the perception of rights is replaced by that of favours stands out in the vast Brazilian literature on citizenship (Covre, 1986; Demo, 1995; Carvalho, 2001; Souza, 2003), mostly characterised by registering its precariousness or its absence, due to the failure of the state in ensuring rights, to the extent to which it reveals the complex cultural mechanism that hinders the increasing of struggles for citizenship in the country.

In problematising states so as to grasp differently citizenship issues, then, we would draw attention to similar dynamics, as previously dominant projects, understandings and principles have to be overcome: incorporated, subordinated, residualised or translated into new alignments (Newman and Clarke, 2009). States – and their specific apparatuses, agencies, personnel and organisational and occupational cultures – form the terrain for negotiation, compromise and even outright conflict as new political projects attempt their reforming missions. For instance, former British Prime Minister Tony Blair once claimed (in characteristically messianic tones) that his attempts to reform public services meant that: 'I bear the scars on my back after two years in government' (Blair, 1999). If such 'blockages' and 'interminglings' of different and successive political projects within state formations are significant, they also link to other arguments, which enable the distancing of oneself from overly abstract or purely institutional understandings of the state(s). In their introduction to their collection on *The anthropology of the state*, Sharma and Gupta argue that the 'conditions for studying the state have shifted', requiring 'new ways of thinking' (2006: 27). The first response, they argue, involves thinking of the state through questions of culture; an argument that is clearly in line with what has been said earlier on the intimate embeddedness of political projects in cultural formations:

> The first analytic move entailed in reconceptualizing states consists of seeing them as culturally embedded and discursively constituted ensembles. Instead of viewing states as preconstituted institutions that perform given functions, we argued that they are produced through everyday practices and encounters and through public cultural representations and performances.... Thinking about how states are culturally constituted, how they are substantiated in people's lives, and about the socio-political and everyday consequences of these constructions, involves moving beyond macro-level institutional analyses of 'the state' to looking at social and bureaucratic practices and encounters and at public cultural texts. It requires conducting institutional ethnographies of specific state bureaucracies, inquiring into the micropolitics and daily practices of such institutions, and seeking to understand their relation to the public (elite or subaltern) that they serve. (Sharma and Gupta, 2006: 27).

States are indeed made up of diverse and differentiated *organisational elements* – departments, levels, functions, places and personnel – whose interrelationships may be more or less tightly coupled and that may be driven by different – and potentially contradictory – articulating principles (eg environmental protection versus business development; social justice versus social discipline). States are also organised according to different 'levels' – federal or central, regional and municipal, for instance – another potential source of heterogeneity, as distinct, even oppositional, projects come to occupy these different levels. There are important implications for citizenship that relate to the different degrees of openness to claims for rights that these different levels of states present, or to how divergent conceptions of what citizenship might be, that are carried by different political projects, are translated into policies and practices. In Brazil, for instance, as the Workers' Party (*Partido dos Trabalhadores* – PT) began its ascension to state power in the late 1980s, first at the city and then at the state (regional) level, experiences such as the Participatory Budgeting of Porto Alegre, through which citizens enlarged their citizenship rights, becoming able to participate in deciding about investment alternatives at the city level, contrasted radically with the situation of neighbouring cities, where repression and authoritarian mechanisms were predominant. When the PT finally reached the federal government in 2002, however, the very alliances with more conservative parties that made possible its election contributed to obstruct the recognition of rights such as, for example, to abortion and to the civil union of homosexual couples. In addition, the distribution of positions in the federal state apparatus among those different parties that have characterised the PT's government since 2002 up to this day accentuated the diversity of orientations and the lack of coherence in the different state institutions.

In a rather different way, the development of community safety as a focus of policing in the UK has mainly been treated as a site of an expanded or authoritarian state, associated with British varieties of neo-liberalism (not least through the recruitment of 'communities' to responsibilities of self-governing). However, a number of authors have pointed to the less than coherent ensemble of institutional arrangements, relationships, principles and practices that result, particularly at different levels of the state. Kevin Stenson, writing about the spread of an authoritarian, neo-liberal and penal approach to crime and community safety in the UK, has demonstrated how a specific set of alliances among different agencies and their staff in one area produced rather different local outcomes. Stenson argues that 'three overlapping networks … powerfully carried and reproduced liberal, universalistic, "social" ideologies and helped insulate against conservative, communitarian, nationalist moral agendas' (2008) in local community safety practices. Thus, local government officers, including community safety ones, had considerable commitment to more holistic, 'social' approaches to community safety, and resisted the narrowness and superficiality of central government crime reduction targets. Second, there were 'progressive' police officers, accountable to the law, which manifested transcendent sovereign authority in relation to sectional local interests, but who were also part of a regional police force with a relatively liberal culture, and hostile to the rhetoric of 'zero tolerance policing'. The third group was the Thames Valley Partnership, a multi-agency network dedicated to a 'progressive, holistic, "social", demographically inclusive approach to community safety' (Stenson, 2008). This alliance developed an approach to policing and community safety that diverged in critical respects from the dominant national agenda.

This particular configuration of agencies and actors might be understood as a site within the state in which it is possible to see *in practice* the distinction – and encounters – between dominant, residual and emergent political-cultural formations. Policies might be understood as enmeshed in, and produced by, several overlapping processes of translation (Shore and Wright, 1997; Smith, 2005; Lendvai and Stubbs, 2007). On one side, policies – the documents of official intention – are themselves the outcome of translations between the objectives or desires of political projects and the existing institutional field (current policies, agencies, agents and understandings). Second, policies themselves become the object of translations, for example, into guidelines, advice, instructions that (re)organise the existing institutional field, bringing into play new objectives to be managed, new organisational structures and systems, new demands on staff, or new forms of liaison with other organisations: what might be called 'the small print' begins to specify what the objectives of a policy are supposed to mean in practice. But such instructions and documents are also translated into practice by agents within the organisations(s) involved – by managers, who may inflect policy to their existing orientations (political, professional, local), and by workers, who try to render policy manageable, usable and survivable, not least by working on the unresolved contradictions, tensions and dilemmas that policies may contain (for different views of dilemmas in public service policy and practice, see, eg, Lipsky, 1980; Hoggett, 2005; Spire, 2005; Newman, 2007). As stated by Shore and Wright:

> Policies are inherently and unequivocally *anthropological* phenomena. They can be read by anthropologists in a number of ways: as cultural texts, as classificatory devices with various meanings, as narratives that serve to justify or condemn the present, or as rhetorical devices and discursive formations that function to empower some people and silence others. Not only do policies codify social norms and values, and articulate fundamental organizing principles of society, they also contain implicit (and sometimes explicit) models of society. (Shore and Wright, 1997: 7)

In the same spirit, Lopez Caballero (2009) insists that the existing variation between the state model (laws, constitution, institutions) and its practical implementation is not a result to be demonstrated but an analytical premise.

Citizenship imaginaries and political projects are undoubtedly part of such processes, and undergo similar 'translations', which also include the translation of contestations into state policies. The idea of translation has been used to describe both how concepts, projects, models and policies move from place to place and how ideas are translated into practices. In these processes of translation, reworkings, slippages, elisions and transformations can be traced – as conceptions of citizenship move from collective inspiration to programmes, from programmes to manifestos, from manifestos to policy statements, from statements to laws, from laws to guidelines for implementation, from guidelines to office regulations, and from regulations to practices/encounters with 'citizens' at the front line/front door of the state (Smith, 2005). At each moment of translation, other logics may be brought into play, which bend, inflect, and concretise the previous idea/conception in different ways. The existing dominant logics may be at work in such processes attempting – in Raymond Williams' terms – to incorporate emergent alternatives ('domesticating' them; or realigning them with the demands of legal codification, economic realism and managerial efficiency). But translation may also involve unlocking and reworking previously dominant conceptions into new configurations, seeking to either bring them into alignment with older (residual) logics or inflect them with newly emergent imaginaries and desires.

During the apogee of neo-liberal years in Brazil, from 1989 to the mid-2000s, redefinitions of citizenship were undertaken given the symbolical and mobilising power that the notion had reached since the late 1970s within the socio-political imaginary of social movements and subaltern sectors. Some of those redefinitions recuperate the traditional liberal conception of citizenship; others are innovative and address new elements of the contemporary political and social configurations in Latin America. Two of their main characteristics are: reducing the collective meaning entailed in the social movements' own redefinition of citizenship to a strictly individualistic understanding of it; and establishing an alluring connection between citizenship and the market. Being a citizen came to mean individual integration into the market, as a consumer and as a producer. Thus, a vast number of projects to enable people to 'acquire citizenship' aim at teaching them how to initiate micro-enterprises, or become qualified for the few jobs still being offered, and so on. In a context where the state progressively withdrew from its role as guarantor of rights, the market is offered as a surrogate instance of citizenship. Hence, social rights ensured in the Brazilian Constitution since the 1940s, for example, have been eliminated under the rationale that they constitute obstacles to the free operation of the dynamics of the market and are therefore restrictive of economic development and modernisation. A peculiar inversion took place: the recognition of rights seen in the recent past as an indicator of modernity is becoming a symbol of 'backwardness', an 'anachronism' that hinders the modernising potential of the market (Telles, 2001). The formulation of social policies towards poverty and inequality provides for yet another dimension of the building of neo-liberal versions of citizenship. A large part of the struggles organised around the demand for equal rights and the extension of citizenship have focused on the definition of such social policies, which were to be formulated with the participation of citizens themselves, as established by the 1988 Constitution. But with the advancement of the neo-liberal project and the reduction in the role of the state, those social policies were increasingly formulated as strictly emergency efforts directed to certain specific sectors of society whose conditions for survival are at extreme risk. The targets of these policies are not seen as citizens entitled to rights, but as 'needy' human beings to be contemplated by public or private charity.

A number of consequences derived from this, which had important impacts on the dispute between the different conceptions of citizenship at stake. A first consequence relates to a displacement of issues such as poverty and inequality: as they are dealt with strictly as issues of technical or philanthropic management, poverty and inequality are being withdrawn from the public (political) arena and from its proper domain, that of justice, equality and citizenship, and reduced to a problem of ensuring minimal conditions for survival. Hyatt makes a somewhat similar analysis in the British context of the 1990s, when she states that:

> Post-welfare policies, like tenant self-management, are thus imbued with the promise that they are able to change 'welfare dependants' into active citizens thereby enfranchising public sector tenants into the world of productive and entrepreneurial activity without any need to invest significant public resources.... Any discussion of poverty as inequality or disadvantage has been effaced from the discourse on housing reform all together. (Hyatt, 1997: 232)

In this sense, Brazil presents one instance of the wider neo-liberal logic of combining market-based individualism with a powerful combination of anti-collectivism and anti-welfarism. Citizenship is thereby 'thinned' and relocated as a responsibility of the citizen to be self-maintaining (see, *inter alia*, on the UK, Clarke, 2005; on the US, Goode and Maskovsky, 2002; on forms of post-welfare provision, Fairbanks, 2009).

Moreover, the new Brazilian solution to such problems as poverty was presented as a moral duty of every individual in society. Thus, the idea of a collective solidarity that underlies the historical reference to rights and citizenship was replaced by an understanding of solidarity as a strictly private moral responsibility. Hence, civil society organisations and individuals were urged to engage in voluntary work and philanthropic actions, under the appeal to a re-signified notion of citizenship now embodied in this particular understanding of solidarity as a moral and individual duty (on the 'moral neo-liberal' in Italy, see also Muehlebach, 2012). Such a re-signification of citizenship and solidarity blocks their possibilities for political mobilisation and erodes the references to a public responsibility and a public interest, so laboriously built through the democratising struggles of Brazil's recent past. As the distribution of social services and benefits tended to occupy the place formerly held by rights and citizenship, the claim for rights has been obstructed since there were no institutional channels for it: through the effort to shrink state responsibilities, social policies were transferred to 'partnerships' with NGOs and private foundations, so that such a distribution would depend only on the goodwill and competence of the involved sectors. Even more dramatic, the very formulation of rights, their enunciation as a public question, became increasingly unable to be realised (Telles, 2001).

The symbolic efficacy of rights in the building of an egalitarian society was thus diluted and the consequence has been a reinforcement of an already powerful privatism as the dominant code orienting social relations. Similar processes have been observed in other contexts, especially by scholars working on development policies and 'good governance'; thus, in her introduction to an issue of the journal *Autrepart*, Atlani-Duault asks about the growing part NGOs are called on to play in development programmes:

> is there not a danger of 'a capture by the best organized interests, using their public accesses to maintain their revenues' (Papadopoulos 2002: 141)?... Does not the growing dependency of these NGOs from the South towards international funding dedicated to the promotion of good governance, and their growing responsibilities in sectors of public life previously managed by the states, question their proximity with those they are supposed to represent, especially when they do not succeed in having their voices heard through representative democracy? (Atlani-Duault, 2005a: 6–7)

In the same issue, Quentin underlines, in her analysis of housing policies in Venezuela and Ecuador, that:

> by placing on a technical level what usually belongs to the political debate, the aim is not any more to discuss about the

> most legitimate actor to guarantee the universality of public
> services, or even about the necessity of such universality,
> but to judge which actor is the more adapted in terms of
> profitability and efficiency. (Quentin, 2005)

Atlani-Duault continues:

> Behind aims – civil society participation, decentralisation,
> privatisation – that correspond to hardly debatable values
> such as solidarity, (participative) democracy, transparency
> and equality, the new political agenda of good governance
> thus offers a particularly efficient tool to the deepening of
> the neoliberal logic. (2005: 8)

Thus, policies and governmental and state practices, in their diversity
and heterogeneity, are as many attempts to implement, propose or
impose new, reworked, different or already-there political projects
of citizenship; they entertain complex relations with those political
projects emerging from mobilisations and social movements, especially
in a period when the borders between states, 'civil societies', NGOs,
international institutions or global cities are blurred, or rather in the
process of being rearranged into new bundlings.

What we might describe as state–citizen encounters are thus
intrinsically heterogeneous, sometimes deceptive and vary from place to
place. They range from delivering rights and services, through enabling
and empowering people, to regulating, policing and disciplining, or
recognising and categorising (see Trouillot, 2001). Indeed, everyday
interactions between people and state agencies often centre on
'recognition' in various ways: as a citizen, as a member of the public,
as worthy/deserving/entitled, as national, as suspicious, as stranger/
foreigner and so on. State–citizen encounters also include moments
of decision when the identity of the person as citizen is accepted,
legitimated, validated and enacted – or questioned, denied and contested.
Such encounters are always moments of indeterminacy in which the
state's empowered agents decide the status of the person (when a specific
form of legal status is what is at stake). Such decisions (enacting legal
citizenship) are always consequential: enabling or denying access to
both material and symbolic value (recognition being the key to forms
of mobility, benefits, services and more). Quotidian encounters with
states both tell people who they are and form the potential settings
for disputation. Because of the frequent conflation of citizenship and
nationality (discussed later), border controls and immigration processing

are among the most visible sites of such decision-making, but many other encounters with and categorisations by agencies and agents of the state act on and through this type of decision (medical care, housing, encounters with the police, etc). For state agents, there is always the possibility of 'discovering' the non-citizen (those whose identities or claims are not 'genuine'), and the search to identify such not-entitled individuals and groups has intensified in countries of the global North as they reassemble the relationships between nationality and citizenship (Balibar, 2002; Clarke, 2004).

Such processes, as well as the heterogeneity of the state, are clearly legible in a 2010 law famously passed by the US state of Arizona (referred to widely as SB1070 for Arizona Senate Bill 1070). SB1070 mandated that all state and local police stop and interrogate anyone they have 'a reasonable suspicion' might be an undocumented migrant. The law specified that the state's 'compelling interest' is to eliminate immigration across its border with Mexico, or 'attrition through enforcement', and made no effort to conceal, obscure or prevent its interpretation as a law targeting Latino/as. The law borrowed the passbook model of population control from apartheid-era South Africa and mandates that everyone in Arizona carry a valid state driver's license, identification card, passport or proof of Native tribal membership. The law criminalised the 'wilful failure to carry' such proof of legal status, with mandatory charges and sentences for all who fail to comply with the law, legal citizens or not. As Latino/a civil rights advocates and even some local law enforcement agencies were quick to point out, SB1070 mandated racial profiling by the police and extended local government's powers into the realm of federal immigration law enforcement. The response to the passage of the law was immediate massive civil disobedience at the state capitol, boycotts by other state governments and nations, and national proliferation of popular expressions such as T-shirts with large letters asking 'Do I look illegal?'. In early July, under tremendous political pressure to respond to the law, US Attorney General Eric Holder filed a complaint in federal court against Arizona and its governor, requesting that the court declare SB1070 unconstitutional and thereby prevent it from taking effect. Three years after its passage, in June 2013, a federal judge ruled that the law's biggest advocate, Sheriff Joe Arpaio of Phoenix and his office were guilty of systematic racial profiling of Latina/os in their patrols and detentions. Despite such challenges, the momentum the law's passage has created against Latinos' and immigrants' claims for rights and equality cannot be understated. After discovering that many of the students protesting the law's passage had taken Chicano Studies classes, the governor immediately announced her intention to outlaw all ethnic studies instruction in public schools and colleges. Several other state governments also quickly introduced similar bills in their own legislatures. And while the US Attorney General argued against the state government's right to interfere in federal matters, including international relations with Mexico, the Obama administration continued meeting its own 1,000 deportations per day quota for its immigration agencies. While states like Arizona criminalised Latina/o people in the name of border enforcement, the federal Immigration Control and Enforcement agency initiated the Secure Communities (S-Comm) programme to integrate local-level law enforcement with federal immigration agencies via the sharing of fingerprints and detaining 'suspected' undocumented persons. While the stated purpose of the programme was to identify and deport 'criminal aliens', approximately three quarters of the over 280,000 people deported under S-Comm by the middle of 2013 had no record of 'Level One' serious crimes and one in three had no criminal record at all. The citizenship questions of civil rights, alienage, divisions of state power, sovereignty and authority are all bound up in this dispute, as well as tensions or antagonisms between different 'state levels' and their respective political projects. The logics of securitisation, criminalisation of publics and increased precarity of rights in wartime are not new, but the extension of surveillance and incarceration regimes across and between levels of government, as well as the degree of integration of for-profit private concerns in the mechanics of enforcement and detention, are noteworthy.

Such situations and examples show the extent to which states' and (non-)citizens' practices and representations should be approached and analysed by considering how states also work at the most local levels – the house, the street, the neighbourhood – and grasp populations through recording, enumerating and categorising them through censuses (see, eg, Chatterjee, 2004; Ruppert, 2007). These are sites of what Painter (2006) calls the 'prosaic geographies of stateness', or Ferguson and Gupta (2002: 981) call 'the everyday practices of spatialising states'. Painter argues – like Sharma and Gupta – for treating the state as an idea or an imaginary that is materialised in a variety of institutional arrangements, personnel and practices:

> Building on Mitchell's and Abrams' interpretations, it makes sense to define 'the state' as an imagined collective actor in whose name individuals are interpellated (implicitly or explicitly) as citizens or subjects, aliens or foreigners,

and which is imagined as the source of central political authority for a national territory. The use of 'imagined' here does not mean that relationships and processes involved are illusory: social imaginaries can have very real effects (Anderson, 1983; Castoriadis, 1987). Moreover, the practices, mechanisms and institutions through which processes of interpellation take place are very real. When I apply for a passport identifying me as a citizen of a state, the passport, the office and the officials that issue it, and the border post through which it allows me to pass all exist. However, the state in whose name they function is neither an aggregation of these elements, nor a separate reality behind them, but a symbolic resource on which they draw to produce their effects. (Painter, 2006: 758)

Fassin has stressed how US-based anthropologists have considered the everyday stuff (*matière*) of states and politics, analysing:

the most harmless (anodyne) but often most decisive, sites and topics.... Through such, sometimes marginal, sites and topics, authors try hard to grasp the 'working state', to understand how it acts on people and how, by so doing, it unveils itself. (Fassin, 2008: 179–80)

Examples include checkpoints in Sri Lanka that allow for a cartography of the state's territorial control, or prisons in Utah that allow for an analysis of the state's punitive policy. In a study of the evolution of the documents required in order to establish someone's French nationality, Asad (2004) shows how, far from being arbitrary, the growing requirements for certificates show the deployment of a state suspicion that undermines the trust mechanisms along which life in society is generally rendered possible. Such an approach centred on the 'working state' allows us to grasp 'the presence of the State not as an abstract entity that would actualize prestigious institutions, but as an actual operator intervening in the way people live' (Fassin, 2008: 180). Indeed, anthropologists have been particularly aware of the need to problematise the notion of 'state', especially in the context of economic globalisation; thus, Trouillot underlines that since the state's presence becomes more deceptive, the relevant strategy would be:

to focus on the multiple sites in which state processes and practices are recognizable through their effects. These effects include (1) *an isolation effect*, that is, the production of atomized individualized subjects molded and modeled for governance as part of an undifferentiated but specific 'public'; (2) *an identification effect*, that is, a realignment of the atomized subjectivities along collective lines within which individuals recognize themselves as the same; (3) *a legibility effect*, that is, the production of both a language and a knowledge for governance and of theoretical and empirical tools that classify and regulate collectivities; and (4) *a spatialization effect*, that is, the production of boundaries and jurisdiction. (Trouillot, 2001: 126)

It is to the exploration and discussion of some of these effects that the next sections and chapter of this book will turn to, focusing the discussion on issues of citizenship processes.

Decentering the state in practice

The gap between the imagined state and the everyday workings of particular states not only is a point of departure for the academic analysis of the state, but provides a resource for popular understandings of the relationship between states and citizenship. Here, too, we find 'decentring' the state in relation to citizenship a useful move. In everyday understandings, practices and projects, the state is rarely a simple or singular object to which citizenship is clearly attached. We think it is worth exploring some of the shifting, ambivalent and contradictory ways in which the state, and/or the government, is envisaged in popular imaginaries of citizenship. As earlier, we stress that 'decentring' is not the same as making the state disappear, but is an issue of relocating it in a field of relationships, practices and projects. We begin with popular doubts and fears about the state, before exploring popular desires, but this distinction needs to be understood as a formal one – in the everyday, popular conceptions of the state are often an ambivalent mixture of such doubts and desires. This ambivalent mixture is also a result of what we said earlier about the heterogeneity and multilayered composition of states: the imaginaries, the different political projects and histories each society, or group of societies, has gone through, if they have produced such heterogeneity, are also to be found in popular/ordinary representations and visions of the state's role towards citizens.

In the US, dominant political discourses articulate a popular anxiety about the state – too big, too intrusive, too expensive – that constrains and inhibits individual freedoms, development, autonomy and so on. The claimed objective is to minimise the costs to citizens' liberty and money/capital, with the exception of expenses aiming at defending the nation, inside and outside, against its enemies, which produces the expanding military, security, police state. Despite an alternative, intermittent, incomplete thinking that what enables the full development, flourishing and so on of all individuals is a level of collective provisioning, protection and guarantees, the dominant emphasis in the US is on 'independence' from the state. The problems of the compromised, imperfect and now increasingly undermined and under-resourced forms of public provision have tended to accentuate popular doubts about the state – since the public realm is equated with impoverished institutions, only suitable for those who have no choice. More generally, the 'big state' is bad and is typically associated with 'socialism' or 'communism'. At the same time, it is important to recognise the ambivalence of the political Right about the state. On the one hand, they distrust the power of the state, are antagonistic to public provision and denounce the 'interference' with the freedoms of the individual and the market. On the other hand, the Right also desire a state, or at least a particular form of the state, that will provide corporate welfare, endow corporations with ever-greater political status, install social order and discipline, and seek to produce ideal citizen-subjects through varying forms of discipline and control.

Popular cynicism about the corruption of government (in bed with the rich and powerful) is both confirmed and transformed by the legitimation of such entanglements of private interests and public institutions: the enthusiasm for doing business with business, the commitment to making corporations citizens and enabling them to be political subjects by granting them rights to free speech, political participation and so on (see, for instance, Isiksel, 2013).

The diverse institutions through which citizens might be recognised (and denied) points to the importance of grasping a complex terrain of relationships, practices and identifications in which citizenship may be enacted. Sharma, writing about Dalit women in India, argues that they mobilise a complex, heteroglossic set of conceptions of rights, entitlements and justice in enacting themselves as citizens:

> They positioned themselves as knowledgeable and deserving citizens, who had been short-changed by a corrupt local administration and who deserved government resources as their right; this was a direct challenge to official caricatures of their identities as unaware, irresponsible, and immoral. Furthermore, they used standard bureaucratic mechanisms,

such as applications, to petition for rights, on the one hand. On the other hand, however, they used the older idiom of 'mai-baap' and the parental duty it invoked, to hold officials accountable. 'Mai-baap' referenced a different time and moral universe where just rulers, like good parents, were ethically bound to care for their wards.

These subaltern women's positioning of the state as a caretaker and direct provider of material benefits as rights for the disenfranchised was in direct contrast to how some officials, such as Vivek Rai in New Delhi, saw the state. Castigating the 'mai-baap' syndrome and 'dole system' that the populist welfare state had fostered, Rai argued that the ideal role of the state was as 'a catalyst, a facilitator' of development and not provider; development, he argued, was the duty of civil society and communities. Nimani's female residents contested such neoliberal renditions of normative state and citizen identities and roles by positioning themselves as informed *yet* victimized citizens-cum-wards of an ideal parental and caring moral state. Nimani's women, like Shyama, spoke a radically particular (Chakrabarty, 2002) language of justice and belonging, as subjects who had been wronged in specific ways and whose oppression could not be addressed in statist legal terms alone. Law, as Chakrabarty suggests, 'can never address the victim … in her own language' (2002, p. 111); it has to be informed by different cultural narratives. In addition to formal, bureaucratic languages, the women in Nimani had to call upon other idioms, including kinship and moral duty, to claim personhood, rights, justice and citizenship as marginalized others. (Sharma, 2011: 974–5; emphasis in original)

Sharma's example offers a reminder that the issue of what sort of institutions (and discourses) populate this landscape is not merely an academic question. Rather, it is important to ask what sorts of institutions are operative in popular imaginaries of citizenship, and which ones (and how and why) are endowed with 'stateness' (Hansen and Steputtat, 2001). Ferguson and Gupta (2002) focus on the 'idea of the state', but is that the only idea that is in circulation? Do (differently located) people imagine spaces of freedom, public spaces, spaces of association and even spaces of action that are other than the state in which citizenly relationships, actions and conduct might take place?

In imagining themselves (or not) as citizens, people enact diverse conceptions of the state, of themselves or of their relationships with state agencies or policies. In her comparison of 'practising democracy' in France and Finland, which we mentioned in the previous chapter, Luhtakiallo found important differences. Among activists in France, 'citizenship' made them think of the state as an institution ruling from above – composed of borders, the political system and national symbolism. In contrast, Finnish activists 'were, all in all, conspicuously comfortable with the notion of citizenship ... they seemed to discern citizenship not as coercive and given, but something that was theirs to define' and the state was not understood as an external and oppressive weight. Luhtakiallo clearly shows how such representations of oneself-as-a-citizen were connected to specific historical conceptions and bundlings as to the relationships between the state and citizens, as mediated or not through forms of association.

So, a variety of sometimes complex resources can be mobilised by citizens and/or subaltern social groups in imagining – and demanding – citizenship; as Sharma shows in the Indian case:

> Subaltern claims on citizenship, articulated from a position of subordination and difference, not equality, and through specific idioms, contest and radically transform the generic and universal slot of personhood that liberalism provides – one that is rational, secular, sovereign, generic and individualistic. Their citizenship claims draw upon multiple discourses, extending well beyond the law, mixing morality and materiality, ethics and politics, and traditional and bureaucratic languages of power, and thereby muddying the very distinctions on which modern citizenship rests. Subaltern struggles over development, thus, force us to reconsider hardened, normative ideas of legal citizenship and to widen the scope through which we look at and think about rights claims, justice, personhood and, indeed, the state in the neoliberal era. (2011: 968)

Posing such questions would allow us to extend the questions of popular ambivalence about the state to the question of the peculiar, liminal status of institutions and organisations that also operate in this space of ambivalence, and may also be equally desired and distrusted (just like the state).

In a growing number of places, popular needs and desires are indeed addressed, and sometimes met, by organisations that work alongside or instead of the state. A variety of institutions and organisations operate in these sites alongside, in the shadow of and against the (nation) state. Some are transnational/international agencies, such as the Catholic Church, providing forms of welfare, education and social provision. Others are insurgent organisations that come to serve as both political and governmental organisations in opposition to the 'official' state, such as Hezbollah in the Lebanon as a welfare organisation (Jawad, 2009) and paramilitary organisations in Peru that provide forms of order and social provision in spaces that the state cannot govern (Nugent, 1997). These different formations appear under the sign of the non-governmental, so starting from an interest in popular understandings opens up a different take on how non-state, para-state, non-governmental, third sector, civil society organisations occupy this liminal space of popular desire and doubt. It is, of course, not a single space, but is always a particular space in a specific social formation. We need to emphasise the diversity of arrangements, relationships and institutionalisations that populate this space that is so simply categorised as 'civil society'. A number of studies in a collection edited by Hann and Dunn (1996) indicate something of this richness, and how the formations exceed – and challenge – conventional Western models of civil society. Some – such as Dunn's (1996) work on American Mormons – emphasise the religious and familial foundations of forms of solidarity; while Anderson (1996) explores the communal practices of resistance to, and negotiation with, the bureaucratic regimes of state collectivism. Anderson also considers how the defence of particular forms of social rights – in the transition from the Soviet regime – might be voiced, paradoxically, through a profoundly ethno-nationalist discourse and forms of political action. In the same collection, Flower and Leonard make a compelling argument that their study of 'civil society' in China might lead to a different conclusion:

> But it would be more fruitful to ask how the Chinese experience might lead us to rethink the idea of civil society itself. This rethinking would have to involve an approach decentred from the western tradition and open to native categories of conceptualising experience. One implication drawn from China is that there is no necessary link between market relations and the nature of civil society. 'Traditional' affective ties are not only capable of engendering a civil space but, in some cases, these are greatly preferred to commoditisation. Another lesson to be gleaned from China is that the state and its agents are considered members of,

rather than mere antagonists to, the civil society. Thus, state-versus-society frameworks need to be broken down to allow room for flexible interactions, and some more nuanced analyses of the blurry, multilayered roles of state agents in civil institutions. (1996: 219–20)

We have tried to indicate something of this complexity of the state – and its agents – in our discussions so far. There are good grounds for loosening the stranglehold of the state–civil society distinction (and variants on it such as Somers' [2008] demarcation of state, market and civil society) in favour of attention to shifting and complexly articulated formations of power (see Ferguson, 2004; Atlani-Duault, 2005b; Petric, 2008). Nevertheless, Hansen and Steppputat point to the continuing salience of the 'myth of the state':

> This myth of the state seems to persist in the face of everyday experiences of the often profoundly violent and ineffective practices of government or outright collapse of states. It persists because the state, or institutionalized sovereign government, remains pivotal in our very imagination of what a society is. Whether we agree on what the state means or not, 'it' is, nonetheless, central to all that is *not* state: civil society, NGOs, the notion of national economy, the market, and the sense of an international community....
>
> Whereas certain forms of state intervention may be loathed and resisted, other and more egalitarian forms of governance, or more benign forms of authority, may at the same time be intensely desired and asked for. Everyday forms of state power, in other words, are always suffused with and mediated by politics: contestation of authority, open defiance, as well as attempts to divert or privatize resources. (Hansen and Steppputat, 2001: 2, 9)

We have tried to stress the importance of unlocking such myths (in academic theory as well as in social life) as a way of stressing that citizenship is practised in mixed and shifting landscapes of institutions and agencies – of which the state's apparatuses form only a part (if a critically visible part). In the UK, there has been a network of NGOs/civil society organisations that provide advice to citizens (this section draws upon an unpublished paper by Clarke). Citizens Advice Bureaux (CABx) are 'local' associations, connected to and supported by national bodies (Citizens Advice and Citizens Advice Scotland). They began in

1939 partly as a response to the anticipated disorders and dislocations for citizens facing war. But they also were a response to the experience of the Depression: the idea of a voluntary advice service was first raised alongside reforms of the Public Assistance system in 1924. By 2009, there were 416 bureaux offering advice from over 3,300 locations in England and Wales and a further 22 bureaux in Northern Ireland and 83 in Scotland, involving around 20,000 volunteers at any one time. CABx have become an institutionalised feature of the organisational landscape: providing independent advice, yet supported by large amounts of public funding (largely from local government but with more specific funding from other public agencies, ranging from health trusts to the Commission for Legal Services).

CABx offer free and independent advice to anyone (whether officially a 'citizen' or not), and the advice is provided in a process that is understood as a *citizen-to-citizen* interaction: the advice work is largely performed by volunteers, supported by specialist advisors in a range of fields: debt, benefits, housing and family, employment and immigration law. The CAB principles stress both the confidentiality of the process and its *independence*: Citizens Advice is explicitly not a state agency, so its conception of citizenship is fundamentally a horizontal one, rather than the vertical one involved in relationships between the state and the citizen as applicant, claimant, supplicant, user, consumer and so on. This independence is important for the service since much advice work involves dealing with, and challenging, state/public bodies on issues such as immigration, benefit entitlements and housing.

Citizens Advice involves a unique conception of citizenship within the UK. There are no other organisations that announce themselves as primarily about *citizens*: there are state and voluntary associations that address people in many other identities (parents, consumers, residents, communities, bearers of special needs, etc), but none that address the generic identity. And although there are many voluntary organisations providing forms of help, advice and services, there are none in which the volunteers are also understood as citizens. Indeed, the name of the organisation does not distinguish between citizens as givers of advice and citizens as recipients of advice. These horizontal encounters set up some interesting questions about the practice of citizenship. First, the bureaux do not apply any sort of citizenship test. That is to say, a person does not have to be a legally recognised citizen to use CAB services or ask for advice. In an era when public agencies are increasingly expected to check the nationality and legal status of people using services, this broad presumption of citizenship is symbolically significant. It is also practically significant given that much of CAB work has involved immigration law and, in some areas, has also involved working with migrant workers to offer advice and legal support. Second, the process is almost wholly 'user-driven', that is, the encounters are inaugurated by people seeking advice. Do people have to recognise themselves as 'citizens' before they make contact with the bureaux? It is not clear if this is necessary, since Citizens Advice advertises itself in both general terms and as offering advice with particular sorts of troubles (housing, immigration, employment, debt, etc). It would be interesting to know to what extent those seeking advice and those providing the service think of themselves – and each other – as citizens (rather than, eg, users and clients).

Citizens Advice is distinctive in its horizontal and egalitarian conception of citizenship. This is both an image and a practice of citizenship that has never been effectively installed in the welfare state, for example. There, citizenship has been more conditional in many ways (subject to a variety of tests and forms of scrutiny). Its conditional character is probably best summed up in the idea of those seeking welfare benefits as 'claimants': those making claims, rather than receiving their entitlements. In the welfare context, citizenship has become increasingly conditional through the last 30 years. The same degradation does not seem to have affected Citizens Advice (although it has certainly generated increased demand for advice).

Nevertheless, it is important not to romanticise this egalitarian conception of citizen-to-citizen encounters. As we know in other contexts, citizenship is located in a complex field of forces in which the commitment to universal and egalitarian relations coexists with forms of social inequality, social difference and social hierarchy. Indeed, the long history of voluntary organisation in the UK is marked by some of these strains. On one side, it can be viewed as expressing a spirit of collective concern or an ethos of solidarity with those in need. On the other side, it can look like a paternal or patrician exercise of philanthropy that locks the poor, needy or unfortunate into relations of personalised dependence and class scrutiny and judgement.

At stake in these examples are two linked issues. First, we can see how states may be decentred in the popular experience as other institutions and organisations occupy the roles – of recognition, provision, regulation and so on – that are conventionally attributed to states. The idea of shared sovereignties is one way of recognising how the terrain of citizenship identities and practices may be occupied by multiple agencies. However, the second issue is perhaps more important than the first, since it calls into question the simplifying category of the popular that we have been using so far in this section. All the agencies we have mentioned – states, religious and political institutions, militias, NGOs of different kinds – may engage with very different people, rather than 'the people' as a singular and homogeneous entity (even if they may address 'the people' in such singular terms).

Dividing and multiplying: reinventing 'the people'

It is perhaps a banal point that the singular people, the nation or the public are political and governmental inventions: they are a made up unity that conceals or temporarily suspends forms of differentiation (on the people of British populism, see, eg, Pozo, 2011). This relation between difference and equivalence (if not equality) has, as we have seen, been a recurring thread in the many projects mobilised through the idea of citizenship. The model of the nation-state that dominated academic and popular thought during the 20th century treated nations as territorially bounded spaces in which people share a common identity, culture and institutions (Gupta and Ferguson, 1992; Clarke, 2004; Clarke and Fink, 2008). As Calhoun notes:

> It is only as nationalist discourse becomes institutionalised in a public sphere that 'nation' or 'people' are constituted as such. Thus nationalist rhetoric shapes the internal discourse of nearly every state … it operates to constitute the nation (the public, the people) as a putative actor – the claimant to ultimate sovereignty – in relation to the state. (1997: 91)

Often, this identity has been racialised, mobilising ideas of a common stock, shared lineage or nation-as-race. Such ideas have dominated European thinking about nations and, through the relations of colonial governance, have circulated well beyond the European region. Ideas of national identities as a reflection of racial/ethnic homogeneity have shaped many approaches to nation-building, from attempts to build a common language and culture to processes of the forced expulsion and murder of specific minority groups (ethnic/racial 'cleansing'). Such processes testify to the powerful dynamics associated with the construction of nations as (supposedly) coherent spaces. In such spaces, heterogeneous cultural, linguistic and religious populations have been brought together, and it has usually required intense governmental efforts to suppress or reconcile such differences. From this viewpoint, hardly anywhere in what is usually taken to be the core of Europe looks like a stable and unified 'nation' and the imagined 'homogeneity' of nations has demanded varieties of repression: military, political, cultural and psychic. The last – the repression of the knowledge of difference – remains a powerful and disturbing force in contemporary debates about diversity and solidarity (Gilroy, 2005). This view of the unity of the nation/people as the *outcome* of political and governing processes points directly to the work that public institutions have done in creating national publics. Mass education systems, investment in health care to develop healthier populations, family policies to manage generational reproduction and expansion, national systems of law and policing, all contribute to the development of distinctive and unifying national public institutions and public cultures in which the unity of the people can be identified. Such unified notions of the nation/people have come under increasing challenge: from repressed internal differences returning to political action; from the unsettling effect of the colony within metropolitan spaces; and from the revived flows of people across borders since the late 20th century. But it must be underlined again that many of these unified notions of 'the people' were more 'state prose' than actually existing entities (Lopez Caballero, 2009); in other words, a significant number of academics engaged in studies of nationalism or national unity on the basis of an uncritical acceptance of such a state prose, while others have clearly showed that such unified visions were often at odds with actual policies, and political processes. Thus, Larcher's work on citizenship claims by the 'free coloured' in Martinique, and on the parliamentary debates around their anthropological 'otherness' and uncivilised mores, shows how 'universal' citizenship rights were diversely applied and equality was denied within the national body politic.

In the process, unifying notions of the nation/people have been challenged as the foundation for identifying citizens. The nation's 'Others' have disrupted unifying imagery and narratives and insisted on their presence with the body politic (despite recurring efforts to expel them from it). Claims-making by excluded, marginalised and subordinated groups is a fundamental feature of the remaking of citizenship – and has been a significant force in the re-energising of the study of citizenship. Here, we want to stress the ways in which such struggles – and the imaginaries of the nation/people that they carry – continue to be significant for contemporary forms of citizenship.

The domestic worker movement in the US embodies the generative potential of a dynamic, ambivalent perspective on citizenship and the state. From one perspective, this movement is a multicultural, multilingual, base-building movement that emphasises horizontal leadership development and the transformation of immigrant women's political subjectivities through civic participation. On the other hand, their principal public campaign objectives focus on legislative and institutional reforms at the state, federal and international levels. They tack back and forth between: efforts to gain basic labour law protections at the state level; alliances with labour unions, disabled and senior citizens, and women's organisations aimed at federal policy reforms; and contributing to the International Labor Organization Convention on Decent Work for Domestic Workers, another source of legitimacy for their moral and political claims on the state. This movement is in the process of doing all the things we think are interesting and difficult. To understand it only as a claims-making process of making demands on the state is to miss the multiplicity of its character. It is not reducible to a single quality, nor is it only about making demands on the state; it is about workers' call on one another, employers and allies to rethink much more deeply the historic, structural legacy of African-American slavery and the sexism underlying cultural disregard for care work and the people who do this work for pay or for their own families. These workers organise across sectors, making explicit links between their goals and claims and those of traditional women's rights group, labour unions and other precarious and contingent groups of both workers and recipients of social services and support. Citing international examples of countries with strong domestic work labour laws and poor practice, US domestic workers and their allied employers, led by disabled people and elders, assert that changing the law is part and parcel of a larger cultural shift that requires struggle over deeply held tensions between independence, traditionally conflated with individualism, and mutuality in American citizenship.

Assembling citizenship

In asserting the need to disentangle citizenship from the state, we do not mean that the state is irrelevant to citizenship, but rather that people's visions of citizenship produce different views of the state as well. These are specific, particular and grounded in regional, local and national histories, imaginaries and political cultures. Citizenship is not only about political relations between the state and individuals; it is also about the co-construction of political subjects, collectivities and disputes over the types of roles and relations differently situated subjects imagine, desire and would like to prevent between citizens and the different faces of states in individual and collective lives; what we called in Chapter One the horizontal dimensions of citizenship.

We might look to the complex articulations of citizenship and states in the post-socialist transitions of the former Soviet bloc. In such changes, people may have identified themselves as citizens, but did so in a project to dismantle or transform their states. In particular, they sought to liberate forms of equality, association and well-being from the control of states and state/party authority. In the process, 'civil society' was valorised as an alternative realm of political and social life. Civil society is a central element of what Charles Taylor (2003) identifies as the 'modern social imaginary'. However, its precise contours are elusive; it tends to be defined by its 'otherness' from both state and market. Gupta (2006) suggests that this makes it a less than helpful concept but we suspect that its political and governmental value derives precisely from this shifting (and contested) quality. In some settings, civil society has formed the terrain on which public and private realms are articulated, rather than being institutionally separated. Civil society is the public domain in which private individuals associate, yet it stands apart from the state. In these terms, it is understood as social, rather than political: an organic, rather than artificial, entity that is inhabited by people (rather than political subjects). It is this liberal imaginary that Michael Walzer articulates when he claims that: 'The words "civil society" name the space of uncoerced human association and also the set of relational networks – formed for the sake of family, faith, interest and ideology – that fill this space' (1995: 7).

This stress on *uncoerced association* typically provides the foundation for the contrast between civil society and the state (treated as institutionalised power that is exercised over people – and therefore always potentially coercive). These liberal conceptions of civil society have strong connections both with communitarian views of social order and libertarian views of individualised freedom (or what Macpherson [1967] called 'possessive individualism'). In recent decades, a variety of political forces and movements have come together in the rediscovery and celebration of civil society. These range from the anti-statism of dissident movements in the former Soviet bloc to the discovery of social capital as a resource for both economic and social development (Putnam, 1993, 2000; Stubbs, 2007). In the former Soviet bloc, the overwhelming power and penetration of the state produced social and political movements that identified civil society as the space of resistance and hope – a space that was beyond and outside the state and its tentacular apparatuses. At the same time, critiques of aid to the South, and Africa in particular, pointed to the institutionalisation of corruption within states (and political parties) as a primary mechanism that prevented the promise of development being realised. International organisations active in aid and development began to look for alternative spaces of possibility in 'receiving' societies. Civil society – in its many facets – offered a possible alternative location for conducting the business of development (Elyachar, 2005; Li, 2007b).

At the same time, states became identified as the agency and the machinery of ethnic domination, turning ethnic and national identities and their imagined 'ownership' of places into what Gregory (2004), writing about Palestine and Israel, calls the 'facts on the ground'. Such developments – the return of repressed national dreams and the invention of new nationalities – supercharged 'ethnicity' as a social and political force and led to a renewed interest in civil society organisations as the site of potential peaceful, integrated or harmonious coexistence, from Northern Ireland to post-Yugoslav countries. If politics, governmental apparatuses and the forces of states were tied up in the ruthless or murderous business of ethno-nationalism, then 'ordinary people', outside of politics, were the bearers of hope (Stubbs, 2007). Such anxieties about the power and effects of states also connect with longer political traditions of anarchism and libertarianism. Whether this is a European anarcho-syndicalism, which saw the state as the repository of power over people, or Gandhian conceptions of popular tradition and self-sufficiency (Sharma, 2008), anti-statism has been a powerful mobilising political philosophy that brings civil society to the fore.

In the process, civil society becomes a pole of opposition to the state. For example, Dagnino argues that in Latin America, it is important to:

> recognize that in some interpretations, the distinction between State and civil society, based on structural determinants, is not only frequently taken as an irreducible given of reality, but also ends up being converted into a relationship of 'natural' opposition, into a premise, a starting point, that exempts us from understanding the political processes that constitute and explain it. Such an understanding is behind the well known and widely disseminated vision of civil society as a 'pole of virtue' and of the State as the 'incarnation of evil'. (2002: 4)

As we have tried to show, there are many routes to arriving at the distinction between the state and civil society. We think it is important to be attentive to these multiple flows of ideas, people and projects since they reveal civil society as something other than simply the creature of global/neo-liberal forces or the 'pole of virtue' that stands for ordinary people against the state. Rather, civil society looks like a keyword that is suffused with multiple possible meanings and values, but which has been given a strong contemporary inflection towards anti-statist and anti-politics movements. This is a key theoretical point that speaks against the tendency to reify 'civil society' as a separate domain. But it is also a practical one that speaks to the diverse popular imaginaries in which terms such as 'state' and 'civil society' are activated or animated. The polysemic quality of civil society reflects the different landscapes in which people mobilise – and the different resources that are put to work in such mobilisations.

For example, in the struggles against the Soviet state and its satellites, there was a recurrent tension between the desire to liberate people from the control of an intrusive state power and the anxieties about loss of state-supported benefits and rights (eg the loss of women's rights in the unification of the two Germanies; see, *inter alia*, Daly, 2000; Poole, 2001; Rosenfeld et al, 2004). In his exploration of the meanings of civil society and citizenship in a Siberian collective farm settlement, Anderson shows that the term for civil society in Russian (*grazhdanskoe obshchetstvo*, literally 'citizen society'):

> tends to connote the everyday world of social entitlements, such as civil law (*grazhdanskii kodeks*), the provision of passenger airline transport (*grazhdanskaia aviatsiia*), or civil work (*grazhdanskaia sluzhba*).... Demokratiia, which nominally means democracy, takes most of its contemporary meaning from the reformers who spearheaded the market reforms under the leadership of President Yeltsin.... The resentment behind the reforms in Khantaiskoe Ozero, like other parts of the former Soviet Union, reflects a claim that the hierarchical civic infrastructure of their recent past was less oppressive than the narrow guarantees of 'democratic citizenship' being enforced today. (Anderson, 1996: 103, 111)

Indeed, there have been persistent anxieties that the 'liberation' of people from the state might well mean their *de facto* abandonment to the rigours of the market (see, eg, Clarke 2005; on Poland, see Kalb, 2005). In Nigeria, for instance, there has been popular opposition to the apparent alignment of the nation-state with the power of global oil capital seeking to exploit the natural resources at the expense of local people. Watts, for example, has argued that:

> Oil has been a centralizing force that has rendered the (oil) state more visible and globalized, underwriting a process of state-building and national community imagining. On the other hand, oil-led development, driven by an unremitting

political logic of ethnic claims-making and staggering corruption by the political classes, has become a force of fragmentation and illegitimacy, radically discrediting the state and its forms of governance. It produced a set of conditions/communities that have compromised, indeed undermined, the very tenets of the modern nation-state....
It also produced forms of governable spaces (the product of what I call political dispersion) that sit uneasily with the very idea of Nigeria – spaces that generated forms of rule, conduct and imagining at cross purposes with one another, antithetical to the very idea of a coherent nation-state that oil, in the mythos of the West at least, represented. (2007: 115; see also Obi and Rustad, 2011)

Such ambivalences about the state and citizenship pose the question of why desires for citizenship, embodied in a strong state, might be revitalised even as people are sceptical about both the excessive power of the state and about its weakness or ineffectiveness in the face of markets, capital and so on. Despite their doubts and suspicions, groups of people may still mobilise around a conception of the national state as collective resource and collective provisioner. As Hansen and Stepputat argue, the 'persistence of the imagination of the state as an embodiment of sovereignty' is essential to understanding the paradox that:

while the authority of the state is constantly questioned and functionally undermined, there are growing pressures on states to confer full-fledged rights and entitlements on ever more citizens, to confer recognition and rights on ever more institutions, movements, or organizations. (2001: 2)

To return to an earlier argument about the ambivalence of popular relationships to states: what do people want and fear from their states? What do people understand citizenship to involve? Again, it is important to remember that we are not dealing with 'the people' in general, but differently located peoples and groups of people. The desire for political and social order – and the sense of security that it might bring – will always be translated into very particular orderings. These often include the projections of some social groups (who identify as citizens) against others (identified as Others, not citizens) for order, rights and justice. For example, Barnes et al (2004) examine how identities of residence and belonging in the UK are converted into claims on political authority and governmental attention in conflicts over Traveller settlement. In such conflicts, they suggest, it is possible to see a citizen identity being:

> used relationally, aggressively and defensively. Moreover, invoking a citizen identity is shown here as a flexible activity carried out in particular local circumstances and relies heavily on the work done by categorization – not only membership categorizations but also location categorizations. (2004: 202)

In yet another context, but also concerning the issue of how figures of citizenship are built through interactions, Hochet underlines that:

> The modern state is not the only one to locate people in a citizenship situation. In West African contexts certain farmer societies propose an infranational frame to regulate the relationships between individuals and the body politic, through the distribution, to 'autochtonous' as well as to 'strangers', of land rights and sociopolitical duties. We are thus confronted by dispositifs that on the one hand allow to think society from a plurality of belongings, and on the other to go beyond these belongings by placing people in a citizenship situation at the local level. (Hochet, 2011: 1041)

Whereas most studies of such societies start from a 'state point of view' according to which there is a clear distinction between *stranger* (a social category) and *alien* (a political one connected to that of citizenship), Hochet clearly shows that 'Minyanka and Bwaba [farmer societies in West Africa] consider as social foreigners (strangers) individuals and groups who for the state are not political foreigners (aliens), but citizens' (Hochet, 2011: 1038), thus highlighting that citizenship can also be envisioned from 'local societies' point of view'.

It should be an obvious point that popular desires and mobilisations do not always deliver the intended outcome, and neither are they always egalitarian; Hochet shows how the local vision of citizenship, if it provides for reciprocal rights and duties for the different groups, also installs a structural inequality between legal citizens. Such desires encounter other political projects, become translated or spoken for by powerful agents, and may be reworked into strategies of governing that bear only a thin relationship to popular imaginings. So, popular desires for security may be translated into the state's project of security. A desire for well-being might be translated into minimalist welfarism, or the self-provisioning 'active citizen'. But it might also mean the struggles for environmental health (Pezzullo, 2012), freedom from Harms (see Hillyard et al, 2004) and the struggle to have and realise rights (Erni, 2011). Such 'desires' for order, security and well-being might be translated in very different ways, used to legitimate state action or state inaction, and deployed to support statist or anti-statist orientations, because this is a profoundly unstable, shifting and contextually specific field of political mobilisations.

We have tried to explore the ways in which popular social imaginaries both decentre and reinvent the state in two critical ways. First, we have drawn attention to the complicated landscapes of institutions, organisations, forms of power and authority in which the state is only ever one element – even if it is a significant element. We have stressed the variability of such popular imaginaries – emerging in specific contexts and reflecting the particular fields of social antagonism, contradiction and tension in which people think and act. Such a view of how 'the idea of the state' is both supplemented and shaped by other ideas about the configuration of social and political power and possibilities is a powerful – and necessary – counter to theories that tend towards a reification of institutions (in which their character and place is known in advance). Second, we have tried to stress the complicated and shifting relationships to the state that are in play in such popular imaginaries. We are tempted by a number of pairings that express popular ambivalence (to the state, but also to other would-be authoritative institutions): cynicism and commitment; distrust and desire; aspiration and anxiety; fantasies and fears. Such combinations say something about the troubled and unstable political-cultural-emotional fields of popular views of states: always hopeful (projecting citizenly futures), and yet always disappointed by compromise and corruption.

The betrayals of politics – and the intrusions of power – form recurrent stories in such popular imaginaries. Such popular understandings are often profoundly cynical or sceptical about the promise of politics, reflected in images of politics (and politicians) as 'dirty', corrupt, self-interested, venal or zealots. Newman and Clarke have explored the different meanings of 'political' that circulate across academic and popular understandings, pointing to the potential for such popular understandings of 'dirty politics' to support populist 'anti-politics' movements or to fuel a withdrawal or retreat from political action that Benson and Kirsch (2010) describe as a 'politics of resignation'. Resignation, they suggest, is a condition that dominant social forces try to inculcate in order to demobilise potential opposition. We would want to stress ambivalence and instability rather than get stuck with one modality as defining a popular sensibility. People move, change their minds, are gripped by new possibilities (like during the recent Arab revolutions or the Indignados movement) or are immobilised by new threats or problems. We think it is important to understand this political-cultural-emotional field as one in which the possibility of imagining (and demanding) citizenship always recurs as a way of imagining how things might be otherwise (see Arditi, 2011). Such imaginings and their associated demands may be ambivalent and conditional, especially, perhaps, when the state is being addressed. But citizenship, in this sense, is always a prefigurative and performative demand – a claim that things could be different; that things should be different. This often, but not always, includes the claim that 'the state should ...', even if one does not believe that it will. Such demands are performative in the sense of making visible problems that must/should be overcome; of imagining collective identities and ways of being that are at stake; and of acting in the name of such collectivities. The making visible is itself a political action (Newman, 2012). It aims to summon a public, it imagines a set of relationships, it announces a future and it forms a critical part of the process of mobilising.

Conclusion: decentering in theory and practice

Critiquing state-centric and nation-centric conceptions of citizenship has involved us in challenging four things: the conception of citizenship as a legal status; over-unified conceptions of the state; the contingent but naturalised entanglement of nation and state; and, finally, the over-identification of citizenship with the state. We briefly review these challenges as a way of pointing forward to Chapter Three.

First, then, our starting point involves unlocking the conventional conception of citizenship as a legal status (ie one grounded in the state). This does not mean arguing that citizenship is *not* also a legal status. On the contrary, both the political and legal construction of citizenship as a status remain critically important focal points for the politics, the analysis and the practices of citizenship. But we think it important to insist that the political and juridical inscriptions of citizenship are the *products* of social, cultural, political and institutional conflicts and struggles. They may be naturalised by states, and reified by commentators, but it is important to make their produced, assembled and contingent character visible because: (1) it draws attention to the specific statuses that are produced in particular places and times (rather than an overly abstracted view of citizenship as a political and juridical status-in-general and as a principle); (2) it enables us to recognise that, even in one place and time, these political and juridical statuses may be multiple rather than singular, 'blurred'; and (3) it underscores the way that the political and juridical status of citizenship is both a product of past struggles and the object of present/future ones. Projects of various kinds seek to revise, remake or transform the statuses, enlarging or narrowing, and so on.

Our second concern is to contest the over-unified and institutionalist conceptions of the state associated with such views of citizenship, viewing the state instead as a heterogeneous assemblage, not ordered by a singular political logic or character (that does not mean that there are not struggles to 'conform' parts of the state, its apparatuses, agencies and agents, to a 'mission', but that is a different story). Also, one might argue, the 'models of citizenship' that they enact are impure, multiply shaped and sourced, contradictory or incoherent. This also implies thinking of states as multiple sites (apparatuses, agencies, agents, places, etc) in which citizenship is enacted, practised, policed, claimed and contested.

The third challenge involves disentangling the 'bundles' in which citizenship is linked with nation as well as state. Our same emphasis on the contingent and contextual character of citizenship needs to apply here, too, precisely because it is the nation that is the most naturalised – and naturalising – reference point for citizenship. The nation – whether or not it is imagined ethnically – is generally the political unit, the geographical space and the 'imagined community' in which citizens are located. We have tried to indicate that the bundlings of citizenship, nation and state are, as Sassen (2005) shows, becoming unsettled and unbundled. She rightly argues that such changes and challenges make the contingent and constructed quality of their connections both more visible and more susceptible to challenge (politically and analytically). We insist on the importance of understanding the nation as one 'imagined community' (among many); on grasping the historically and politically contingent hyphenation of the nation-state (and its variable relations); and on understanding how looking for citizenship in sites, settings and forms that are not those of nation and state is a critical endeavour. This is all the more important given that such visions are profoundly Euro-centric, and that including in the frame of discussion and analysis other contexts, such as those of China or West Africa mentioned earlier, allows the opening up the possibilities of arrangements to much more diversity and complexity, thus questioning the dominant framings and forms that are too readily taken for granted.

Finally, we have tried to challenge the residualisation of social and political relations and practices of citizenship 'beyond the state'. We have started to make visible the other domains in which people are engaged socially, politically and culturally by the promises and problems of citizenship. Citizenship is imagined, sought, enacted and practised in settings beyond the state and at critical points of intersection between people and the apparatuses of states – individually in transactions with state agents, in mobilised groups being managed or demanding, and in struggles for political projects that will transform the state, citizenship and the relationships between them. It is this promise – and this challenge – to which we turn in Chapter Three.

CHAPTER THREE

Imagining the 'communities' of citizenship

In this chapter, we explore the 'imagined communities' of citizenship. One of the potent qualities of the idea of citizenship is its capacity to serve as a term through which different sorts of collectivities of people and connections between people may be imagined, mobilised and brought into being. Such imagined communities are constructed and elaborated in many different sites and settings, although this diversity is overshadowed by the persistent articulation of citizenship as a national question (both in academic theory and governmental practice). We begin, then, with questions about these national articulations, launching ourselves from Benedict Anderson's (1983) famous understanding of the nation as an 'imagined community'. This conception of imagined communities guides us in three directions during the chapter. First, we examine the implications of treating the nation as an imagined community for reflections on citizenship. This leads us to recent debates about the fate of the national character of citizenship in what has been described as a 'post-national' world.

Second, we consider the ways in which the nation is equated with the 'national level' as a privileged site of citizenship. Here, we encounter arguments that citizenship is both identification with the political community of the nation and practised in relation to national-level institutions, processes and issues. In contrast, we consider such nationalising logics to be part of a form of 'scalar thinking' that naturalises a specific ordering of social and political arrangements and, in the process, diminishes the salience of other sites and scales of social organisation (seeing them as encompassed by the national and the global). In such views, the local is always 'merely local'. We explore alternative approaches to the politics of scale: asking how scales are imagined and institutionalised, and how they are contested by alternative political projects.

Third, and most importantly, we turn to the diverse imagined communities that citizenship can articulate. We stress the importance of citizenship as an idea – a keyword – through which collectivities can be imagined and brought into being. Drawing on earlier arguments, we insist that the diversity of communities: are imagined and enacted in heterogeneous sites and settings; not only take place at different scales, but also bring with them new sets of connections between scales; and, of course, are mobilised around diverse identities and issues. Such different concerns and claims have kept citizenship at the heart of political projects across time and space.

Benedict Anderson (1983) famously described nations as 'imagined communities'. At the core of his path-breaking work is the claim that the nation 'is an imagined political community – and imagined as both inherently limited and sovereign' (1983: 6). He goes on to argue that 'It is imagined because the members of even the smallest nation will never know most of their fellow-members, meet them, or even hear of them, yet in the minds of each lives the image of their communion' (1983: 6). Here, we wish to borrow his idea and take it a little further in two particular directions. First, by asserting that nations are not the only communities to which people, as citizens, imagine themselves as belonging. Anderson also knew this, noting that the idea of an 'imagined community' should not be located in a binary distinction between true and false, rather 'all communities larger than primordial villages of face-to-face contact (and perhaps even these) are imagined. Communities are to be distinguished, not by their falsity/genuineness, but by the style in which they are imagined' (1983: 6). Two decades later, the concepts of imagined and imaginary have come to play a rather larger role in the social sciences, but Anderson's view of the nation (and the difficult terms associated with it – 'nationality' and 'nation-ness', for instance) remains a critical point of departure for us. Indeed, much contemporary scholarship of affiliation, attachment and identification stresses the multiple connections through which people see themselves as articulated: multiplicity and heterogeneity seems to mark the terrain of these imagined relationships, and this also applies to the field of citizenship.

Second, we will enlarge Anderson's conception of how communities are imagined, insisting that all aspects of social life combine imaginaries with relations and practices, and that such imaginaries are also mobilised in and by political projects that may offer contested and opposed conceptions of conflict and connection, division and solidarity. Citizenship is recurrently attached to questions of nation (the citizen is imagined – and inscribed – as a legitimate member of the imagined national community), particularly as nations are enacted and institutionalised by states. Nevertheless, it is important to insist on the multiplicity of identifications and imagined connections that might be in play in struggles over citizenship. It is thus worth directing particular attention to the contested ways of connecting state and nation, since the 'national community' is one of the most frequent ways to conceive of the 'community of citizens'. Many writers on citizenship have drawn attention to the increasingly unsettled and contested relationship between nation, state and citizenship (eg Bauböck, 1999; Kofman et al, 2000; Morrisens and Sainsbury, 2005; Bosniak, 2007; Castles and Miller, 2009). Indeed, other collectivities can be addressed, summoned or built, including by the state(s), when such a community is envisioned or enacted (Newman and Clarke, 2009). The question of collectivities that do not have the state at the centre of their political vision, or even do not have it at all, is also significant.

Indeed, communities can also be defined and lived as 'forms of collective *experience* in which individuals with plural identities find ways to agree and end up, maybe, forging something like a common identity, without this aspect being a principal and priority goal' (Bourdeaux and Flipo, 2011: 87; emphasis added). Such a 'communalist' conception of community is the opposite of the communitarian one, according to which a community can only exist under the condition of previously sharing cultural traits. It allows for the possibility of envisioning communities not from the point of view of identities, but starting from (material) common objects, 'from which we can build a community that is never given, never inherited' (Bourdeaux and Flipo, 2011: 87). Such an approach to communities as based on sharing commons seems particularly important when one considers citizenship processes, especially since it allows for a reflexive and critical discussion on the links between citizenship and 'culture'; Rosaldo's notion of cultural citizenship in a sense connects to it by stressing the possibility of sharing such commons without building a 'communitarian' community.

As Balibar rightly underlines:

> The question of the community of citizens ... thus has no once and for all defined or definable solution, neither in the form of an *empirical community* (such society, such culture, such State) nor in the form of an *ideal community* (for instance 'the republican nation', but also the 'post-national' federation). It neither has an univocal 'logical site', contrary to what Habermas seems to think, but rather a moving historical site, both sociological and symbolic: a meeting point between processes of work division's transformation, populations' movements, revolution of customs, and emancipation or solidarity dynamics. (Balibar, 2001: 125–6; emphasis in original)

We concur with Balibar's analytical position, seeing citizenship as marking the site of constant struggles – in both theory and practice – to unlock the naturalised and naturalising connections between citizenship, nation and state, and as constituting the support for inventing other (communal) types of communities, based on both commons (*des communs*) and dissensus, as argued by Rancière (1998, 2000).

Nationalising and naturalising citizenship

Our experience of working collaboratively on citizenship processes and practices has shed a stark light on the troubled and troubling relationships between states, nations and citizenships. One specific aspect of these issues has to be restated here, since it does have an impact on this work and how it might be read. This book has been written in a language that is not the first language of two of the authors. This is also a language in which 'citizenship' can be read with at least three meanings, and it is not always easy, or even possible, to decide which one is meant by its users. In English-written literature, 'citizenship' can be read as 'nationality': the legal dimension of an individual's state membership in the context of an interstate system (see, *inter alia*, Sassen, 2006; Fahrmeir, 2007; Bosniak, 2008). It can also be read as referring to sets of rights and connected obligations, and to the rules and procedures through which they can be accessed. For example, Bosniak's (2008) *The citizen and the alien* examines the question of citizenship, nationality and alienage; while Somers' *Genealogies of citizenship*, published in the same year, explicitly focuses on what she calls the 'inside/interior' dynamics of citizenship's dynamics of inclusion and exclusion (2008: 20).

In such cases, the difference between nationality and citizenship can be very blurred. Alternatively, citizenship can refer to participation in the public sphere, to the process of becoming political subjects (Isin, 2002). These different usages articulate different meanings of the idea of 'membership in a political community'. The first two take membership as being a legal matter, a question of status, and are both state-centric and nation-centric. The third takes participation in a political community as the fundamental relation of citizenship. Bosniak observes the effect of these elisions when she points to the problem of:

> the analytical and normative nationalism that characterizes discussions of citizenship in mainstream constitutional and political theory. Most such discussions presume that citizenship is enacted within bounded national societies. Ordinarily, these presumptions are unspoken and

unacknowledged: theorists tend to treat both a national setting and a state of boundedness as already satisfied conditions for the practices and institutions and experiences of citizenship. Making these assumptions permits them to focus their attention on what citizenship requires and entails in substantive terms within these pre-given boundaries.

More often than not, in fact, this literature appears to presume not merely that citizenship is national as a matter of current fact, but also that it is national as a matter of necessity or nature. One of the arguments I make ... is that the automatic correspondence commonly presumed between citizenship and nation-state is unfounded. Citizenship's intimate relationship to the nation-state is not intrinsic but contingent and historical, and the forms and locations of citizenship, as we conventionally understand the term, are more varied than ordinarily acknowledged. Citizenship has been, can be, and arguably should sometimes be enacted not merely within national borders but beyond and across them, as well. (Bosniak, 2008: 5)

We continue to find this 'nationalisation' of citizenship in the English-language academic literature troubling – analytically and politically. It is not just a question of translation. It is that each term carries with it an accreted weight of meanings, and attachment to particular social, political and theoretical imaginaries, that differ both within the same language used in different contexts, and between different languages. Thus, Sassen considers that:

Today the terms citizenship and nationality both refer to the national state. In a technical legal sense, while essentially the same concept, each term reflects a different legal framework. Both identify the legal status of an individual in terms of state membership. But citizenship is largely confined to the national dimension, while nationality refers to the international legal dimension in the context of an interstate system. (2005: 81)

But are citizenship and nationality really 'essentially the same concept' even in a technical legal sense, 'generally' speaking? Is 'citizenship' really confined to the national dimension? Thus, for instance, Canadian immigration documents ask 'What is your "citizenship/citoyenneté"?', meaning by that your legal international state membership, where equivalent French documents will ask for your 'nationalité'. Alternatively, the Mexican Constitution defines all Mexican men and women as *possessing nationality* but not *ciudadania/citizenship* until they reach 18 years of age and live honestly ('*tener un modo honesto de vivir*'). Mexican nationality by birth adheres to the person; citizenship is revocable. The conditions of full inclusion in the definition of nationality and citizenship have changed along with the Mexican Republic and Constitutions (Ortíz Leroux, 2007). We have spent a lot of time in this book contesting the view that citizenship is (only) a legal status vis-à-vis the state – and this applies equally to the tendency to equate or elide it with nationality, or claim any stability in either category.

Sassen claims that both terms – 'citizenship' and 'nationality' – refer to the 'national' level, where national seems to mean the 'state'; this is a further example of the ambiguously naturalised connection between states and nations when 'national' becomes a way to designate a *level*, as opposed to 'local', for instance. But what is to be learnt from their confusion and conflation, or from the apparently not only commonsensical, but also academic and governmental, facility with which these terms are used interchangeably? It seems to us that attention to the fluctuation in uses and meanings, in different contexts, is a central issue when discussing the decentring of states and nations in relation to citizenship processes. Exploring such fluctuations – and particularly unsettled moments – is one of the ways through which to unlock relationships that are often taken for granted as conventional, natural or normal. Our emphasis here is on the need to problematise and decentre the often-assumed connection between nationality, nation-ness and citizenship(s), and to question the practice of treating the 'national community' as the only or the natural way to imagine the 'community of citizens'.

The resulting elisions between 'the nation of citizens' and 'the nation of compatriots' (Habermas, 1992), and the troubled connections between nation-ness (feeling of belonging to a shared identity), nationality (as a legal status linking an individual to the state) and citizenship (as political subjectification and membership), are commonly found, as stated earlier, in the multiple uses of the term 'citizenship' in the English-language literature; also, as evoked in Chapter One, similar 'slips' in meanings can be observed in French, as well as in German. We discussed earlier the need to include theories of citizenship themselves in the 'thick contextualisation' of citizenship, and the same goes for the ways through which contingent crystallisations of the connections between nation-ness, nationality and citizenship achieved the status of 'abstract models'. Thus, for instance, the classic and naturalised dichotomy between 'the French' conception of the civic, political and contractual nation (nation of citizens) and 'the German' one of the ethnic and cultural nation (nation of compatriots) was produced in specific historical circumstances in the 1870s, when the aim was for each country's philosophers and politicians to prove their legitimate right on Alsace-Lorraine. As Balibar rightly suggests:

> It is time to get out of perspectives limited by stereotyped antithesis between 'citoyenneté à la française' and the fairly caricatural figures of 'anglo-saxon communitarianism' and of 'ethnic nation' of besides the Rhine or further East, to reject binary oppositions ... and look for more complex formulations. (2001: 207)

The process of working transnationally has been productive for making these issues more visible, since looking at other contexts and the different 'bundlings' that they produce enables some critical distance from the recurrent, if rarely examined, English-language conflation of nationality and citizenship. Relationships between citizenship, nationality and national identity are indeed historically and politically variable and always 'under construction' (or reconstruction) as political projects to govern the 'nation' shift. In Brazil, the emphasis on the state's definition of citizenship through the category of 'worker' is intimately connected with efforts directed at developing national identity from the 1930 Revolution onwards, where the Brazilian focal concerns were expressed in the terms *unidade nacional* (national unity) and *construção da Nação* (nation-building). Concerns with the centrality of culture in that process made the *construção da cultura nacional* a focus of the Brazilian 'state ideological production', which played a powerful role in establishing a common ground between state intellectuals and others, including those not aligned with the authoritarian bias that presided over the state's projects and who, in fact, opposed them strongly. One strong reason for the recognition of workers as citizens was the need to include them in the nation, whose very existence was seen as fragmented by different cleavages, among which the non-citizenship of popular sectors and poor people was culturally and politically significant. This nation-building work is often primarily associated with 'new nations' – marking a particular phase of forming and establishing the nation (which is then transcended when nations become 'mature'). We would prefer to see it as a recurrent issue for nations – and their states.

What Anderson (1983: 13) calls 'nation-ness' (to distinguish it from the more formal/legal sense of nationality) is one of the forms through which states try to organise – and naturalise – the relationships between people, place and politics. The nation is imagined simultaneously as: a bounded space (the territory claimed by the nation-state); a people (the inhabitants of that space); and a polity (in which people, government and state form a symbolic unity). As analysed by Neveu and Filippova (2011), in the Russian case, the two terms *načional'nost'* (usually translated as nationality/nationalité) and *grazhdanstvo* (citizenship) have very different meanings. The first means 'ethnic belonging' (very close to Anderson's notion of *nation-ness*), while the second refers to membership in a political/state-based community. Until 1997, Soviet internal passports (officially named 'Soviet Citizen's passport') had a *načional'nost'* entry that provided information on a person's ethnicity (eg Russian, Tatar, Yakut, etc, but also 'Jewish', which had been considered a national [in the sense of people] rather than religious identification). Nowadays, in Russia and in some of the New Independent States, the *načional'nost'* entry is excluded from passport and personal data files; a change that manifests, to some extent, a 'privatisation of ethnicity', although individuals are still questioned about their 'nationality' during population censuses. So the blurring here is rather different: between 'nationality' and 'ethnicity', rather than between 'nationality' and 'citizenship'. According to this logic, the nation is not a political entity, but rather just one of many possible forms of ethnic community; during the Soviet era, the 'Soviet Nation' was never an issue, there was a 'Soviet People', officially defined as 'a new historical community', composed of many 'nations' (*načii*), 'peoples' (*narody*) and 'nationalities' (*narodnosty*).

Relations between nation-ness, nationality and citizenship are thus not 'natural' ones; they are built in the face of specific stakes and aims, and need significant cultural and political work to be deployed to make them come true. One example of such work is the extent to which, in a period that has seen the development of analysis underlining the potential emergence of 'post-national' forms of citizenship (see later), the relationship between citizenship and the 'national question' has been re-dramatised in states of the North in recent decades (Balibar, 2002; Sassen, 2006). Thus, the 2007 Goldsmith review of citizenship for the UK government examined and articulated links between questions of Britishness and national identity, legal discourses of residence and nationality, and the contemporary framing of citizenship in terms of the rebalancing of 'rights and responsibilities'. This is political work in the large sense (Edgar, 2008), addressing the dilemmas of governing the nation, in which questions of nationality and citizenship are understood as traversed and troubled by migration and social/ethnic diversity (see, *inter alia*, Yuval-Davis, 1997; Parekh, 2000; Johnson, 2008; Kannabiran et al, 2007; Wetherell et al, 2007).

States serve as privileged sites for organising the nation and the national culture. This 'national' conception of culture involves a particular understanding of culture as something that nations and other groupings can possess: it is grasped as the distinctive shared, stable and inalienable property of a people that binds them to a place (Clarke, 2009). Critiquing essentialised views of the state–nation connection should not lead us to lose sight of the ways in which states are recurrently involved in making up, revising and enforcing aspects of nation-ness. For example, states (as ensembles of policies, practices and people) involve themselves in the management of the relationship between citizenship and nationality, in small and large ways. In 2007, the French government created a Ministry of Immigration, National Identity, Integration and Co-development that brought these issues together in very state-like ways. These concerns with constructing nation-ness are also visible in the invention (and reinvention) and institutionalisation of national culture and its relationship to other cultures. Nation-building and -rebuilding projects typically involve the reinvention and institutionalisation of national identity.

So far, we have argued for the need to dissolve 'the semantic link between citizenship and national identity' (Habermas 1998: 69), which means that to a claimed cultural identity does not necessarily correspond a political identity' (Bayart, 1996: 12). Indeed, not all feelings of nation-ness or national identity necessarily have state sovereignty as their aim, making it important to question this 'article of faith' according to which state sovereignty would be the natural continuation and only mark of success for sentiments of national identity. Although there are many arguments that globalising dynamics have unsettled previously stable configurations of people, places and polities, it is important to remember that both the past and the present show more complex and contested alignments than the imagined unities of nation would allow (Clarke and Fink, 2008). For example, settler societies have produced complex – and unequal – alignments of peoples, places and political systems, including matters of national identity and national sovereignty (eg Cattelino, 2008).

The entangled qualities of nation, national identity and political institutionalisations are also visible in the history and contemporary situation of the French West Indies. Thus, as analysed by Zander (2010), the aspiration to, and assertion of, a Martiniquese 'national identity' does not politically translate into a claim for state sovereignty, but is inscribed within a desire for recognition as both equal (French) citizens and a different people. 'Feelings of belonging' might be expressed, towards the idea of 'France' as a 'community of citizens', towards the Republic as a political community, but not towards 'France' as a 'nation of compatriots'. Such feelings and aspirations, observed in the recent period by Zander, have a longer history. According to Giraud, slave insurrections in the West Indies were 'citizens' revolutions', revolutions that demanded the equality of free citizens. So, instead of separating or distancing the colonies from the metropole, they brought colonies much closer to it at a time when the French people supported, and partly enacted, values that corresponded to the most profound aspirations of insurgent slaves:

> A convergence, or even a community of values, [that] was perfectly illustrated by the highly symbolic and surprising fact that when the San Domingo slaves launched their assault on French expeditionary troops, a little before Haitian independence, they did so brandishing the [French] Tricolour flag and singing the Marsellaise. So, too, did the victorious slave insurrectionists in Martinique, half a century later on the 22nd of May, 1848. (Giraud, 2005: 97)

He goes on to argue that, in more recent times, the desire for 'integration' within the Republic, considered by some as a particularly pernicious brand of 'Uncle-Tomism', has significance as a response to:

> the self-maintained illusion of so many metropolitan authorities that what is, for West Indians, precisely a hunger for citizenship, would for them be synonymous with a desire of the nation. [De Gaulle in 1964] ... mistook, following many others, the choice of values the French nation accidentally supported in history, with love for that nation, the signified universal message with the particular 'national framework' signifying it, in short, drunkenness with the bottle (*l'ivresse avec la bouteille*). (Giraud, 2005: 98–9)

According to him:

> At stake was not to be rendered similar but to be considered as equals.... When wishing to acquire citizenship of France, peoples of the 'old' colonies did not want, in their large

majority, to melt in 'the French cultural identity', but to work suppressing colonial injustice by giving themselves the means to benefit, on an equal footing with the other French citizens, from the rights that this citizenship is supposed to guarantee. (Giraud, 2005: 99)

This assertion of a will to be part of a 'community of citizens' defined alongside a political project of equality has been read by officials as a will for cultural assimilation. At the core of the project to be part of a political, rather than a national, 'community of citizens' was a critical distinction between issues of national identity/nation-ness and issues of citizenship.

There are thus feelings of nation-ness that do not aim at being translated into forms of state sovereignty, and desires of citizenship that are clearly disconnected from any assimilation in a common identity; however, as has been evoked earlier, a significant number of state policies have tried, and are still trying, to 'naturalise' both the connection between citizenship and nation-ness, and membership in the second. Indeed, such aspirations to become at last fully part of a 'nation of citizens' while maintaining different cultural identifications (and the same analysis could be made with regards to the 1983 March for Equality in France, see Chapter One) are always confronted with processes of naturalisation of national identity that go further than asserting the need for 'cultural homogeneity' or for a single shared 'nation-ness' for citizenship to actually have meaning and efficiency. If one wishes to problematise more clearly the complex knot linking issues of citizenship and identifications, this first line of analysis must be connected to processes of 'naturalisation'. Indeed:

> Even when the state grants citizenship to non-indigenous individuals, it aspires to turn them into *naturalized* citizens. More precisely, the state invites these individuals to conform their subjectivity 'to the *nature* of the society that grants them citizenship, *a nature that allows for their subjectivity to be nationalized*' (Gourgouris 1996: 33, emphasis in the original). (Tzanelli, 2006: 31)

Thus, in the French context, the official discourse about a civic and republican model of belonging to the 'community of citizens' seems to have progressively drifted towards a process of naturalisation, of essentialisation. Catherine Neveu (1994) has previously argued for a reading of the 1993 debate on the French Nationality Act's reform as having highlighted the weight of an 'autochtony myth'. According to Loraux's (1989) work on ancient Athens, an essential dimension of this myth is that 'one is born an Athenian and cannot become one'; if the *poiétoi*, that is, artificial citizen (adopted children or naturalised citizens), is apparently part of the city, 'he is not always perceived as such, since his patronym still designates his father as of foreign origins' (Loraux, 1989: 19). The 1993 Nationality Act reform showed troubling similarities with this myth: only those French becoming nationals through *jus soli* were forced to formally manifest their will to become/to be French nationals. A suspicion was thus thrown on the 'Frenchness' of certain nationals, since only *jus soli* ones had to express this will, which was taken to be innate among *jus sanguini* nationals. As Raissiguier (2010) argues, this double movement around national belonging locates migrants in France as 'impossible subjects':

> I use the concept of impossibility to conjure up the complex mechanisms (both material and discursive) that establish impossible subject positions within the French nation. These mechanisms include discursive practices that turn certain immigrants into unthinkable members of the national body, as well as material and legal practices that locate them in spaces of impossibility. In addition, I deploy the term *impossible* to suggest the unnerving and unruly forms of political intervention that these mechanisms elicit … the ways in which immigrants are involved in political practices that question nation-based understandings of civil membership, and to show how they invent new ways to stake their claims and stage their battles. (2010: 4–5; emphasis in original)

Fifteen years after the introduction of the Nationality Act, Fassin referred to the same kind of process when he states that:

> It became clear that inequalities had to be analysed not simply in terms of traditional categories of social class, profession, or even nationality, but also from the point of view of the origin, real or presumed, as identified through skin colour or foreign sounding names.… Discrimination is directed not so much against foreigners as against people seen as illegitimate members of French society, whatever their nationality (the majority of them are French and born in France). (Fassin, 2006: 18)

Lorcerie also stresses the extent to which the contemporary development of research on 'race' in France 'must not evade a critical thought on the nation' (Lorcerie, 2007: 304), and especially of what she describes, following Geertz, as 'national primordialism … this cognitive scheme nourished with an animal feeling of 'home' (*chez nous*) and with an ethno-racial imaginary' (2007: 327). According to her, the word 'immigré' is thus:

> an appellation designating a non-natural belonging – persons to whom this word is applied to are perceived and treated as different in an 'ineffable' way, while they can be born in this country and have its legal nationality. 'Immigrés' are those who are not the 'depository/trustee of the nation' and, as a result, risk being treated in social relationships as 'undesirable'. (Lorcerie, 2007: 306)

In the process, citizens of migrant origin, or even all non-white citizens, are summoned to forget their 'particularity' so as to be considered as 'really' French citizens, while all the time being constantly reminded of, and suspected because of, their particularities and having their 'Frenchness' questioned. Giraud argues that:

> [In metropolitan France,] since neither their citizenship nor their close relation to the French history and culture have been for them [French West Indians] a guarantee against discriminations and practices of exclusion, and this while they are constantly reminded that they are *de jure* fully French, those with backgrounds in French Overseas Departments living in metropolitan France discover they are thus indeed, according to Aimé Césaire's formulation, 'fully apart French', and that while not being strictly speaking aliens, they are not considered as being completely from the nation. If it is about 'national framework', the frame is empty and the nation very narrow indeed! (2005: 101).

As for Lorcerie, she underlines the extent to which in the contemporary French context, 'the tension between Republican principles and a non-avowed primordialism is a major mode of conflictuality' (2007: 303). Such conflicts and debates are distinctively French and yet share much in common with other colonial nations of the North, for whom nationality, national identity and race/ethnicity are entangled in powerful ways (eg Gilroy, 2002, 2005). The model of the nation-state that dominated academic and popular thought during the 20th century treated nations as territorially bounded spaces in which people shared a common identity, culture and institutions (Gupta and Ferguson, 1992; Clarke, 2004; Clarke and Fink, 2008). Often, this identity has been racialised, mobilising ideas of a common stock, shared lineage or nation-as-race. Such ideas have dominated European thinking about nations and, through the relations of colonial governance, have circulated well beyond the European region. Images of national identities as a matter of racial/ethnic homogeneity have shaped approaches to nation-building, from attempts to build a common language and culture to processes of forced expulsion and murder of specific 'non-national' minorities – those who could not be assimilated to the nation. This naturalisation of national identity has a strong association with racialised versions of 'culture', and thus to forms of essentialisation in which 'culture' often comes to stand for 'race' (Clarke, 2009). This remains a tangled ground for European states attempting to manage heterogeneous populations after colonialism (Balibar, 2006).

Becoming post-national?

In Chapter One, we explored the 'unbundling' of established connections forged between nationality, nation-ness and citizenship, but here we take the problematisation of the connections between 'the national/nation' and citizenship a step further. The turbulent times of citizenship and nation-states – the destabilisation of established 'bundles' in Sassen's terms or what Malkki (1995) calls changes in the 'national order of things' – have fuelled debates about the emergence of 'post-national' forms of citizenship (see, eg, Soysal, 1994, 2012; Wind, 2009; Olsen, 2012). While many of the arguments developed about these new forms are of political-philosophical inspiration, a number of them are inspired by actual evolutions, particularly the development of inter- or supranational institutions, together with the changing practices of international migrants, economic globalisation or 'cultural denationalisation' (Tambini, 2001). In line with some of the earlier discussions around 'national citizenship', issues of legal rights and arrangements, of sovereignty, and of identifications are often intermingled and conflated. As a result, it is hardly surprising that debates have emerged around questions of 'post-national' forms, sites and practices of citizenship, entangled in very diverse understandings of what the post-national might designate (from Delanty's [2001] denationalised global cosmopolitan citizenship, through Soysal's [1994] view of emerging post-national citizenship in the European space, to the work of Raissiguier and others [Raissiguier, 2010; see also, Coll, 2011] on migrant claims to citizenship). This diversity of concepts reflects different understandings of the nation: as political-juridical institutions; as a shared ethnicised or culturalised identity; as a territorial assemblage; or as a primordial community.

In the European context, many discussions of post-national citizenship have been connected to the emergence of a European Union (EU)-based legal citizenship, which has been seen by some as a unique historical opportunity to 'free' citizenship(s) from its 'national' limits and limitations, that is, to create a citizenship at the European level that would thus be disconnected from 'identities', which would remain attached to the national level. Meanwhile, Habermas (2000) has pleaded for ethno-nationally defined citizenship to be replaced by 'constitutional patriotism' as a basis of political belonging. Conversely a number of theorists have mobilised 'in defence of national citizenship', arguing that it had to be rescued as the only viable and efficient form of citizenship (Schnapper, 1997; for a critical discussion of these arguments, see Tambini, 2001). Yasemin Soysal's conception of post-national citizenship connects with our previous discussion about the contemporary unbundlings of state, rights and identity:

> My inquiry … challenges the predominant assumption, both scholarly and popular, that national citizenship is imperative to membership in a polity. As I show in the case of postwar migrants in Europe, incorporation into a system of membership rights does not inevitably require incorporation into the national collectivity.… The recent guestworker experience reflects a time when national citizenship is losing ground to a more universal model of citizenship, anchored in deterritorialized notions of person's rights. (Soysal, 1994: 3)

According to some authors, since (nation-)states are no longer the sole purveyors and/or guarantors of rights, the national level would only remain relevant in terms of identity and not in terms of citizenship rights. The usual ambiguities around 'the national' are at work here: is it referring to an institutional level, that is, the central state, or to nation-ness as a necessary component of this specific level? Is the 'national collectivity' understood as a political one (the nation of citizens) or a 'cultural' one (the nation of compatriots)? As to the ground lost by 'national citizenship', we think this remains to be empirically substantiated. Many rights remain institutionalised within national legal, political and welfare systems. At the same time, the purchase of international or supranational political and juridical powers has proven to be limited in a number of cases (see the discussions of Muslim mobilisations through the European Court of Human Rights in Edmunds [2012], or human rights in relation to Guantanamo detainees in Russell [2005]). As noted earlier, while the relationship between citizenship, state and nation has been disturbed and brought into question, there are also attempts to construct new national settlements – new bundles, so to speak – in which citizenship, nation and state are reassembled. Such attempts are again found to be enacted by a variety of actors: state agencies and policies, social movements and academia. Tambini convincingly analyses this last domain when he observes that:

> Thus, the argument [of the 'new national agenda in liberal philosophy'] is that in the absence of the nation as the embodiment of the public good, and with no recognizable identity, civic culture, or project, citizenship is impossible. At best, individuals can only engage in self-serving, instrumental behaviour; at worst, they are so disorientated by the lack of common culture that they cannot exercise any agency at all. (Tambini, 2001: 204)

The shift to a universal model of individuals as bearers of human rights thus remains a much-debated change. For some commentators, the model of the rights-bearing individual provides a critical political foundation for a cosmopolitan model of global civil society, in which individuals escape the confines of identity and nation (eg Delanty, 2001). Critics of such a view challenge it on a range of different fronts: its foundation in a culturally and politically specific Northern universalism; its rhetorical rather than practical character; the absence of institutions that implement or enforce such rights; and the persistence of nation-states as both guarantors and obstructors of rights for most people (eg Koopmans and Statham, 1999; Russell, 2005; Maas, 2008). Recently, Zivi (2012) has challenged the philosophical or normative character of the debate on human rights for its abstraction from the practices of rights claiming. She argues that taking such practices seriously through a performative view of the practice of claiming leads to a view of rights claiming as a fundamental practice of 'democratic citizenship'. The last point – that it is inseparable from 'democratic citizenship' – is asserted, rather than demonstrated, and citizenship itself goes sadly undiscussed in these arguments. A rather different approach has been developed by John Erni (2011, 2012) in the context of Chinese struggles to name and claim human rights. Erni grounds his approach in a cultural analysis of law, stressing its contextualised and contested construction and practice. This opens up questions of how transnational repertoires (such as rights discourse) both travel and become grounded in specific social formations, with particular forms and sites of juridicalised practice.

Exploring the potential and/or actual emergence of post-national or transnational forms of citizenship requires us to take into account both institutional arrangements and regulations, and the practices of a variety of actors, especially the transnational or even diasporic ones of migrants – the mobilities, identifications and affiliations that connect them with more than one geopolitical and cultural place, such that they built differently their relationships and involvement in the communities they inhabit (eg Levitt, 2001; Tarrius, 2002; Erel, 2009; Raissiguier, 2010). These seem to us to be a distinctive dimension for the ways in which the national is being troubled, dismantled and sometimes reassembled. We return to these issues later. If certain authors capture vividly the multiple sources for such changes (state policies and agencies, migrants, voluntary groups etc; see Basch et al, 1994), others, like Soysal, tend to show relatively little interest indeed in the daily conditions and relationships in which such post-national citizenship is enacted and lived by citizens themselves. We feel that there is something strangely abstracted about these individuals who bear rights but do not live their lives in strained, contested and unequal societies in which citizenship may be imposed, withheld, practised and enacted in a range of different ways that go far beyond the legal specification of rights and duties. Many approaches seriously underplay what is, for us, a central dimension of citizenship processes: the weight of representations and the play of actual social relationships, what Poche (1992) describes as the sphere of recognition and the sharing of the *topos* (for more on that central issue, see later). Even in more conventional citizenship terms, Soysal has little to say about the conditions of access to political (especially voting) rights, viewing such access as a secondary issue (in contrast, see Coll, 2011). In other words, such approaches pay little attention to the fact that individuals, although endowed with rights that might be guaranteed by supranational institutions, live complex lives, in contradictory places and in shifting relationships.

Instead of postulating a global move towards new (post-national) forms of citizenship, it seems to us that what is worth analysing is the diversity of arrangements, struggles and reorganisations that can be observed in a diversity of contexts, and the volume and type of political work being done to try and circulate new schemes, emancipatory as well as not, for citizenship. If the national and its articulations with states and forms of citizenship have been destabilised or unsettled, it persists as both a site of attempted identifications, affiliations and forms of belonging, and as a significant level or scale in the organisation of political authority. At the same time, new forms of bundlings emerge. As Tambini suggests:

> If the current decline of national citizenship continues, we should not try to bury our heads in the sands of nineteenth-century liberal nationalism, calling for the preservation of an institution that is no longer able to fulfil its former roles. Rather, we should be aware of the complex variety of functions that the nation has served, and seek new institutions to serve them – institutions that reflect the reality of a world that is both globalizing and fragmenting. (Tambini, 2001: 212)

These have been variously described, for example: not just post-national, but also transnational; the contradictory processes of denationalisation and renationalisation of citizenship; post-nationalist politics; migrant multinational citizenships; and more. This diversity reflects something of what is set loose, and put into play, when the 'unbundling' processes begin to destabilise the normalised and naturalised formations of nation, nationality and citizenship.

However, we think that it is important to insert a note of historical caution about the intellectual and political enthusiasm that surrounds the contemporary unbundlings and destabilisations of nation, state and citizenship. There is danger of seeing only the present flux, innovation and possibilities for people to live their relationships with these arrangements differently. But the fact that nation–state–citizenship were temporarily stabilised formations should not lead us to ignore the ways in which they were always inhabited and contested in important ways. For example, the long contested history of forms of citizenship or our earlier discussions about colonial rebellions and their complex and contradictory relationships to the metropole (its identities and political representations) warn us against a simplified view of the past as stable and the present as unstable (Clarke and Fink, 2008).

We need to attend to at least three dynamics that are at stake in the idea of the post-national. The first is the destabilisation of taken-for-granted notions of the imagined political, cultural, economic and territorial unity of the nation. This contemporary sense of destabilisation perhaps bears most tellingly on the societies of the global North – those that had the luxury of imagining their inviolate unity – as opposed to the colonised territories of the South that always knew they were not 'closed' or tightly bounded, even if that image of closure and unity became an aspiration for nation-building projects. The second is the increase in – and increasing visibility of – transnational relationships, flows, processes and practices that traverse national boundaries (albeit unevenly), in which the transnational and trans-local connective practices of migrants remake national spaces. In the process, as Coll (2010, 2011), Raissiguier (2010) and others have shown, migrants may remake the meaning and substance of citizenship. Third, the 'post-national' also marks the site of the reassertion and remaking of the national, whether in the revitalisation of nationalist, exclusionary and racist discourses and practice of the nation or in the willingness of governments and academics to re-imagine nations and their territory in order either to capture money, people and resources apparently located 'elsewhere' (see, eg, Basch et al, 1994; Larner, 2007), or because they hold to national citizenship as the only viable and relevant form of citizenship. In the following section, we consider some of the ways in which the communities of citizens have been re-imagined.

Reinventing the 'communities' of citizens

In this section, we first explore what the 'national' is being made to mean in these 'post-national' times. Does it involve new bundlings between identifications and status/territory? Or does it imply new conceptions of how to organise the government of the people? Certainly, both of these have been the sites of intense governmental work, as political projects seek to redefine and re-establish the relationships between territory, people and government. However, at the same time, not all imagined 'communities of citizens' are national ones. Indeed, many imaginings of political community intentionally refuse the unifying constraints of the national identification, while social practices of migrants have changed and modified certain bundlings or formations of place and identification and the ideas of borders and boundaries on which they rest. In what follows, we explore some of these attempts to reinvent the communities of citizens.

We begin by exploring the idea of community itself as a site for reinventing the nation. In the UK in recent decades, the state has named neighbourhoods or communities as administrative, governmental and political sites; has sought out, addressed and recognised their 'members' and 'representatives'; has allocated different forms of resources to them; and has held them accountable or responsible for desired policy outcomes. In such relationships, forms of citizenship may be implicated, produced and practised: for example, identity checking, negotiating over rights to services and contesting principles and practices of inclusion and exclusion. Community has a long lineage as an imaginary relation in very different UK political formations: for example, in 'golden age' Conservatism, communitarian political philosophy, Fabianism, British colonial government and the community development projects of the 1980s. These different roots have enabled the concept to be highly elastic, allowing its recruitment in support of projects and policies of community care, community governance, community development, community capacity-building, community policing, community safety, community enterprise, community schools, community cohesion and many others. This proliferation of policy concepts suggests how far community has become implicated in the business of reforming government, especially, but not only, in the UK (see, eg, Joseph, 2002; Creed, 2007; Craig, 2007; Mooney and Neal, 2008).

In a multi-ethnic society, community has also become one means of mapping – and managing – forms of social difference in new processes of governing the social (Rose, 1999; Clarke, forthcoming). Community is, at one and the same time, the *object* of governance (governing agencies seek to act on communities), the *desired outcome* of governance (dysfunctional areas/people need to become communities) and the *subject* of governance (communities who govern themselves). Such governmentalised communities are invested with authority and capacity, and are imagined as moral agents. They need the attention, respect and engagement of (local) government agencies and personnel through consultation, participation and 'co-governing'. At the same time, communities are seen as the storehouses of values, commitments, resources and capacities that might be 'activated' in these process of co-governing. Once activated, such desirable qualities may help reduce the costs of public provisioning by providing resources that substitute for public expenditure (HM Treasury, 2002, 2005). This image of society beyond the state has been revised and renewed in the 2010 Coalition government's enthusiasm to reduce public spending and govern through the 'Big Society'. Conservative Prime Minister David Cameron described this as follows:

> The first step must be a new focus on empowering and enabling individuals, families and communities to take control of their lives so we create the avenues through which responsibility and opportunity can develop. This is especially vital in what is today the front line of the fight against poverty and inequality: education....

> The era of big government has run its course.
> Poverty and inequality have got worse, despite Labour's massive expansion of the state. We need new answers now, and they will only come from a bigger society, not bigger government. (Cameron, 2009: 1, 11)

Two extracts from earlier (New Labour) UK government documents give some idea of the multiple significance of community. The first ties citizenship and community directly together:

> There is a deal for citizenship. This is a country of liberty and tolerance, opportunity and diversity – and these values are reinforced by the expectation that all who live here should learn our language, play by the rules, obey the law and contribute to the community. (Home Office, 2008: 5)

Here, community stands for the nation – the national political community – to whom citizens (now referring to newly arrived or naturalised citizens) owe a series of obligations over and above their loyalty to the nation-state and its institutions (including the monarchy). Citizenship and its implied membership of the community offers one means of restoring the nation and the national identity in the face of the perceived threats and dangers of a post-national world – especially those posed by migration (the phrase 'those who live here should learn *our* language' marks the problem of restoring the nation). Community has also been a major focus for producing new sites of governing below the national/central level, including the commitment in the New Labour years to promoting 'community cohesion' in the face of ethnic-cultural divisions and antagonisms:

> Communities that are strong and inclusive lead to a better quality of life, a stronger sense of identity and belonging, and mutual respect and equality. This is central to the idea of a civil society on which democracy rests....
> A cohesive community is one where:
> * there is a common vision and a sense of belonging for all communities;
> * the diversity of people's different backgrounds and circumstances are appreciated and positively valued;
> * those from different backgrounds have similar life opportunities;

- strong and positive relationships are being developed between people from different backgrounds in the workplace, in schools and within neighbourhoods. (From: http://www.gos.gov.uk/gone/peopleandsustcomms/ community_cohesion/ [accessed 14 November 2007])

'Community' has played a central role in these attempted realignments of government, governance, the state and civil society (Mooney and Neal, 2008). It provides a way of imagining living together that invokes much older – and nostalgic – ways of life based on neighbourliness and local solidarities. It is central to the rescaling processes of sites and forms of governing, and part of the re-imagining of places, practices and identities within – and beyond – the nation. But it is also a way of reframing social diversity, with 'minority ethnic communities' taking their place alongside other supposed communities, fracturing and displacing the idea of wider public solidarity (Clarke and Newman, 2012). The turn to 'community' as a governing strategy both seeks to accommodate diversity and, at the same time, separate it from the politics that identified difference, inequality and exclusion as political issues. Similarly, the idea of the nation as a 'community of communities' provides a way of governing difference while, at the same time, erasing the kinds of difference that might challenge the current political–cultural project. The UK's obsession with community, denoting both forms of affiliation or identification and a local scale, is one particular variant of changing patterns of state formation and citizenship specification.

In contrast with the UK obsession, we should remember that the 'imagined' communities of citizenship are in no sense limited to nations or collectivities within nations. On the contrary, even if nation-states remain significant sites for, and guarantors of, juridical citizenship, Soysal's other aspect of 'post-national' citizenship is a profoundly important site of 'imagined communities' that span national boundaries (Soysal, 1994; but, on different examples of transnational or diasporic citizenship, see also Evergeti and Zontini, 2006; Ong, 1999b; Caldwell et al, 2009; Coll, 2010; for 'new cosmopolites' who organise their lives with a rather detached relation to their countries of 'passage', see Tarrius, 2002). Sometimes, such connections are grasped in terms of the material and symbolic connections that link people across places (care chains, remittances or even trans-local politics); at others, they raise questions of formal citizenship – dual citizenship (nationality), citizenship choices and so on. In both senses, they are tangled in forms of 'imagined community' that span national borders. Forms of connection, solidarity and even stretched sociality (stretched across time and space) are imagined in multinational and multi-local 'communities' (Tarrius, 2002). Furthermore, despite the excesses of cosmopolitan celebrations of 'global civil society' (Kaldor, 2003; Keane, 2003; Held, 2004), there are other forms of transnational connection, alliance, network and movement that connect 'citizens of the world' in forms and practices of international solidarity (eg Santos and Rodrigues-Garavito, 2005; on global justice, see also Fraser, 2005). It is important to stress how such imagined communities reframe ideas and practices of citizenship in non-national ways. People may imagine themselves as members of communities that exist beyond and below the nation. Such imaginings of citizenship are important for their capacity to break the ties that seem to bind citizenship to nation and state. This reminds us of Lochak's view of the French revolutionary nation as a political community, rather than a territorial one, which we discussed in Chapter One. It is an important reminder because, as we argued earlier, the temptation is to treat current post-, supra- or transnational imaginaries of community, collectivity and citizenship as temporally associated with the break-up of the nation-state constellation. But a variety of colonial movements – in the Caribbean and India, for instance – have involved imagined communities of citizens that traverse national boundaries (and the exclusionary and divisive politics of imperial citizenship; see Mamdani, 1996). Banerjee's work on movements for 'imperial citizenship' in Victorian India explores the 'naturalization of a vocabulary of rights', borrowed and translated from British origins, but in ways that 'exceeded the question of sovereign promise or imperial benevolence' (2010: 192). She argues that:

> The naturalization of the new vocabulary took place in different venues and through diverse routes, which often extended beyond the realm of the juridico-political. Tracing the multiple strands of citizenship and their complex affective and imaginative ideations ... makes clear that the history of citizenship has multiple bearings and points of provenance, which not only exceed the compartmentalization of citizenship into discrete civil, social and political units, but also call for an entwining of legal history with social process, political negotiations with their cultural and affective imaginings. It points to how the category of citizenship is hardly self-evident. Prying citizenship apart from the nation-state in fact allows for a capacious reading of these histories of citizenship. It keeps

alive the ties between citizenship as defined – and denied
– by the state and its intimate links with notions of civil
liberty and civil society. (Banerjee, 2010: 192)

Banerjee points to the different – and contested – imaginings of
citizenship that were being mobilised in this period: conceptions
and practices that affirmed national boundaries, reinvented them and
spanned them in subaltern geographies of empire. Her study underlines
the capacity of citizenship to function as a keyword through which
different sorts of 'community' or collectivity may be imagined. Much
writing on citizenship has stressed the double dynamic of inclusion and
exclusion: the 'belonging' to a political community paralleled by the
refusal or denial of such 'membership'. We have seen how territorial
conceptions of belonging can provide a foundation for citizenship
claims in both local and national terms. The recent destabilisations of
the established citizenship–nation–state bundlings (Sassen, 2005) have
called such territorial conceptions into question. They have unsettled
the 'imagined geographies' in which people and place are mapped and
which underpin notions of people being 'out of place' such that 'this
place' does not belong to them, and they do not belong 'here'. In one
sense, this reflects the collapse of the imagined colonial geographies
that linked 'race and place' in apparently stable or sedimented forms.
Such imagined geographies ranged from national to local spaces,
where dense conceptions of attachment, belonging and ownership
are condensed (Wemyss, 2006). We have seen the emergence of
governmental strategies for governing populations where formations
of ethnic/cultural differentiation have become intensely politicised
in transnational, national and local forms (Lewis, 2000; Parekh, 2000;
Hesse, 2001; Modood, 2005). New governance arrangements that
are structured by this multi-ness aim to accommodate or contain
potential social and political antagonisms. Multi-ethnic/cultural
governance creates zones of containment that may also be the sites
of accommodating differences or producing practices of cohabitation
or conviviality (Gilroy, 2005). The contemporary flux of differences
constructed around national identities, ethnic identities and religious/
faith affiliations – and the attempts to make them align with one
another – marks a difficult, shifting and troubling field of conflicted
and contested identifications. In the process, such histories of 'place
and race' connect senses of attachment and identification, ownership
claims, and ideas of belonging in ways that create a distinctive field of
governance problems.

The problem is that there are profoundly contested claims to spaces and places, which are mobilised through citizenship discourses and representations. These might crudely be characterised as exclusionary or expansive struggles. So, claims to exclusive belonging have been mobilised against 'immigrants' or mobile people (Roma, Travellers, etc) in the name of belonging: we, the citizens, have established rights of belonging to places, rights and so on. In difficult times, citizenship has become the focus of governmental attempts to shrink its scale and scope, to make citizens more 'active' and 'responsible', and to reset the conditions of nationality – in different ways in different places. Such retrenchment has also made ethno-nationalist and exclusivist conceptions of citizenship a more potent popular discourse and practice (Kalb, 2005). However, at the same time, new citizenship claims are made, new expansive imaginaries are identified as the ground for new solidarities, new practices of 'being citizenly' are brought into being – and the closures, retrenchments and exclusions are (unevenly) contested. Citizenship, then, remains '*imparfaite*' – still in the (contested) process of being made and remade.

In the previous chapters, we argued for the need to both recentre and decentre citizenship, seeking in the process to disentangle it from its taken-for-granted locations, and instead attend to its relationships to political projects and cultural formations. In advancing these arguments, we have drawn on a variety of citizenship projects and practices that illuminate the contentious and contingent character of citizenship. We now want to trace the heterogeneous *locations* of citizenship: the multiple sites, scales and settings in which citizenship is imagined, demanded, refused, negotiated and enacted. We will be arguing that citizenship *takes place*, and this 'taking place' has to be understood not only as a metaphor (denoting an event happening), but also as consequential in spatial terms. Citizenship happens in places; citizens act in places; citizenship is practised (or not) in particular places. We begin from an interest in why some places (sites, scales, settings) are deemed (by states, social movements, citizens, etc) to be 'proper' ones for citizenship, while others are not.

Sites and scales of citizenship

Given the centrality of the nation-state to conceptions of citizenship, it is perhaps hardly surprising that it is often identified as a privileged *level* of analysis. However, the view that citizenship(s) can solely be formed and practised at, or addressed to, the level of the (national) state has to be critically examined. We argue that, on the contrary, citizenship entails practices at different levels and takes shape in projects that connect different levels. Thus, rather than an established structure or hierarchical order of levels or scales, scales are themselves a political product: their ordering is the outcome of particular projects and struggles. Considering the heterogeneous sites and settings in which citizenship 'takes place' allows us to develop a view of the shifting scalar and spatial dynamics of citizenship. Thus, if the heterogeneity of states produces a multiplicity of sites in which states and citizens encounter one another, it is important to address the fact that state sites and spaces do not exhaust the possible sites and spaces of the practice or performance of citizenship. The notion of 'horizontal citizenship', discussed in Chapter One, is intended to allow for such a multiplicity. Hence, it is vital to recognise that commonly defined sites of citizenship in parts of academic research (elections, institutional politics and education, to mention the most common) are not the only ones. The unruly practices of popular innovation and imagination that are expressed in citizenship practices spill over the conventional boundaries of 'politics' or state, and disrupt the distinctions between public and private, or between places of residence, attachment and legal membership. Indeed, it is the variety of daily, routine or more exceptional practices of citizenship that make it possible and desirable to think through citizenship across a diversity of levels, sites and places that are differently connected. Examining how citizenship 'takes place' both enlarges the study of citizenship, and identifies citizenship as a critical dimension in the politics of scale and space. Citizenship projects are connective: linking people, places and power in distinctive – and very different – ways.

Citizenship provides one of the more fruitful vantage points from which to critically discuss what Ferguson and Gupta (2002) analyse as 'the vertical topography of power', and Isin (2007) calls 'scalar thought'. Indeed, geographical and spatial metaphors of 'up there', 'grassroots', 'bottom up' and 'top down' are plentiful in the social sciences, in both conventional and critical modes. Writing about ideas of the state, Ferguson and Gupta stress the:

> Two images [that] come together in popular and academic discourses on the state: those of *verticality and encompassment*. *Verticality refers* to the central and pervasive idea of the state as *an* institution somehow 'above' civil society, community, and family. Thus, state planning is inherently 'top down' and state actions are efforts to manipulate and plan 'from above,' while 'the grassroots' contrasts with the state precisely in that

it is 'below,' closer to the ground, more authentic, and more 'rooted.' The second image is that of *encompassment*: Here the state (conceptually fused with the nation) is located within an ever widening series of circles that begins with family and local community and ends with the system of nation-states. This is a profoundly consequential understanding of scale, one in which the locality is encompassed by the region, the region by the nation-state, and the nation-state by the international community. These two metaphors work together to produce a taken-for-granted spatial and scalar image of a state that both sits above and contains its localities, regions, and communities. (Ferguson and Gupta, 2002: 982; see also Isin, 2007)

For some analysts, there would be different ways to be a citizen (or the impossibility of even being one) according to the 'level' at which one acts; we would argue that configurations connecting qualities, competencies and levels depend not on these levels, but on the political projects at play and their politics of scale. It is such sets of presuppositions that we intend to challenge, relocating them in a more general discussion about the 'topographic imaginations of politics' underlying them, which, today, constitute an obstacle to the analysis of a growing number of processes.

According to Isin, 'the scalar thought that underlies our understanding of modern political entities (cities, regions, nations, states …) assumes exclusive, hierarchical and ahistorical relations among and between these entities, and conceals their multiple, fluid and overlapping forms of existence' (Isin, 2007: 211). In terms of citizenship, such scalar thought implies that there is one, and only one, level of belonging and loyalty, that is, the nation-state level. Because of its exclusive and encompassing logic, the scalar thought implies an exclusive thought of citizenship itself, as being essentially connected to the state as the only producer of identification, belonging and engagement. A critical analysis of such conceptions is, then, a precondition to grasp the very complexity of citizenship, and the diversity of its sites, levels and spaces of production and enactments. The approach to citizenship we have been developing here is one that stresses its debated, contested and always-in-the-making character, and includes in the frame its horizontal dimensions and the fact that not all citizens are legally recognised ones. It is thus because we hold a view of citizenship(s) as manufactured through a multiplicity of processes and by a diversity of agents, and as necessarily contextual, that we came to critically question the comfortable dichotomies and exclusive, hierarchical order of the 'scalar thought'. Indeed, 'as soon as we begin to shift the question of rights and obligations from the juridico-legal site into social, cultural, ethical, aesthetic and indeed political sites, scalar thought comes up against severe limitations' (Isin, 2007: 218).

While the legal and institutional arrangements of citizenship differ from one context to another, the notion that the citizen is (or should be) principally attached to the central state is still a very powerful one, for instance, when new practices of citizenship(s) and statuses of double nationality are seen as a threat to such attachment or 'loyalty'. Meanwhile, such visions tend to underestimate the fact that even the 'level' referred to in such discussions might differ according to constitutional arrangements; thus, in Switzerland, to take just one example, access to nationality is not dealt with by the federal state level, but follows a complex circulation from the 'local' (*commune*) level to the federal state one, through the *canton* (see Centlivres et al, 1991). As shown by Tambini (2001; see also Balibar, 2001) among others, this is largely due to how 'national citizenship' evolved as a general 'form' during the last two centuries. The important point here is that both this 'vertical topography of power' and 'scalar thought' are 'state visions', that is, they are produced from the state standpoint and through its 'prose on itself' (Lopez Caballero, 2009), even if they are often 'internalised' by people, including researchers, as the 'normal state' of things. In his discussion of the scalar thought, Isin stresses the extent to which it underlies our understanding of modern political entities (cities, regions, nations and, above all, states): 'The early modern and modern politico-legal thought, by instituting the state as the supreme artificial person, created a scalar relationship between the state and other bodies politic and corporate that was exclusive, hierarchical and ahistorical' (Isin, 2007: 215). He locates the emergence of such thought in the development of the modern state and its will 'to reduce the chaotic, disorderly and constantly changing social reality to something closer to the administrative frame of its observations' (Scott, 1998: 81–2, quoted in Isin, 2007: 214). As we argued above, challenging such scalar essentialism is vital for the study of citizenship, because it is one of the forms in which citizenship and the nation-state are posed as inextricably combined. Although we are troubled by such 'scalar essentialism', we recognise that it is a powerful and widespread way of thinking about the structuring of political life, especially in dominant conceptions of relationships between the state and society. Indeed, the effects of such a mechanical connection between levels and practices, where the local is conceived of as if not merely parochial, then at least as a space where '*montée en généralité*' (increasing abstraction) cannot happen and thus where larger, 'really' political issues cannot be engaged with, are visible in two related examples from France.

In the French context, as in many others, research dealing with citizenship issues is rarely empirically based and anthropological research on citizenship processes is indeed rare (see Neveu, 2009). Conversely, the now important literature dealing with 'participatory democracy' practices rarely mentions 'citizenship' or 'citizens' as relevant categories. This could indeed be explained by the fact that such words are relatively underused in these practices or more generally at the local level (Neveu, 2011). But on closer examination, another explanation could be found for such an absence in both cases, which is connected to the level at which these studies are made, or, more precisely, to a set of representations concerning 'the local', the main level at which 'participatory democracy' practices are managed and anthropological research on this issue is conducted. In the French context, 'the local' remains relatively ill-defined, mostly referring to that which is not the national/central/state level. Meanwhile, it is endowed with specific characteristics that are used, paradoxically, to both justify the implementation at that level of a series of public policies and delegitimise the possibility that 'the local' can be a level at which *political* decisions could be made. 'The local', generally in the guise of urban neighbourhoods, is thus typically constituted, in academic literature as well as in policies, as the privileged space of actual and authentic relationships, and for solidarity and 'social cohesion' to (re)develop. In the same move and for the same reasons, this 'localist local' is generally conceived of as a pragmatic space, devoid of the qualities and characteristics of an actual 'political' level or space (see also Freeman, 2001; Massey, 2004). Thus, when Crowley (2003) considers 'the local' as a level for bargaining about resources, and contrasts such a bargaining with 'properly political deliberation', which, according to him, can only take place at the national (or, more exactly, central state) level, he implicitly mobilises a purely pragmatic reading of bargaining on the one hand, and a specific conception of politics on the other. Indeed, one could question the conception that such bargaining practices have as their sole basis the defence of and negotiations about particular interests; as research on EU institutions has clearly shown, bargaining is also about accommodating a diversity of 'political cultures', that is, about discussing and negotiating compromises not as much on concrete resources as on worldviews and ways to describe and qualify them (Abélès, 2005). Bargaining, in this view, involves practices that identify, construct and negotiate political issues and relationships, rather than refusing their political character.

It is essential here to underline the extent to which such a vertical/ hierarchical encasement logic distinguishes specific publics for each of its levels. Analysing participatory democracy practices in France, Blondiaux thus stressed how publics are called upon:

> sometimes as users to whom services are delivered; sometimes as residents whose advice is sought but who are assigned to a territory and whose deliberations are maintained within the confine of the neighbourhood; much more rarely as citizens to whom the possibility would be given to express themselves on the very opportunity of projects, to raise the discussion to a more general level, i.e. to simply do politics. (Blondiaux, 2002: 9)

Here, users, residents and citizens are indeed identified as categories connected to specific processes and issues (service delivery, consultation, 'politics'), to which specific levels are assigned. Such representations are common, according to which different categorisations are connected to specific levels and endowed with specific competencies and attributes. In the French context, it is more than common to speak of 'inhabitants' at the local level and of 'citizens' at the national/ central one. Political processes and projects are also thus designated or envisioned: 'inhabitants' would contribute to the development of participatory democracy, while 'citizens' would belong to the world (and level) of representative democracy. The former would engage in actual and concrete stakes while the latter would belong to abstraction; the former would speak from their 'users' expertise', and/or their local rootedness, while citizens should abstract themselves from their social determinations and from their other forms of belonging to anything other than the national/central level in order to deliberate as equals in the public sphere (Neveu, 2011).

Such conceptions are both mechanical (attaching a category and a type of process to each scale) and hierarchised; they also carry specific conceptions of politics, and of citizenship. They are indeed shot through with the dominant conception of the citizen as an abstract individual, acting in the public sphere from a position of detachment from any kind of belonging, identification or interest (local, cultural, gendered, social). Thus, opposing 'the citizen', defined as an individual able to abstract him/herself from social and localised rootedness, and 'the resident', defined as a localised expert, and referring these two categories to distinct levels, qualities and competencies, only maintains an easy dichotomy that forbids any critical discussion of these very notions

(Neveu, 2005, 2011). Is 'the citizen', indeed, necessarily a disembodied being who speaks clearly and rationally, is s/he really this being without qualities who deliberates in the public sphere by abstracting him/herself from his/her connections and belongings, and would this be the only way to think a 'general interest' (Boullier, 2009)? Does the expertise of 'the residents' derive only from a particular spatial closeness that may often be disconnected from their own actual practices, relationships and networks?

What is striking here is, first, how the different 'publics' are related to different sites: users to their services; inhabitants to their neighbourhoods; and citizens to 'politics'. But it is also specific competencies that are thus valorised and connected to such levels, legitimating these publics' contributions: 'expert knowledge' for users; 'ordinary expertise' gained through their routine uses of the neighbourhood for inhabitants; and capacity of abstraction for citizens. This kind of work thus reflects political processes and projects of citizenship(s): 'inhabitants' would be located within participatory democracy, while citizens would belong to representative democracy; the former would be involved in actual and tangible stakes, while the latter would go for abstraction; the former would speak from their expert knowledge and 'local' belonging (therefore positively seen), while the latter should abstract themselves from their social determinations and belongings (negatively considered) in order to deliberate among equals in the political public sphere.

In a related instance, when the elected local authorities (*conseil municipal*) of Tours decided to launch a '*démocratie de proximité*' ('propinquity democracy') initiative, they opted for the creation of four *Conseils de la Vie Locale* (CVL; local life councils), each covering a quarter of the city's territory and population; a much larger level than that of the 'traditional' neighbourhood. If practical and tactical arguments were given to explain this choice (see Neveu, 2008b), more fundamental reasons were also evoked to justify it. This choice of a 'grander scale' was indeed presented as one the major innovations introduced by this scheme. Dividing the city into four sectors for CVLs was presented by the *1er adjoint* as resulting 'from a philosophical or political, as you want, choice, that consists in saying that a city is a whole, and not a sheer juxtaposition of neighbourhoods seated in the shade of their parish churches' (Neveu, 2008b: 71): the local is (merely) parochial. Even more importantly, creating *ex nihilo* such sectors was seen as allowing to get rid of local 'identity reflexes', of parochialism, by forcing residents to get out of their usual environment and confront themselves with 'larger stakes'. The implicit idea was thus that by some kind of mechanical effect, new practices and behaviours would automatically flow from simply modifying the size of the area concerned. Changing scale was thus seen as a propaedeutic exercise, as the condition for more 'abstracted' and detached discussions, and citizens, to be created.

This mapping of types of subjects, sets of practices and sites and scales of action is both common (scalar distribution is not only French, as we shall see), but also distinctively framed by a particular politics of scale, in which citizenship is equated with being interested in what some define as the 'legitimate political sphere' (having an opinion, showing interest in politicians, parties and their programmes, and voting), which is then equated with the central-national state level. Indeed, it is sometimes argued that politics – and citizenship in this sense – can only take place at the central-national level because the local is merely local or even parochial, or a level at which only 'bargaining' around specific interests can exist. The capacity for 'abstraction' or 'generalisation' that is considered as the key characteristic of this type of citizen requires them to transcend, or leave behind, their particular identities and attachments – including their local affiliations. Neveu's work has demonstrated clearly that dominant understandings of citizenship in France view it as a status and relationship that operates at an exclusively national state level, linking individuals and the state, individuals abstracting themselves and rising above merely local and/or particular issues, interests and identities. Such a capacity of abstraction is indeed seen as the very condition for citizenship, and politics, to actually exist and be practised as such.

This somewhat mechanical model of scale creation might be usefully contrasted with the innovation of the Participatory Budget in Porto Alegre, Brazil. Implemented in 1989, the city has been divided into 16 regions, with plenary assemblies and representatives of their own. Since the objective was to produce a budget proposal for the whole city, after the first year of operation, there was a collective decision that those representatives visit the 16 regions in order to know and assess their needs and, when choosing the priorities to be contemplated by the budget each year, thus be able to make decisions not limited to favour strictly the demands of their own regions. Here, too, there is a concern to create a stronger 'general interest' for the city as a whole, but we would want to draw attention to two key points. First, the conception of participatory budgeting itself aimed to change the *politics* of the 'local', involving people of the city in its budgetary decisions. Second, attention was given to the processes of interaction and exchange through which such a politics might be built, constructing the relations of exchange and interaction through which common interests and identities might be formed – or at least argued over. Meanwhile the 'levels' of these politics are still determined by powers in place; decentralisation in Mali presented an even more radical departure from such level playing fields, since inhabitants of villages themselves were to decide about the shape, size and composition of the newly created 'communes'; in some cases, sites that were not physically close were built as a 'commune' because of existing networks and relationships (see Lima, 2006).

Such forms of scalar thought – and particularly the reification of the central-national level of the state – evoke different critical responses, two of which need to be briefly mentioned here. The first typically involves an inversion of the central-national fixation and celebrates the 'local' as the organic location of 'real' or 'popular' politics (sometimes as 'grassroots' organisations; sometimes as 'bottom-up' processes). We will have more to say about the local and its multiple significance for the politics of citizenship in later sections, but here we want to note a couple of problems with such reifications and romanticisations of the local. They are also a version of scalar thought and of politics of scales: reifying the local as a fixed level within a hierarchical order, although they valorise it differently. They also tend to give its political value a distinctly romantic and rosy cast: the local acts as a guarantor of political virtue, championing 'ordinary people' against the state/power bloc (Ferguson, 1994; Massey, 2004; on 'ordinary people', see also Clarke, 2010). We will instead explore how the politics of scale – including the contested place of the local – and the politics of citizenship are entwined.

The second response to state-centric scale has been the idea of 'multi-level governance', which was developed in the European context as part of the debate about the decline of the nation-state itself. Multi-level governance approaches are sometimes associated with the idea that the nation-state has been 'hollowed out' by changes that move governing power and processes 'above' and 'below' the nation-state (Rhodes, 1997). So, multi-level governance points to the role of international or supranational agencies and institutions usurping or constraining national decision-making power (the International Monetary Fund [IMF], World Trade Organization [WTO] and the EU), while processes of decentralisation or devolution have dispersed power to levels below the national (eg Bache and Flinders, 2004). This view of multiple levels has also been applied to citizenship. For example, Bauböck and Guiraudon have argued that:

> While earlier generations of citizenship theorists still operated with models of closed national societies, the

focus of present debates is often on boundary transgressing phenomena – such as migration – and on multilevel citizenship that combines sub-state with supranational modes of membership and rights. (2009: 439)

We have already indicated the importance of 'boundary-transgressing' or blurring processes, we are less persuaded about the value of 'multi-levelness' (but see Maas, 2013). Our problem is that the multi-level approach tends to multiply the number of levels, while continuing to understand them as existing in a fixed order – from top to bottom, or nested, as Massey puts it, in a sort of 'Russian doll' model in which each level is encompassed by the (larger) one above it (Massey, 2004: 9). Similarly, Stubbs has argued that:

In many ways, the concept of multi-level governance relies on a taken-for-granted notion of geographical scales – supranational, national, and local as well as various regional scales. A different approach, a fusion of post-modernist and critical political geography, points to the contingency, complexity, and, above all, the socially and politically constructed nature of scale. (2005: 76)

In the following section, we turn to the significance of a 'politics of scale' for studying citizenship.

The commitment to recentring and decentring citizenship thus requires us to take into account its multiple sites and spaces of enactment, and to pay attention to the always diverse arrangements that connect a variety of 'levels'; one could even want to do without the very notion of 'level' that almost automatically results in organising and hierarchising them. Analysing spaces and sites, and eventually examining whether or not they are thought of or lived as 'levels', therefore seems to us to be a more fruitful approach in that it also allows for the grasping and understanding of what politics of scale are at work.

A politics of scale?

We develop our concern with levels and scale through an exploration of a series of representations, as powerful as they are rendered invisible, which impregnate most conceptions of politics, citizenship and scales/levels we are brought to use. It is part of a wider move that questions a 'common sense cartography of the social and political space', which mainly relies on a 'vertical topography of power' (Ferguson,

2004: 383–4). Drawing on an in-depth analysis of the contemporary uses and success of the notion of 'civil society' in anthropological research in Africa, Ferguson stresses the existence of a specific spatial imaginary, in which the state is located in a universal 'up there', with a civil society sandwiched between it and the family, which is 'down here'. And this vertical topography of power is consequential since its very verticality is connected with representations about the 'local' (as authentic, rooted, actual) and grassroots social movements on the one hand, and the state and the global (as abstract, artificial) on the other (on the nesting of levels and places in a 'Russian doll' model, see Massey, 2004). Interestingly enough, Ferguson also underlines the extent to which the success of 'civil society' as a virtuous opposite of the 'bad and corrupted' state is a new way to frame what used to be a reversed opposition, between a modern state that was to bring modernity and progress and a parochial and backward 'local'. Both 'topographies' are politics of scales that valorise differently the state/central and the local/ civil society 'levels'.

As with citizenship, so too with questions of scale: we are committed to a view that treats aspects of social formations as both the objects and the outcomes of contending political projects. So, in attending to the politics of scale – and its relation to the politics of citizenship – we move through three steps. First, we contrast the conception of a fixed scalar hierarchy with practices that 'jump scales'. Second, we insist that both specific scales and the orderings of their interrelationship are the result of political and cultural work. The apparent 'facticity' of particular scales and their order has to be understood as an accomplishment – the effectivity of a form of scalar thought – rather than a universal and permanent arrangement. The local, we suggest, emerges in varying configurations and through different fields of relationships. Finally, we point to the ways in which citizenship is entangled in these scalar and spatial imaginaries, as articulations of people and place.

Even within established hierarchies of scale, citizenship is often imagined and practised in ways that 'jump scales'. Most evidently in the experiences and practices of migrants, there are complex connections between different levels and locales of citizenship. So migrants have sometimes acted as forging horizontal connections between two (or more) national levels, thus connecting spaces and levels that are not physically or politically contiguous. As has been explored earlier, the links between citizenship and territory have conventionally been conceived as exclusive; as a status managed by states, citizenship was supposed to be attached only to their own territory. Public policies in France that deal separately with 'integration' on the one hand and 'development' on the other (even though migrants' practices have long since been in a different dynamic connecting the two; see, among others, Tarrius, 2002) are a result of such a conception, which is quite often formulated as a summons to choose between the two sites/ spaces (France or the country of origin), or even between two sets of references (and this is yet another example of scalar thought). But many practices developed by migrants and their children connect, sometimes in paradoxical ways, diverse and disconnected territories and spaces, thus subverting the traditional limits of citizenship. Such practices and forms of public engagement could thus be read as prefiguring differently 'global' cities, global not because of their capacity to attract and manage global financial flows, but because of their inhabitants' practices, circulations and networks (Massey, 2004).

For more than 50 years, migrants from the Senegal river valley in France have been financially and otherwise involved in multiple development projects (Gonin et al, 2011). Too often, such projects are viewed as initiatives the aim of which would be for their bearers to prepare their return in their country of origin. However, not only did they not 'return home', but such development projects have indeed worked as powerful tools for them to envision differently their citizenship, both in France and in Senegal or Mali. While these migrants have not yet succeeded in gaining a right to vote in France, even in local elections, they nevertheless claim and assert, through these many projects and actions 'out there', original forms of spatial and social belonging, rendered even more important with the birth and socialisation of their children in France.

These migrants from the Senegal river valley have thus progressively settled in specific forms of migratory circulations and citizenship practices (Gonin and Kotlok, 2013). Far from being disconnected, this type of double involvement contributes to a move towards a dynamic and complex articulation connecting territories, identities and mobilities. Such practices have been explored by Cartiaux (2008) in her analysis of the practices and discourses of members of voluntary groups created by Senegal river valley migrants and their children; she locates three ways to conceive of and practise the relationships between France and West Africa. The first one she calls 'translation' (as a notion of geometry), that is, the transfer of persons or resources from one site to another (usually from a village to the hostel where migrants in France live and organise); while sites and spaces are not directly connected through translation, practices and relationships in one site have effects in the other, for instance, in terms of changing social relationships within 'traditional' peer or age groups. Another model of connection between these distant sites is 'conjunction', a different one in that it includes something common to the two concerned territories (an administrative level as when two cities are connected, or the capital city of one of the countries when it is used as a site for meetings and exchanges). When there is 'conjunction', citizenship practices connect sets of agents involved in common projects, mostly at the local level, and only refer to the state level when specific support or planning authorisation is required. The third conception is 'enlargement', an enlargement that can rely on a thematic approach to concerns expressed in the Senegal river valley (ie health or education, but also mining; in that case, the sites connected include not only concerned neighbourhoods or voluntary groups in France and Senegal-Mali, but other sites where similar issues are debated – in the case of gold mining, contacts have been made with Canadian groups). But such thematic enlargement also flows from concerns in France, such as access to employment, the fight against discrimination and asserting legitimate belonging to French society despite/because of one's origins. For instance, Cartiaux shows how agents involved in voluntary groups (in social, economic or cultural activities) in French cities' neighbourhoods link these territories with those of the origin of their inhabitants, thus introducing new coherence in their action. Such initiatives then create a 'spider web' connecting a local space (a neighbourhood or a city) to multiple other territories that are close to it, not geographically, but through social and cultural networks; a connection that is then 'horizontal', that is, that does not follow the previously discussed 'Russian doll' logic, but creates space for citizenship practices and representations that connect sites located at different levels (villages, capital cities, regions, states …). Cartiaux concludes her analysis by stressing that:

> the territorial configurations expressed in voluntary groups … are complex, they trifle with scales…. But in all these configurations, the French state appears somehow absent (*en creux*), and dynamic citizenly positions are not directly confronted with the statutory or normative rules it has the power to concede (Cartiaux, 2008: 124).

Holding dual nationality, acting as citizens in two different states or demanding forms of citizenship in a second space (Ong, 1999b) are other forms through which such connections and reconfigurations of sites of citizenship can be enacted or fought for. Coll's (2011) study of local voting demands in Cambridge, Massachusetts illuminates how citizenship attachment may be imagined and demanded locally in a public meeting over local voting rights:

> It was an elaborate, ritualized, and well-coordinated performance that discursively placed non-citizen community members at the heart of city life and politics. It also claimed the place for this locality in global debates over the boundaries of the state, the meaning of sovereignty and the reconfiguring of citizenship. (Coll, 2011: 995)

Migrants have also connected forms of citizenship in different places: campaigning politically in both diasporic and original settings; acting as 'economic citizens' through the practices of remittance; and organising practices of intimate citizenship 'at a distance'. Luin Goldrin's work on Mexican migrants filling in for the state by funding the infrastructural needs and basic services through their Hometown Associations in the US and Canada is a revealing example of such practices. These migrants effectively become 'supercitizens', with the capital and authority to do what they feel local government at home should be doing. While they might be described in the literature as 'transnationals', their primary affiliations are indeed *trans-local* (for another example, see Besserer, 2002).

If there have always been forms of circulation between different levels and sites in citizenship-making processes, with 'models', changes, practices and influences travelling from one site to another (see, for instance, Herzog, 2003), there is an important question of how, in these processes of circulation and exchange, the role of some sites and/or 'levels' became forgotten and denied, while that of others (and especially the central/national state one) was underlined, made central and reified, and what processes make for the rise to predominance or for the retreat of any given level (be it in discourses and representations or in practices). This is the core issue of 'the politics of scale': not taking for granted, or only criticising, representations and analyses that rely on scalar hierarchisation, but paying attention to how such issues are connected and argued about, as particular embodiments of political projects and governmental strategies (Neveu, 2013a). This is all the more important as a number of historical approaches tend to explore past periods and processes as if words had the same meanings through time, as if the same nominal categories referred to the same processes and/or groups. Cerutti's (2012) work on early 18th-century northern Italian states very clearly shows the extent to which the contemporary notion of 'foreigners' is at odds with its more 'ancient' figures; the reasons for being considered a 'foreigner' (*étranger*) were many, but they could be experimented with by any individual, whatever his/her origin or background. Her analysis thus changed Cerutti's research object from the foreigner to the condition of extraneity (*extranéité*), from a *status* to an *experimented* condition. Her historical approach is indeed very close to the one we have adopted concerning citizenship, since this shift from status to processes and experiences flows from a resolutely empirical approach, and from taking seriously (whether today or yesterday) practices and meanings-in-use.

This brings us closer to a question of how the 'rescaling' of government, states and citizenship happens. If we do not accept the hierarchical ordering of scales as fixed, then a number of authors have pointed to processes of 'rescaling', particularly as they affect states (Brenner et al, 2003; Brenner, 2004). Such arguments have tended to focus on core political economic transitions – for example, towards post-Fordism or neo-liberalism (Peck, 2001; Jessop, 2002) – and have stressed the double dynamic of scales above and below the nation. Such arguments still tend towards a relatively fixed view of levels, concentrating more on how political projects seek to redistribute power, authority and capacity to different levels. Here, too, we encounter problems with the concept of levels – and the view that they are tidily nested within successively larger spatial containers (see, eg, Ferguson and Gupta, 2002; Allen, 2003; Stubbs, 2005; Clarke, 2009). Rather than focusing on the multi-level character of governing, we might want to think about the ways in which political or governmental projects (as well as practices by other actors) bring new spaces into being, or make new framings of space and scale visible, such as 'South East Europe' (Stubbs, 2005) or the 'local health economy' (Aldred, 2007). In the former, South East Europe has to be imagined, mapped and produced – made into a reality – by the very institutions that name themselves as governing the area, just as 'Europe' itself has to be imagined and enacted in the process of its governance through the EU (Walters, 2004a; Clarke, 2005). Such a perspective stresses the political processes by which scales are assembled, rather than being pre-existing sites that become the focus of new mechanisms of governing. Allen and Cochrane's work on the constitution of regional tiers of governance in the UK suggests that:

> The sense in which these are 'regional' assemblages, rather than geographically tiered hierarchies of decision-making, lies with the tangle of interactions and capabilities within which power is negotiated and played out.... There is, as the authors have tried to indicate, an interplay of forces where

a range of actors mobilize, enrol, translate, channel, broker
and bridge in ways that make different kinds of government
possible. (2007: 1171)

We think that this view of the assemblage of regions as spaces to be
governed is helpful. The emphasis on sites as constructed outcomes,
rather than having a pre-given character (whether this is their scale,
territorial reach or institutional type), allows a more productive
engagement with both the current paradoxical and multiple dynamics
of change, and the problems of thinking about their political effects.
Escaping the fixation on the national level as the appropriate site and
scale of citizenship opens up both the potential significance of other
sites and scales, and the ways in which they are themselves being
imagined and sometimes, but not always, successfully institutionalised
as governing arrangements in which citizenship may be implicated.
Ferguson and Gupta consider that:

> The force of metaphors of verticality and encompassment
> results both from the fact that they are embedded in the
> everyday practices of state institutions and from the fact
> that the routine operation of state institutions *produces*
> spatial and scalar hierarchies…. Because state practices are
> co-implicated with spatial orders and metaphors, an analysis
> of the imaginary of the state must include not only explicit
> discursive representations of the state, but also implicit,
> unmarked, signifying practices. These mundane practices
> often slip below the threshold of discursivity but profoundly
> alter how bodies are oriented, how lives are lived, and how
> subjects are formed. (Ferguson and Gupta, 2002: 983)

While we agree that states are among the principal agencies through
which sites and scales are ordered and institutionalised, we want to
insist that they are not the only agencies engaged in the politics of
scale, as some of the situations discussed earlier have clearly shown.
Social movements, political projects and mobilised networks also seek
to organise spaces and scales in ways that sometimes disrupt – and
sometimes confirm – existing arrangements. Analysing the practices
of youth associations in Roubaix, Neveu highlighted such a 'politics
of scale' being enacted by other actors than state agencies. Feeling
trapped by the logics of public policies, which they felt had denatured
their initial collective project, voluntary youth groups' members opted
for a strategy of 'circumventing the obstacle'. They first distinguished

between, on the one hand, the micro-local level (the neighbourhood youth group) where they would develop their own project, and, on the other, the city level (Federation of Youth Groups [FAJ]) that would be dedicated to negotiation with local authorities. After a while, dissatisfied with this arrangement, they created two city-level structures (the FAJ and the Roubaix Coordination of Youth Groups [CRAJ]) (see Neveu, 2003), thus trying to organise as completely separated spaces the one where they would confront and work with local authorities (FAJ), and an autonomous 'counter-public' where they would engage with their own projects and debates (CRAJ). Such an organisation could be analysed as an example of how:

> certain dominated, structurally disadvantaged by the functioning logics of the public space, social groups, can also find in the creation of socialising and discussion spaces, that temporarily function as … means to express uneases and claims, and to formalise their interests. (François and Neveu, 1999: 29)

The lack of success of this strategic move can be partly explained by endogenous factors within these groups. But the main conclusion drawn by these youth groups' members was that it was clearly incoherent to try to create a space where collective meanings could be produced, a 'place where a meaning of action in a given situation is elaborated' (Biarez, 1999: 280), without questioning at the same time the prevalence within their own local groups, and in their relations with local institutions, of consumerist social action practices that were denying their public any capacity to act as citizens. In other words, these young people made the double observation that: first, the implementation of a public policy (technical dimension) could not avoid a reflection on the meaning and parts agents were attributed with (ethical dimension); and, second, that a minimal coherence between processes at play at different levels was necessary. While the attempts of these Roubaix youth groups to create another 'politics of scale' were not fully successful, they nevertheless are clear testimony to the capacity of social movements to engage in 'politics of scale' that are not purely dictated by those of state agencies.

As we will see in the next section, such reconfigurations may involve asserting the authority of the 'local', but they may also lay claim to emergent spaces and scales of citizenship in innovative ways – or at least in ways not imagined or intended by authoritative agencies. Andrijasevic et al (2010) have described how a mobilisation of sex workers addressed the European Parliament and, in doing so, disrupted the dominant understandings of European citizenship. They crossed borders (including those of the EU itself) and traversed symbolic boundaries (translating their 'damaged' or 'stigmatised' identities into collective citizens). They also acted in *activist* ways that overran the implicit European norms (and limits) of 'active citizenship' (see also Newman and Tonkens, 2011). Similar processes have been explored by Collomb (2011); analysing the different 'stages' through which French Guyana's indigenous populations envisioned (and practised) their citizenships, he clearly shows how the largely fictitious dimension of the French legal citizenship granted in the 1970s drew them, alongside other indigenous movements, to mobilise in order to be recognised as an autonomous collectivity endowed with a specific status. While this mobilisation allowed them to be granted certain limited collective land rights, these populations then opted for another strategy, relying more on a 'delocalised citizenship' that connected them to the global indigenous movement in Latin America and elsewhere. Yet another 'level' and/or type of citizenship was later called upon, closer to Rosaldo's notion of cultural citizenship. As Collomb underlines:

> This capacity to build different figures of citizenship, beyond or beside the rule model of French legal citizenship, and to play between them with a certain strategic skilfulness, allowed Amerindians to propose their own reading of the 'Amerindian fact' in the political and social space of [French] Guyana. The willingly used whim 'I am Amerindian, Guyanese, French and European' evokes those different registers between which they learnt how to move – a 'legal' citizenship, an 'autochthonous' one and a 'cultural' one, through successive simultaneous changes in conjunctural and contextual levels. (Collomb, 2011: 989)

Such examples point to the ways in which citizenship 'takes place': its practices are always socially and spatially located and may involve reworking the taken-for-granted arrangements of people and places.

In the following section, we return to the ways in which citizenship 'takes place'. We focus particularly on the ambiguous role played by the 'local' in the politics and practices of citizenship. In doing so, we wish to underline two things: first, that scalar thought typically implies a *spatial* imaginary, such that scales (the global, national, local, private, etc) are equated with types of territory, such that encompassing scales are also bigger spaces. Second, we will take up the point made in passing earlier that the 'local' is not everywhere the same, and may indeed be mobilised for very different political purposes. But we also want to stress the concrete, material dimensions of citizenship practices, the actual places in and through which they are enacted.

Locations and localisations

Conceptions of the local seem to oscillate between its characterisation as residual (or merely parochial) and its celebration as the site of authentic human conduct and politics, or as sites of resistance against globalisation, whether such resistance is described as parochial and backward or as emancipatory. We have argued against the former version earlier in this chapter, suggesting that it over-valorises or reifies the national (and sometimes the global) as the scale at which 'real politics' takes place. But it is important not to simply invert this characterisation and replace it with a romanticised view of the local. Such a view draws generally on a positive appreciation of the 'natural' virtues of the small scale in which the quarter/neighbourhood/locality is relatively systematically associated with a romantic/pastoral vision of the village in the city, including all aspects of the life cycle and offering face-to-face encounters. This is an image of the local society (or the community) of a small size that feeds the European imaginary of the 'natural' state of things (Abram, 2002).

Despite this, we are struck by a variety of discourses that constitute the 'local' as a new terrain (a new promised land?) of citizenship, democracy and/or political renewal, and often insisting anew on a positive connection between identity (this time, local) and citizenship. Such an approach leads to a reactivation of a problematic triple register that combines: a romantic vision of the local as a justification for proximity as the central device of political engagement; an understanding (derived from a communitarian view of political collectivity) that a shared identity could function as a powerful factor in the revival/renewal/reactivation of citizenship action; and a consensualist view of citizenship itself, which ignores its inherently disputatious character. 'Rather than begin with the premise that locality and community are obvious, that their recognition and affective power flow automatically out of direct sensory experience and face-to-face encounters' (Gupta and Ferguson, 1999: 7), it seems preferable to follow Gupta's suggestion to interrogate the processes of place-making and people-making and how they are articulated.

We are not the first – and will not be the last – to argue that such consensualist views of locality as a community are problematic. They underpin versions of citizenship and forms of rights claims that are exclusivist in different ways. In the UK, for example, the local has been mobilised as a site of belonging against 'outsiders'. Neveu's study of Spitalfields (Neveu, 1993), for example, showed how representations about the right to housing were connected to different conceptions of the right level in which the agents' legitimacy was grounded: white residents considered that they had more rights because of their 'ancient' residence in and identification with the neighbourhood; while residents of Bangladeshi origins grounded their claims on both needs (*necesidades*) and equality, referring to their legal status as British citizens. The 'imagined community' of citizens that was called upon to legitimise rights was thus different: the neighbourhood in the first case; the state in the second. This appropriation of the local – as a site of historic belonging – has continued to be a powerful force in British conflicts about citizenship – especially ones centred on the East End of London (see Wemyss, 2009).

In a more recent East End study, Dench, Gavron and Young (2006) explored the disaffection of (white) 'Bethnal Greeners' and, in doing so, made 'community' play a characteristic double role – moving unproblematically between ideas of community as culture/ethnicity and community as place/locality. They see that increasing competition for council-provided housing and its allocation on principles of need rather than historic residence 'also had the effect of breaking up long-established East End family and community links' by failing to give priority to applicants with 'local and community connections'. Here, the 'community' is represented as both *local* and *historical*: people and place are viewed as being tied together over generations. History links the East End's celebrated place in the Second World War (the docks serving as Britain's lifeline, and being the focus of intensive civilian bombing) and the promise of social reconstruction after the war. Many of Dench, Gavron and Young's interviewees connect this conception of *belonging and entitlement* to a sense of 'broken promises':

> We did our war service and now they do not want to know us. But if you are an immigrant you get the top brick off the chimney. (Retired driver).

> Let us have some priorities. Our parents fought a war for us. When the Bengalis come here they get full pensions. My wife has just been informed after years of paying full contributions she will only get a £1.59 pension when she retires. Why do they get it when they've contributed nothing? (Publican).

Old people now are scrimping and saving. They don't get half of what they should get. Those who fought in the war would turn in their graves if they knew that Asians were getting everything. Years ago when you had lots of kids you had to support yourself. Now the state keeps you. (Market trader). (Dench et al, 2006: 215–16)

In sharp contrast to the view articulated by Dench, Gavron and Young, Wemyss's study of Tower Hamlets in the mid-1990s argues that 'white, working-class people were normalised as being the natural and historically legitimate occupiers of East End spaces in the discourses of the local and national media. They were at the top of the "hierarchy of belonging"' (2006: 228). This conception of belonging was constructed through identifying and deploying local histories stretching back across generations. By contrast, Bangladeshi migrants and their descendants are made to appear history-less: they are in, but not of, the locality and cannot belong to this version of community. Having such a 'history' naturalises the connection and conflation of race and place. In this case, 'localness' simultaneously expresses and denies a racialised understanding of community and belonging. Gail Lewis (2000) has called it the 'now you see it, now you don't' flickering character of racism in contemporary Britain.

At stake in such uses of the local is a question of *belonging*. Belonging has two meanings: a feeling of attachment ('I belong here'); and a sentiment of proprietorialism or ownership ('this belongs to me'). Localist claims on citizenship in the East End of London conflate these two meanings – such that the feeling of attachment is also a proprietorial claim: this place should belong to us (and not them). Locality is one very powerful way of grounding citizenship claims, but is not necessarily associated with exclusionary or regressive political relations. Localities can be sites of solidarity; they can be sites of challenges to state or economic power that comes 'from the outside' ('community gardening' versus supermarket development; or campaigns to save local public services or facilities such as hospitals). The local is, in that sense, politically indeterminate: it does not have any pre-given political character.

On 5 May 2003, the City Council Chambers of Cambridge, Massachusetts were filled with local residents including immigrants from Africa, the Middle East, South Asia, Latin America, the Caribbean and Europe. Dozens of working people, stay-at-home mothers and professionals had shown up on a Monday evening to testify on behalf of a proposal to grant all local residents the right to vote in local elections.

Even elected city councillors who disagreed with the measure sat attentively as speaker after speaker testified as to the number of years that they had been waiting to naturalise, what it felt like to be unable to vote for School Committees when their children were attending local public schools and how they identified with colonial Boston Tea Party activists in their frustration at their own experiences of taxation without representation. Residents spoke of colonial American traditions of immigrant voting without naturalisation and pointed to new international norms of democratic practice that allow for universal local suffrage. It was an elaborate, ritualised performance that discursively located non-citizen community members at the heart of community life and politics; indeed, at the centre of what it means to be a citizen in the 21st century. At the end of the debate, the majority of the City Council voted to support the measure and send it to the state legislature for approval (Coll, 2011).

The process of claiming and struggling became the act of citizenship itself because over 20 years of intermittent campaigning on this issue, none of the three locales in Massachusetts managed to get the state legislature to approach their proposals to enfranchise non-citizens at the local level. Attention to the politics of scale entails that we pay attention to the terms of people's demands, such as their invocation of specific narratives of national history and international norms of democratic practice. Their claims may be broad and even couched in universalist terms but they take place in city halls and the very small-scale context of struggle for specific legal reforms.

Another distinctive example is presented in the in-depth analysis of naturalisation processes in Switzerland by Centlivres et al (1991). They underline the extent to which 'local' residents might agree for someone to become a national citizen, but not locally:

> [members of] local families were saying 'we have nothing against Ms S. [a woman of Spanish background who has always lived in the village] ... but she cannot be a Confignon native, she must go to a big city [to get naturalised]'.... These families were absolutely not denying her the right to be Swiss, but not from Confignon. (Centlivres et al, 1991: 42–3)

Here, we have people who, while being ready to share the local turf (Massey, 2004) with a 'non-native' Swiss national, consider that such a legal transmutation – the process of becoming a (national) citizen – has to take place in the 'big city'. Indeed, for them, being a Swiss national in Confignon required being a Confignon native, so that the *right* to become Swiss is not denied, but the place/site where this *change of nature* takes place matters. Here, again, we can see the mobilisation of the different meanings of belonging in which the local is claimed to belong to those who have been born in the place.

The example from Switzerland also provides an important reminder that the local is not everywhere the same, particularly in terms of its qualities as a level of social and political action; again, an example of different politics of scales being enacted. The local is always specifically located, both in time and space, and grasping the diversity of sites where citizenship is enacted and contested requires us to register both the diversity of institutional arrangements of scales and spaces (and the meanings they are endowed with) in relation to citizenship processes, and how alternative conceptions and practices can be developed by agents. This means attending to several issues. First, the organisation of governmental and institutional levels differs considerably, even in the settings that we know. So the national state and its relation to local and/or regional levels of politics differ considerably between the central state-centric example of France and the strong federalism of Brazil. In Switzerland, naturalisation procedures place the local level at the centre: 'in order to acquire Swiss nationality, the candidate must first of all prove his/her rootedness and established relations at the local level. It is the local level of sociability, work or leisure that is determining' (Centlivres et al, 1991: 237); if the canton level has a word to say (and the federal one is only an administrative level), recognition of belonging belongs to the local council's decisions. Meanwhile, US federalism entails that states have authority to determine their own conditions of citizenship, including social entitlements and voting practices at state and local levels (Article 2 of the US Constitution). This is how, in the post-Civil War South, white people at the state level were granted impunity (*de facto*, by the refusal of the federal government to intervene) to terrorise the newly enfranchised black community. The exercise of violence and the threat of further violence were effective weapons in undermining the possibilities of practising citizenship, leading the black community to give up the vote and surrender many of the gains of Reconstruction, including multiracial representative governance, land ownership, labour rights, public health and public education. In contrast, again, the UK contains a shifting complexity of levels, from the partly devolved 'nation regions' of Scotland, Wales and Northern Ireland to very different incarnations of the local – local government (municipalities), zones, neighbourhoods, communities and so on. Decentralisation has sometimes taken place to local authorities but, sometimes (especially since the 1980s), beyond local authorities to individual institutions (eg schools) and to local communities. The result is a patchwork of levels, whose interrelationships have been frequently reordered in a kaleidoscopic way. In yet other contexts, local conceptions of citizenship and belonging might develop parallel to state-defined ones, as Hochet (2011) demonstrated in his work on Burkina Faso, or as Jacob and Le Meur (2010) did in the introduction to their edited book on land ownership and belonging politics.

Second, the spatial scope of the local may also be highly variable – covering everything from a few streets (the neighbourhood) through the quarter/*quartier* to the city space (and some forms of 'local government' are territorially still larger). The question of identification and attachment is thus always potentially problematic. For example, in debates about the reform of police governance in England and Wales, one report observed that people do not identify with an area larger than their street: 'people are most interested in issues at the very local (their own street) level and in how they are treated' (Flanagan, 2008: 83). At other times – and around other issues – people's spatial identifications may be both larger and more complex than this view implies, including the 'global' scale – imagining themselves as connected through ties of care, responsibility, solidarity or affinity with those 'elsewhere'. In the case of Roubaix analysed by Neveu (2003), some members of the youth associations, in order to free themselves from sometimes complex relationships with local policies and politics, proposed and practised a 'geographical dissociation' between their spaces of work and of political engagement (they decided to live and be engaged in one location, and work elsewhere). Such a practice underlines the necessity of not making simple or naturalised equivalences between sites of engagement and sites of attachment or identification (Neveu, 2003). It also indicates the importance of avoiding thinking that all types of engagement (social, political, professional) necessarily combine in a single geographical space/place. This points to the sort of study conducted by Sencébé (2004), where her analysis of different relationships to space in Diois leads her to distinguish four types of 'belonging' (*appartenance*), thus underlining how people, places, practices and representations may connect in a diversity of ways, and stressing that there is no 'natural' causality or clear isomorphism between the places people live or work in, feel they belong to, and want to get involved with.

Third, and underlying the other points, we want to think of these forms of spatial organisation in relational terms. Places are made out of the multiple relations that connect them to their elsewheres – their many social, personal, political, cultural and economic relationships that enable 'this place' to be (and to change). We borrow this view of the relational character of space and place from Doreen Massey (2005), with a particular emphasis on her ideas of 'geographies of responsibility' (2004). And, as always, we insist that such relations are often entangled with questions of citizenship. They make possible the exclusive claims to the local (and the national) that we have discussed earlier. But they also make possible the lines of connection in which citizens can imagine themselves and their relationships with others – both within particular places (in which we owe responsibilities to one another) and across places to others with whom we might share responsibilities, affiliations and obligations.

The 'local' can also be seen and conceived of as a pedagogic space where people learn to be (national) citizens through participation in officially recognised practices of being a citizen. For instance, town meeting practices in the US have been considered as essential to the development of a democratic spirit, as a breeding ground for the 'good American citizen'. However, the manner of previous and contemporary localised attempts at redefining citizenship (as far as voting rights are concerned) so as to include non-citizens have not been paid much attention (Coll, 2011). However, such processes of becoming may not stay within the conventional limits. As Coll has shown, in one western Massachusetts college town, non-citizen university affiliates and long-term town residents had the *de facto* right and ability to participate in the Town Meeting governance process. However, they also sought the right to vote for city councillors for legal immigrants like themselves. In another eastern Massachusetts city that was too large to be governed by Town Meetings, Haitian activists led a multiracial coalition of immigrants and allies to demand the right to vote for school boards and the City Council for all city residents. Despite the differences between these two local movements, they both drew on similar legal historical scholarship that demonstrated a history of local 'alien' voting since colonial times, and examples from other states and locales where the practice was already in place, to defend the practicality of their claims. While assuring local policymakers of the limited 'scale' of their project, they also mobilised the anti-colonial slogan of 'no taxation without representation' and aligned themselves with the normative representation of American citizens as hard-working, law-abiding, home/business-owning, responsible neighbours and family people.

Ideas about this 'pedagogical' role of the local in terms of 'becoming (good) citizens', then, have to be connected to wider sets of representations about politics and democracy. We mentioned earlier Crowley's analysis of the local as a space for sheer bargaining, politics only taking place at the central/state level; in this case, the local could be envisioned as a propaedeutic space where people could progressively 'learn' about real politics by acquiring capacities for '*montée en généralité*' (increasing abstraction). In her analysis of local participatory democracy schemes, however, Carrel (2007) provides for a more in-depth analysis, and shows the extent to which 'the local' can be used differently according to the conception of democracy (representative or deliberative) held by the organisers and of their visions of how local poor people should be included (equal or differentiated treatment).

We want to underline the ways in which local practices and representations of citizenship are not merely the object or effect of scalar destabilisations in which the national has become less taken for granted, but also actively engaged in the 'politics of scale' – from projects and practices that imagine citizenship in 'local' forms to the projects to connect people to supranational, transnational or global citizenship questions, relations, identities and demands. These range from the trans-local practices of citizenship that connect diasporic or migrant groups to their points of departure; to the 'scale jumping' of some citizenly demands (eg reaching beyond the 'national' governmental or state level to the European Court of Human Rights or connecting distant places through networks and representations); or to the summoning of 'global citizens' to respond to an environmental crisis, which is always local, national and global simultaneously; or, indeed, to very ordinary practices in which the local is endowed with political meanings.

Citizenship taking place

We have discussed earlier how the 'communities of citizenship(s)' could be imagined by different agents and at different times; we now want to come back to an often underestimated dimensions of such 'communities': their spatial dimensions. Citizenship 'takes place' in a variety of sites and settings and, indeed, as we have suggested, is a mobilising term that can connect different sites and settings. This is true for both 'official' forms of citizenship, enacted by states, and for alternative citizenship projects. Holston (2008) describes the distinction between entrenched and insurgent forms of citizenship in his study of Brazil, in which he pays particular attention to the sites in which citizenship was re-imagined. In paying attention to the social geography of the struggles over Brazilian citizenship, Holston argues that:

> The city is not merely the context of citizenship struggles.
> Its wraps of asphalt, concrete and stucco, its infrastructure
> of electricity and plumbing also provide the substance.

The peripheries provide a space of city builders and their pioneering citizenship. Through autoconstruction, the working classes transformed the unoccupied hinterlands of 1940 into the densely populated, socially organized and urbanized peripheries of 1990 in all major Brazilian cities. They made them not only their principal residential space within Brazil's city-regions, but also a new kind of political and symbolic space within Brazil's social geography. In particular, residential illegality galvanized a new civic participation and practice of rights: the conditions it created mobilized residents to demand full membership of the legal city that had expelled them through the legalization of their property claims and the provision of urban services.

Thus I argue that in the development of the autoconstructed peripheries, the very same historical sites of differentiation – political rights, access to land, illegality, servility – fuelled the irruption of an insurgent citizenship that destabilized the differentiated. Although these elements continue to sustain the regime of differentiated citizenship, they are also the conditions of its subversion, as the urban poor gained political rights, became landowners, made law an asset, created new public spheres of participation, achieved rights to the city, and became modern consumers. In such ways, the lived experiences of the peripheries became both the context and the substance of a new urban citizenship. In turn, this insurgence of the local transformed national democratization. (2008: 8–9)

This testifies to one potent version of citizenship 'taking place'. The sites and settings in which citizenship is imagined, claimed and practised are not merely a passive context or backdrop against which the action takes place; nor are spatial metaphors purely that, since people's practices actually 'take place' in a very material sense. Rather, the social and spatial contexts animate citizenship – the located experiences of actors fuel desires and demands and create the possibilities for imagining themselves as citizens, and physical places and spaces play a role in those imaginings. The locations of citizenship are heterogeneous – the word can be appropriated and translated into a variety of locations, and can be used to imagine diverse forms of collectivity and solidarity. But what is particularly attractive about Holston's formulation is the way in which it refuses to divide the world into good and bad places; instead, he insists that the places – the city peripheries of Brazil – are both the site of exclusion, inequality and oppression (the 'entrenched' division of Brazilian society) and the site of insurgent alternatives. This dialectical view of space refuses simplifying mappings, whether the scalar imaginary of hierarchical levels or the imagined topographies that separate state and civil society (see, eg, Somers, 2008).

The experience of *Assembléia do Povo*, a *favelado* movement that emerged in Campinas, S. Paulo, Brazil, in 1978, offers a good example of how an old and obscure juridical clause about the 'social use of public land' has been used in order to claim land rights that had emerged at the local level. The claim was directed to the city government, which had the power to assign the land to be used by *favelados*, thus ensuring their housing rights. Although the legislature rejected the city government proposal, the local strategy adopted by *favelados* of Campinas became a national practice among similar social movements throughout the country, ending up by finally becoming accepted by different state agencies across the country.

Another example of this 'travelling' between locations is the inclusion of 'direct participation' as a basic central principle in the Constitution of 1988 in Brazil. Such a claim clearly originated first at local levels, inspiring several experiments in different cities during the late 1970s and 1980s, and later assumed national and even continental dimensions. Between the early 1990s and the early 2000s, 19 countries in Latin America have included some provision for citizen participation in their legal–institutional frameworks (Hevia, 2006). The origins of the participatory claim are very diverse in a number of different contexts: if it is clear in some cases that the initiative came from original local struggles that developed into national claims, in others, the inclusion of that participation was merely a nominal adhesion by dominant sectors to a 'fashionable' discourse, without significant practical consequences. The building of this 'fashionable' discourse also results from 'travelling' processes. On the one hand, it expresses a 'demonstration effect' among countries of the region, through which social movements in different countries learned from each other's experiences (which included governments' responses to participatory claims). On the other hand, it expresses the dominant sectors' incorporation (Williams, 1977) of it, sometimes even *avant la lettre*, in a pre-emptive effort to contain such claims. The travelling quality of such participatory models now extends well beyond Latin America, as very different political and governmental projects have sought to absorb and implement them (with very different aims and ambitions; see Neveu, 2007).

States themselves are materialised in offices, personnel and practices that are 'everywhere'. The national state occupies specific places (the buildings and networks that embody them in Brasilia, Washington DC, Paris, London), but the departments of the state also materialise unevenly within and beyond the national territory (as embassies and armies, or the local offices of government bureaucracies). Such state spaces form settings for enacting citizenship: getting documentation (and being 'recognised'); applying for, and possibly receiving, benefits and services as someone who is entitled; being processed by bureaucracies and legal apparatuses; and attending rallies, going to meetings and voting. Such official, governmental or state spaces blur into the landscape of public spaces – parks, squares and streets – which may also provide conditions for performing citizenship. Of course, the use of such spaces – both the governmental and the public – is itself a matter of contestation, as the recent occupation of Taxim Square in Istanbul clearly showed, after those of Tahrir.

Such places and spaces are always the product of attempts to order them: to organise them in ways that make them function as the authorities would like. So, official buildings may be guarded and may exclude certain members of the public (or large groups of them) who are deemed inappropriate or potentially threatening. Their internal organisation announces the divisions of labour between state officials (behind desks or windows; behind closed doors) and citizens (standing in queues; sitting in fixed or bolted chairs; waiting for the state's attention). Equally, public spaces are also regulated, managed and policed in different ways to ensure the preservation of 'public order' and 'public decency'. It is not accidental, we think, that Piero della Francesca's famous painting of the Ideal City contains no people in its public spaces.[1] The challenge of keeping the public realm tidy often seems most likely to be accomplished by excluding unruly people from its spaces. Conceptions of order and decency vary across time and place, of course. So, too, do the modes of regulating them – and, of course, the challenges to them.

These places – and their contested uses – reveal *architectures* of public power and authority in which the intended relationships of citizens, publics and states are inscribed, as well as (re-)appropriations of spaces by citizens. For instance, the *Piazza del campo* (public square) of Siena architecturalises the ideal or intended relationship between subjects and rulers, organising the public space into a banked rectangle from which all citizens of the commune should be able to see their leaders addressing them from the balcony of the *Palazzo Pubblico* (for similar reflections in a different context, see Neveu, 2008b). But this is not just a matter of the architecture of power in a simple sense: the openness of public places and spaces is variable and, of course, contested in demonstrations, occupations and invasions. When the citizens of the former German Democratic Republic stepped out from the 'shadow of the state' in December 1989, they headed for the offices of the STASI (the former state's secret police) – and forcibly opened the offices and the files to 'the public' (Funder, 2003). Nacira Guénif-Souilamas (2012) traced the complex history of the building that now houses *La Cité nationale de l'histoire de l'immigration* (national museum of the history of immigration). The former *Palais de la Porte Dorée* was constructed for the Paris Colonial Exposition of 1931 and was subsequently devoted to colonial ethnography. Guénif-Souilamas argues that the shift in use to a museum of immigration left both the history and symbolic decoration of the building (including bas-reliefs of 'natives') unremarked. More strikingly, the building's history was differently evoked when it was occupied by *sans papiers* in 2010 (see: http://www.collectif12.com/spip.php?article183). Practising citizenship sometimes mobilises people to act against the conventions that govern public places and spaces, not least 'the streets', to both demand and embody different social and political relationships. From feminist 'Reclaim the Night' marches to gay festivals; from anti-capitalist demonstrations to peace camps around nuclear bases; from demonstrations of solidarity with '*sans papiers*' to street theatre in front of banks – people have found ways of making orderly spaces and places disorderly. Marches, demonstrations and performances – at all sorts of scales – dramatise and publicise possibilities, desires and needs. The Occupy movements, Arab revolutions and Indignados in Spain, as well as the students' movement in Chile in 2011, have been here particularly revealing of such processes (see, among others, Arditi, 2011). Caldeira (2000) also shows that the multiplication of 'gated communities' in Brazil can be seen as an attack on public space that could erode, and in many ways is already eroding, the very conditions for democracy and citizenship; social inequality thus not just creates and reinforces spatial segregation, but can, in its spatialised, material forms, be a threat to citizenship itself.

Returning to Holston's analysis of the 'dangerous spaces of citizenship', he traces the contradictory and contested dynamics of public space in Brazil (including the attempts to regulate, order and even privatise such spaces). It is echoed by Jerram's (2011) account of 'Streetlife' in 20th-century Europe, which explored the ways in which politics were both created and enacted in urbanising public spaces – such as streets and squares. Such settings – and the factories, shops, bars and houses that constituted the fabric of such spaces – were, he argues, the sites in which other futures were imagined and demanded, even as existing orders were reasserted. Thus, if spaces and places have always been possible settings for the assertion of the state's presence and power, for the framing of expected citizenly attitudes or their control, they have also always been resources for citizens in their search for recognition, or equality. While public demonstrations or mobilisations can and do use the city squares, parks and streets to assert their belonging or publicise their claims, it is also in more mundane, ordinary and daily uses of such spaces that citizenship practices can be built and observed. Analysing the organisation of a political street festival, *Débattons dans les rues* ('let's debate on the streets', but the phrase in French also carries strong assonances with 'let's put sticks in the wheels', *des bâtons dans les roues*), Neveu (2008a, 2008b) highlighted how the public and collective actions developed during this festival were connected to more ordinary practices enacted in the participants' daily lives. In other words, the political uses to which public urban space was put were not limited to the week during which the festival was held, but were part of its organisers' daily life.

Public and/or urban spaces are also sites where opposed conceptions of belonging and citizenship can be enacted by different movements; 'reclaiming the streets' is not always an emancipatory act performed by excluded groups, but can be a tool for exclusionary visions of citizenship to be enacted – Dematteo (2008) clearly showed how local policies about parks and squares in Northern Italy were used as a way to reassert the exclusive ownership of them by the 'local' indigenous population against immigrants (on similar issues, see also Coman, 2008). Echoing Holston's view of the experience of urban spaces being the condition for people imagining themselves as citizens, a recent study by Boudreau et al examines how the possibility of political action – participating in protests and demonstrations – is intimately linked to the routines and practices of everyday urban life (rather than being an abrupt rupture from them). Boudreau et al explore how the experiences of 'taking the bus daily' as a quotidian activity for migrant women working in Los Angeles created the conditions of possibility for taking part in demonstrations against immigration laws:

> To return to the analysis of continuities in the emotions felt during the *Gran Marcha* and those experienced in everyday life, women talked about trust. They could project their everyday trust for others who, like them, rely on mutual assistance to cope with difficult conditions, onto the feeling of trust experienced during the demonstration. Similarly, everyday struggles for respect and the angst associated with those struggles were transferred to a collective struggle for

respect during the protest event. Sometimes, in their routine, women feel resentment towards their boss. This resentment is projected, in event time, onto white authorities. Similarly, everyday feelings of fear towards deportation or aggression were collectively felt during the protest.

Continuities in practices, modalities and emotions between everyday life and the protest event have influenced these women's decision to participate in the demonstration and feel comfortable during the event. The mechanism through which everyday practices influence the decision to participate could be synthesized as the deployment of skills, whereas the passage from everyday emotions to participation in a protest can be understood as self-confidence. Similar modalities between the demonstration and everyday life bring to the forefront another mechanism, that of familiarity. Familiarity, skills and self-confidence enabled these women to participate in the demonstration. Even though they made the decision to go out on the street, for most of them, they had no idea what to expect and what role they would play. In other words, the translation of practices and emotions into political action most of the time does not proceed from a rational decision. (Boudreau et al, 2009: 343)

Recent uprisings in Brazil in June 2013 began in S. Paulo around a reaction against the increase in public transportation fares and rapidly spread to include an impressive variety of demands, taking millions of people onto the streets of many cities across the whole country in the following days. Inspiration from similar movements in Europe and in the Arab countries was evident. Hasty communication through social networks brought together individuals holding their handmade banners expressing the difficulties and problems they felt in their everyday life: the poor quality of public transportation, public health services and schools, police violence, gay marriage, high taxes, domestic violence against women, high investments in the financing of events such as the World Cup and the Olympics, environmental questions, corruption, dirty politicians, and ineffective political parties. The need for a political reform, postponed by the Congress for more than seven years, was a significant claim. A thorough and exhaustive diagnosis of life in Brazil, produced by its own ordinary citizens, occupied the cities' streets for days in a row with unparalleled support from the population, and was rapidly and selectively reproduced by the media. Larger cities were literally paralysed for a whole week by the protests, combined with looting and the invasion of public buildings and violent reaction by the police, which only contributed to fuelling the protests. Over the unprecedented diversity of demands and their holders, one common theme was at stake: they wanted their voices to be heard, they wanted to ensure their right to participate in political decisions and they wanted to affirm their condition as citizens: 'Pardon the inconvenience, we are changing the country'.

We have tried to work 'anthropologically' in thinking about citizenship taking place. By this, we mean two things (rather than that we have all become anthropologists). We have tried to be attentive to the specific contexts in which citizenship arises: the places in which citizenship takes place are both specific and constitutive. They are not merely the sites in which citizenship is played out, as though some general script is picked up by a group of local actors and performed more or less well in local costumes. Anthropology has been more careful than most other disciplines about the ways in which contexts matter – the locations and localisations of citizenship produce connected but distinct enactments of citizenship. So, *where* citizenship is imagined and practised is significant for *how* it is imagined and practised.

Second, however, attention to the local and particular is significant for how we have come to think about citizenship. Whether dealing with popular transformations of citizenship in Brazil, migrant imaginings of themselves as US citizens or the struggles in colonial societies to reinvent the framings of imperial citizenship, we are conscious of something other than the 'variations on a theme' view of non-metropolitan places. Either directly or by implication, such practices speak back to the dominant, conventional European 'models' of citizenship and call them into question. They unsettle the dominant conceptions of citizenship – and their conventionalised bundlings of people, places and power. In 'provincialising' European models of citizenship, they open spaces of possibility in which social and political life might be reordered (Chakrabarty, 2001). As a consequence, they also call into question – make available for disputation, perhaps – Eurocentric theorising about citizenship. So, observing 'other' local or particular practices of citizenship is never just a matter of accumulating interesting examples. Rather, they open the spaces of possibility for thinking citizenship differently by decentring the established dominant modes of citizenship and modes of thinking about them.

Conclusion: citizenship as connective

Whether we consider the 'unruly spaces' identified by Holston in Brazil or the struggles by *sans papiers* to not be 'out of place' in France (Raissiguier, 2010); whether we consider the movements that have laid claim to public spaces to make them sites of politics (from feminist demonstrations to 'Reclaim the Streets' to contemporary anti-capitalist occupations, Occupy, Indignados and the Arab revolutions); whether we consider struggles for access to citizenship (right to vote movements) or new solidarities being constructed across apparently intractable social differences – the proliferation of citizenship struggles demands out attention. It is not just that 'citizenship is everywhere', but that citizenship is everywhere being re-imagined. In multiple sites, settings and forms, citizenship is being actively disputed. Such disputes demand an approach to studying citizenship that places dispute at its heart, rather than seeing such practices as mere variations on a theme.

But it is not just a question of noticing the many sites and forms in which citizenship is being re-imagined; it is the capacity of citizenship to function as a connective symbol or device. Citizenship – in the many examples that we have explored in this book – functions as a way of imagining and enacting connections between people, between people and places, and between people and institutions. Perhaps too much attention is focused on the exclusionary effects of various forms of citizenship. These are undoubtedly significant and often become the focus for new mobilisations to challenge them. Yet, citizenship is more than a simple system of inclusion and exclusion, it is powerfully connective. Even in its conventionally binary forms, citizenship imagines and enacts connections between different groups of people (eg making a national citizenry out of different classes); it makes connections between those groups and a place (the national territory) and institutions (the apparatuses of the nation-state). Disputes around citizenship are always about bringing new sets of connections into being: making new citizens and making citizenship anew. The re-imaginings and remakings of citizenship inscribe connections – between people, places and institutions – making new social and political landscapes and new ways of living in them.

Everyday experiences and uses of spaces can thus provide the conditions for political action, particularly where it involves a degree of recognition of connections and commonalities. Coll (2004, 2010) has also explored the conditions of mutual recognition in exchanges between migrant women – in this case, in encounters between Chinese and Latina migrants. She suggests that three keywords emerged as marking commonalities – *convivencia, necesidades* and *problemas* (conviviality, needs and problems) – that women found in their everyday lives and were points of translation between personal and citizenship struggles. Citizenship is thus a form through which connection and commonality can be imagined and spoken. In such settings, citizenship does not abolish differences; rather, it may be seen as a way of suspending some differences (here, of ethnicity) while foregrounding shared experiences and the shared desire for solutions to *necesidades* and *problemas*.

On 1 May 2006, as tens of thousands of white-shirted demonstrators filled the streets of downtown San Francisco, they both wrote themselves into a specific local history and acted as part of a national mobilisation, work stoppage and consumer boycott called 'A Day Without Immigrants' by some and 'The Great American Boycott' by others. Some Latino demonstrators who had never participated in a US May Day greeted white radicals with smiles and thanks for joining in 'their' march. Red, white and blue signs proclaimed 'America, we are your people!' Immigrant women pushed babies in strollers alongside older children boycotting school for the day and behind banners demanding equal labour protections for domestic workers. Men draped Mexican as well as American flags around their heads, and the Nicaraguan consular officers hung their flag out of the consulate's high-rise window. Signs ranged from the pragmatic 'Stop HR 4437' to the pointed 'You like our food, why don't you want our people?'.

The synchronised marching of the uniformed honour guard of the Longshoremen's Union elicited cheers from the crowd and was a reminder to all who know local history of how militant longshoremen had led the last general strike in San Francisco in 1934. This historically union city was proud of having been the first to shut down in a labour action that paralysed ports from San Diego to Seattle that summer. However, in 2006, the militancy of the marching male and female longshoremen was matched by the light-hearted spirit of protesters who squatted down and jumped up in concert to make long waves up and down Market Street from City Hall and the Civic Center to the Ferry Building at the Port of San Francisco. The first national walkout of this scale for immigrant rights reclaimed the international celebration of organised labour for a new American workforce. If the contemporary global order denies the dignity of labour and seeks to define us by what we consume, these demonstrators embodied the message that not all workers are men, not all consumers are adults and not all voters are white and native-born. In the words of one banner, 'Today we march, tomorrow we vote'. The marchers' actions echoed the tradition of each new generation of US immigrants learning to wield influence in electoral politics. However, they also demanded recognition of their difference along with inclusion. By claiming equal rights and democratic protections for all, even for those excised from the body politic by law or by custom, they challenged fundamental assumptions of membership and belonging in the country.

Such actions also point to a very different conclusion from those who see Americans to be increasingly 'bowling alone' instead of building civic institutions (Putnam, 2000). Formulations that focus on the dismantling of familiar white and middle-class forms of sociability tend to erase the contributions, indeed, the personhood, of the people who may be the most active in building community and social life in many parts of the US today. If shared political heritage is the product of plural contributions, dispute and struggle between groups and citizens, then attention to the politics of scale and cultural meanings of citizenship acts such as 1 May 2006 offers us new resources for understanding some of the dynamics and dilemmas of American citizenship in a post-industrial, late-capitalist, increasingly culturally diverse and economically stratified city like San Francisco.

In short, citizenship 'takes place' in sites, settings and locations: it is imagined, practised and enacted in quotidian practices, as well as spectacular mobilisations. In the process, citizens make places different: they change their meanings, their possibilities and their uses. Citizens – understood in the broadest sense – struggle to make places for themselves and, sometimes, for others. In the same process, citizenship is both deployed and reinvented. It is deployed by political projects because of its accreted meanings, sentiments, implications and political-cultural echoes (as much as it is for the formal or substantive rights that it may announce). Political projects lay claim to citizenship – and do so in particular places and with a particular and selective re-imagining of its meaning. As we said earlier, attending to the diversity of places in which citizenship takes place is not just a matter of recording that diversity or noting the plurality of forms, sites and scales in which citizenship is brought into being, demanded, granted or refused. The examples that we have traced here underline the continuing value of citizenship as a potent political signifier. They illustrate the settings in which people come to imagine themselves as citizens. They illuminate the interplay between places and projects as actors come to see themselves as actual or potential citizens. Most importantly, they reveal the sites in which people not only imagine themselves as citizens, but also re-imagine citizenship itself.

What some of the examples explored here also point to is the extent to which the vision of the citizen as a pure being of 'reason', devoid of emotions, identifications and attachments (to people and/or places) is indeed a very specific one; its predominance has made for such dimensions of citizenship processes to be underestimated, or described as 'pathological' or deviant. Taking into account the spatial and material dimensions of citizenship processes is thus also about (re-)including these dimensions in our analysis instead of simply disqualifying them as irrelevant or an obstacle to citizenship. Rosaldo's discussion of cultural citizenship is part of such a re-evaluation, as is a certain line of research that examines how strong feelings of attachment towards a place, a landscape or an atmosphere can be resources to which people can 'hold' in becoming political (see, among others, Boullier, 2009; GRAC, 2009; Carrel and Neveu, 2013).

That leads us to a final comment about citizenship 'taking place'. Places, as we have argued, need to be understood relationally, not merely as isolated physical locations. Citizenship 'takes place' in that double sense: it happens in specific settings and it reconfigures the relationships that make places. As a result, it is not helpful to view citizenship through analytical frameworks that divide up the social world into different spheres: the public versus the private; the state versus society; or even the state, market and civil society. While such spheres may be imagined and institutionalised as separate (such that the state stands above society, or the public stands outside the private), they are always entangled in practice. Binary (or occasionally trinary) framings that enforce such separations produce strange reifying and romanticising effects: the state as the root of all evil; the all-consuming or all-powerful market; and civil society as the fountainhead of virtue, civility and popular mobilisations (see Dagnino, 2002; Dagnino et al, 2006). Writing about 'insurgent citizenship' in Brazil, Holston also resists these reifying separations:

> I do not study these developments ... by separating civil society and state. Nor do I view the mobilization of social movements as the resistance of the former and their demobilization as cooption by the latter. I avoid such dichotomies by focusing on citizenship as a relation of state and society, and I study its processes to reveal the entanglements of the two that motivate social movements to emerge and subside. I examine these processes as they appear in the practices of citizens. That is, I emphasize the experiences of citizens with the elements – such as property,

illegality, courts, associations and ideologies – that constitute the discursive and contextual construction of relations called citizenship and that indicate not only particular attributes of belonging in society but also the political imagination that both produces and disrupts that citizenship. (2008: 12–13)

Perhaps more than most other studies, Holston's seems particularly addressed to the shifting entanglements and disjunctions of citizenship: its capacity to address, contain and redress formations of difference and inequality; its ability to institutionalise structures of power and to challenge them; and its role in establishing arrangements of order, discipline and hierarchy and in disputing them. The forms of insurgent citizenship that he explores make the practices of taking place central to the analysis: in the shifting and contested spaces of the urban peripheries in which citizenship is re-imagined; in the challenges to institutionalised forms of authority and conduct that rule public spaces; and in the challenges to the ordering of public and private space (in which property, inequality and entrenched forms of authority are articulated). 'Insurgent citizenship' re-imagines places and the relations they embody, and presents the possibility of new connections between people that challenge the established expectation that they will 'know their place'.

It is precisely because citizenship as a keyword contains these connective possibilities – the chance to imagine the relationships between people, places and power differently – that it continues to fascinate and attract. It is a keyword for political projects because of what can be spoken through it. It is a word that carries an accretion of meanings and references (rights, belonging, equality, membership, commonality, civility) that can be deployed, translated and revitalised by political projects that seek to change things – or to keep things the same. The same qualities ensure that it exercises its fascination on scholars of citizenship, too.

Note

[1] In the collection of the *Palazzo Ducale* of Urbino, Italy. Available at: commons. wikimedia/org/wiki/File:Piero_della_Francesca_Ideal_City.jpg

Conclusion: Disputing citizenship

We are conscious that we have written a rather strange book. It has been disputatious, wrestling with approaches to, and conceptions of, citizenship that we find unhelpful. It has been 'all over the place' as we have traced different sites, settings and forms in which citizenship has been – and continues to be – disputed. It has tried to liberate citizenship from the ties that bind it to particular normative, institutional or political formations, and instead to make its mobility and mutability a central rather than a secondary feature. We have tried to take seriously Etienne Balibar's wonderful and productive insistence that citizenship (*citoyenneté*) is '*imparfaite*' – always unfinished, always in the process of being imagined, made or enacted. It is a conception that illuminates both the multiple ways in which citizenship is open to dispute, to being imagined, demanded, mobilised and practised, and the desire of so many (different) political projects to perfect and finish citizenship: the striving to make it come true. The book is also, we think, strange because we have tried to write from our differences – of place, language and intellectual and political formation – to articulate a common project without forcing a false consensus. All of these forms of strangeness make writing a conclusion difficult.

In particular, the last two – the unfinished quality of citizenship and writing out of difference – imply something other than a conventional approach to a conclusion. We cannot, for example, produce an elegant summary of the basic truths about citizenship, nor a last-chapter revelation of what 'citizenship is *really* about'. Neither can we put away the differences that have been both productive and difficult for our collaborative work on citizenship. Such strategies might make it easier to get to the end. They might even make it a tidier conclusion for the exhausted reader. However, they would certainly divert the orientation, the argument and the practice away from what we believe in. As a result, this strange book gets a strange conclusion: one that reflects our commitment to the unfinished and disputatious character of citizenship (and the process of studying it). The first part of the conclusion reviews some of the ways in which we have approached citizenship. We intend to offer an *approach to* citizenship, rather than a *theory of* citizenship. We try to underscore why it matters to decentre citizenship from its conventional and apparently fixed moorings; why it matters to see it taking place in heterogeneous locations; why it is a continually disputed – and re-imagined – keyword and *condition* (Cerutti, 2012). In the final part of the conclusion we turn to our own 'unfinished business': the disputes that have animated our collective engagement. Writing the book has been hard in many ways, but one critical problem has been how to make visible to readers the fundamentally conversational, argumentative and disputatious practices in which it was born, imagined and practised.

Citizenship in the making

Our work together began with a set of puzzles that centred on the mismatch between dominant theories and conceptions of citizenship and the diverse practices and projects in which we encountered citizenship 'in the making'. We were fascinated by the growing list of sites or forms of citizenship: cultural citizenship, environmental citizenship, intimate citizenship, sexual citizenship or the citizenship claims of hitherto excluded groups (disabled people, incarcerated people, children, etc). Such a proliferation of citizenships indicated – at least – that lots of people thought that there was something important about citizenship that made it worth claiming. But such lists also induce a temptation to see this as a process of 'filling out' citizenship – extending its substance and reach (see the discussion in Lister, 2007). This temptation rests on a view of citizenship as an established phenomenon to which groups are actively adding new sorts of rights or to which they are gaining access. We had the sense that this view rather underestimated two other dynamics that were significant for us.

First, these processes need to be seen as taking place alongside the remaking of dominant versions of citizenship, which indicates that the established understandings and institutionalisations of citizenship cannot be taken for granted as a permanent baseline to which additions can be made. On the contrary, the reworking of citizenship's articulations with nationality (not least in relation to migration and particularly the movement of refugees) by states and international organisations has diminished, or has made increasingly conditional, access to citizenship. At the same time, governments in the global North have attached new conditionalities to the legal, political and social rights that were celebrated in Marshall's evolutionary account of citizenship. Over the past three decades, welfare has been retrenched, made more conditional on the 'performance' of active citizens (in relation to paid work especially). More recently, the crisis of finance capital has led to increased precarity and inaugurated regimes of austerity (Clarke and Newman, 2012). The 'rebalancing' of rights and responsibilities has tended to increase the responsibilities of citizens while diminishing their rights (thus reducing the 'burden' on governments). In certain societies, such as Greece, it is even the very shape and foundations of what Castells (1997) called 'the salaried society' that is being dismantled, leaving people on the moving, and threatening, ground of a complete change of all reference points. While Castells argued that such structures and cultures of employment were being transformed in the emergence of the network society, the dislocations of national economies and social formations resulting from the nationalisation of the crisis of finance capital have deepened the speed and scope of those transformations (Castells, 2012). Meanwhile, marketising dynamics have changed relations between states and citizens in individualising, privatising and de-socialising ways. As a result, it is important to attend to the ways in which dominant forms of citizenship are not stable incarnations or crystallisations of citizenship. If, as Balibar points out, the re-imagining and remaking of citizenship is a process driven by marginalised, subordinate, excluded or insurgent forces, it is always in complex relationships with these dominant projects, hence the need to critically question all approaches that maintain rigid conceptions of what, where or who are the 'centre' and 'margins'.

Second, we are increasingly drawn to the importance of seeing citizenship as being constantly re-imagined and reinvented, rather than merely extended. In itself, the demand for 'inclusion' by an excluded grouping usually troubles and often transforms the taken-for-granted assumptions on which a particular institutionalised formation of citizenship rests. Events such as the Arab revolutions, the Occupy Movement, the recent massive uprisings in Brazil and other mass mobilisations signal a rejuvenation of more engaged, collective citizenship. If they also signal the precariousness of insurgent democratic practices and institutions, these always leave 'traces' and signs that can be reinvested by future groups and mobilisations (Arditi, 2011). Reworking the underpinning models of personhood that identify some types of people as having the 'right stuff' to be citizens (property, male genitalia, self-possession, etc) not only reworks the relationship between particular individuals and their state, but also redraws the existing social body (identity, belonging, power, solidarities) as well as the body politic (rights, entitlements, etc). In a wonderful discussion of such mappings in the context of colonial relations between Jamaica and England, Catherine Hall has argued that:

> Marking differences was a way of classifying, of categorising, of constructing boundaries for the body politic and the body social. Processes of differentiation, positioning men and women, colonisers and colonised, as if these divisions

were natural, were constantly in the making, in conflicts of power.... The mapping of difference, I suggest, the constant discursive work of creating, bringing into being, or reworking these hieratic categories, was always a matter of historical contingency. The map constantly shifted, the categories faltered, as different colonial sites came into the metropolitan focus, as conflicts of power produced new configurations in one place or another. (2002: 17, 20; on the same issue, see also Cerutti, 2012)

Citizenship is one of the privileged sites for such mappings (and for their constant contestation). Particular institutionalisations of citizenship (formalised in specific places at particular times) turn one mapping into law and usually imply the naturalisation and normalisation of that set of particularities. Each institutionalisation runs the risk of becoming disputed, since it formalises and attempts to reify a particular mapping of the social body and thus solidify a particular formation of difference, inequality and power. Because citizenship occupies that precisely contentious location at the conjunction of the political and the social, it is hardly surprising that it persists as a focus for projects that seek to re-imagine and remake it.

Contested meanings: what is at stake in citizenship?

Our view of citizenship as disputed brings to the fore the question of what citizenship means, or, more precisely, how citizenship is made to mean different things in different contexts. The remaking of citizenship always involves revisions to, or reworkings of, its existing meanings. Here, we return again to Lister's observation that citizenship is 'an essentially contested concept' (2005: 2). It can only be essentially contested because it has no essential meaning: there is no essence that can be used to limit the substantive uses to which it can be put. This, of course, does not mean that there are no such attempts – both in academic and political settings, there are always attempts to police the meaning and use of citizenship that run counter to struggles to transform, redefine and remake it. But, as Williams well knew, these efforts to define the reality of citizenship have to be seen as the strategies and tactics of struggle, rather than the abstract or disinterested truths that they claim to be. Instead, both the multiple and complicated real politics of citizenship and our orientation to meanings and practices, to meanings-in-use (as intrinsically entangled with politics and power), necessitate an understanding of citizenship as open to multiple meanings: as polysemic or polyvalent.

Yet, this is only a general orientation to the problem of contested meaning: it is a statement of possibility, rather than a description of permanent and continuing flux in the field of meanings. On the contrary, citizenship – like many other concepts – often looks deeply solidified, entrenched and institutionalised (eg think of those unbroken historical arcs that – apparently – link us directly to the ancient Greeks and Romans, possibly via the French Revolution). But if we are to make our way between over-essentialised and overly fluid understandings of the polysemic character of citizenship, we may need some intermediary concepts that allow us to think about the different combinations of contestation and solidification that are visible in specific contexts. One of these is the idea of 'temporary crystallisations' (Neveu, 2005), which denotes the ways in which particular meanings come to fill out and specify the idea of citizenship, which become installed as the dominant meanings, which become embodied in institutional policies and practices, which circulate in political and public discourse, and which become the naturalised norms of the particular society. The metaphor of crystallisation evokes the transition from flux and fluidity to a moment when a particular formation takes shape, solidifies and becomes a social, political and cultural 'fact'. It is, however, important that this idea also includes the word 'temporary': such crystallisations always become the object of further contestations that seek to rework them into new formations. Elsewhere, Clarke has talked about the value of Gramsci's idea of 'a series of unstable equilibria' for capturing just this double sense of dynamics of settlement and unsettling (Clarke, 2004: 25). This implies close attention to the spatio-temporal specificities of citizenship – the forms in which it 'crystallises' and becomes contested – rather than dealing in abstracted 'models of citizenship'.

Such a radically contextual approach to citizenship places a premium on empirical attention to the ways in which citizenship is imagined and inhabited, crystallised and contested. But such an emphasis on the particularity of contexts cannot be pursued in a way that separates contexts. Particular crystallisations of citizenship become sedimented and leave traces that travel across both space and time. The question of historical sedimentation is an important one for dealing with the excessive voluntarism that can sometimes attach to culturalist or post-structuralist conceptions of meaning as polysemic, arbitrary or contested. Lister hints at the consequences of such a view losing sight of any 'distinctive meaning(s)':

> The breadth of the field represents one of its strengths, for it offers an exciting terrain for scholars from a range of disciplines to engage with this 'momentum concept'. However, there are times when perhaps the notion of citizenship is stretched too far so as to lose its distinctive meaning(s) or when it is sprinkled indiscriminately simply to add conceptual spice. (Lister, 2007: 58)

How can we think of citizenship as an object of meaning in a way that neither leaves it as an 'empty' signifier, apparently vulnerable to any meaning that comes along, nor sees it as an 'overloaded' signifier, bent under the weight of every meaning that has ever been attached to it? We began with Raymond Williams' conception of 'historical semantics' that he introduced in his study of 'keywords' (1983 [1976]) and we return to it here as one way of locating the problem of meaning analytically. He argued that, rather than a search for the 'proper meaning' of words', we should be attentive to:

> a history and complexity of meanings, conscious changes, or consciously different uses; innovation, obsolescence, specialization, extension, overlap, transfer; or changes which are masked by a nominal continuity so that words which seem to have been there for centuries, with continuous general meanings, have in fact come to express radically different or radically variable, yet sometimes hardly noticed, meanings and implications of meaning. (Williams, 1983 [1976]: 17)

But in the process of these shifting and contested meanings, some meanings become sedimented or leave their traces on the word despite subsequent changes. Ideas of traces, sediments, deposits or accretions are useful in suggesting that the work of changing meanings of keywords is not a simple matter of invention or innovation. Unlocking or disassembling established or consolidated meanings is a process of struggle, and established meanings often prove recalcitrant. They have to be worked on, and against, in the process of re-articulation. They may also leave their traces attached to the word even as it is given new meaning. Citizenship is one such keyword, having acquired sedimentations and accretions through its mobilisation in political-cultural projects over generations. Each effort to rework it, to attach it to new projects and possibilities, both draws selectively on these historic sedimentations and attempts to create a new 'crystallisation' of meanings. The accumulated accretions of meaning make 'citizenship' an object of political-cultural desire for many – both in everyday life and in political projects. Citizenship carries political, cultural and affective value because of these accretions and associations.

In what might be called liberal-democratic societies, new political projects have to engage with the question of citizenship and inflect its meaning in specific ways. It is a keyword in the sense that it is recurrently used to announce the existence of desired social, political and cultural relationships, or at least the social imaginaries in which the principles of citizenship are central themes. Expansive as well as reductive projects have to work with – and through – citizenship. Transformative projects of different kinds also have to negotiate the historically accreted weight of meanings of citizenship in order to bring about new social, political and cultural orders. So, 'neo-liberal' projects seek both to reduce key aspects of citizenship while also transforming the social and political relationships in which it has been embedded. In the process, though, they must negotiate central associations – citizenship's articulation with questions of rights, equality, difference, democracy and participation.

Even neo-liberal political projects that strive to reorder relations between the economy and social order, to diminish the scope and reach of democratic authority, and to revitalise inequality as a principle of dynamism have to deal with 'citizenship'. The result may be a diminished field of rights (centred on the right to 'spend one's own money'), a shallow conception of participation and the regeneration of forms of private rather than public authority – but such neo-liberal projects have worked through, rather than around citizenship, marking its centrality to the contemporary political-cultural field. As Dagnino has argued elsewhere, such neo-liberal reworkings of citizenship can create a 'perverse confluence', where new projects for domination come to occupy the same political and cultural terrain as insurgent or popular projects. Neo-liberalism did not invent (and does not own) terms such as 'choice', 'freedom' and 'civil society' or sentiments of anti-statism or anti-authoritarianism. Rather, it has tried to re-articulate those keywords and powerful sentiments, aiming to inscribe them into a specific political project of economic, social and political domination. In the process, the confluence (the shared cultural terms and figures) becomes perverse to the extent that popular vocabularies and orientations (which underpinned popular struggles for citizenship in Latin America, in particular) are re-articulated into a new (and neo-liberal) common sense. This common sense delivers (at least) a partial alignment with the reconstruction of political, economic and social power into new relations of exploitation, domination and inequality. In the process, neo-liberal projects have colonised and translated key concerns with equality, freedom and diversity and appropriated ideas of civil society as a domain of mutuality, respect and solidarity to reinvent philanthropy and diminish the state. Such projects also coexist in many settings with a revived and regressive nationalism (Kalb, 2005), as nationally based political projects attempt to both manage the processes of 'insertion' into a global economy and contain popular discontents and antagonisms arising from those processes. Although the example here concerns the neo-liberal project (Peck, 2010), this is just one example of the ways in which dominant projects continually seek to renew and reinvent themselves in the face of opposition, obstacles and the threat of emergent alternatives.

Citizenship occupies a distinctive place in these struggles for dominance and hegemony, because it is always a 'Janus-faced' relationship. It can both, in successive periods or simultaneously, empower and discipline, liberate and oppress, endow with rights and burden with responsibilities. It can – simultaneously – evoke vertical relationships with authorities and horizontal relationships with 'fellow' citizens. It can individualise social relations (making them appear as the domain of separated 'private' subjects); but it can also animate individuals, giving them the powers, vocabularies and fields of connection through which they can act. However, while citizenship has sedimented associations with equality, difference, rights, democracy and participation, the meaning of those terms is also always particular, subject to revision and reworking. The substance of any of them – and their mutual articulation – remains the focus of political-cultural conflicts. Citizenship also articulates them with shifting understandings and practices of nation, nationality and nationalism, as well as with issues of individuation. Nationality – the conditions of membership of a nation – has been a powerful force among the various conditionalities of citizenship, providing a dynamic of exclusion and inclusion. This dynamic operates in both formal-juridical and everyday or practical registers, such as the processes of attributing national membership at work in the official practices of nationalisation, border control and immigration management. Constructing connections between citizenship and nationality is also at work in the everyday business of state apparatuses and agencies, sifting and identifying likely nationals and non-nationals 'at a glance'. In the everyday, too, social relations between citizens may be overdetermined by questions of nationality and belonging, particularly where these are interwoven with formations of race and ethnicity. But if citizenship definitely carries connections with 'communities' of very different types (of which the national, as discussed earlier, is just one), it has to be stressed that it has also been through time a powerful emancipatory tool for individuals. Indeed, as this might be yet another version of the Janus-faced character of citizenship processes, citizenship as 'becoming political' has been, and can still be, a powerful way for individuals to question and refuse the constraints of oppressive communities. Here, again, it would be a problematic stand to consider individuation from the sole point of view of its (neo-)liberal contemporary version (see Ferguson's [2013] critique of liberal models of individuated personhood).

Citizenship, then, is constructed and contested, enacted and experienced, through multiple processes at different levels of social formations. It is always in process and is brought to life by being enacted in many different practices. It remains an 'object of desire' for many political projects as they attempt to mobilise popular support in the name of imagined and improved social orders. It remains a potent element in everyday understandings of social and political life – desired and defended in different ways. To borrow Paul Smith's phrase, citizenship is the site of contested visions of who can be 'subjects of value' and 'valued subjects' – those who can be recognised (through different political-cultural lenses) and rewarded (with very different kinds of material and symbolic resources). Citizenship is the common term around which divergent political projects coalesce, as well as being a potent site of exchange between governmental discourse and popular sentiments. Citizenship is disputed precisely because its whole functioning relies on conflict and dispute (Rancière, 1998), and not on consensus, agreement and unique belonging.

The unfinished

In our arguments throughout this book, we have returned time and again to Etienne Balibar's conception of citizenship as '*imparfaite*' – unfinished. From the early days of our collaboration, we have found this an indispensable way of marking the way citizenship is always 'in the making' (*en travaux*). The disputes, conflicts and struggles that swirl around citizenship, that indeed *make* citizenship – and the social and political imaginaries that it contains and expresses – make it a 'keyword'. As a consequence, however, we have no sense that this book can – or should – be the 'last word' on citizenship. Because citizenship is always in dispute – in theory as well as practice – we expect to have to think again about it. Our objective has been to articulate and share a way of thinking about citizenship that resists the many temptations to reify, reduce or romanticise it. Instead, we have worked through the idea of 'disputing' it as a way of characterising the political contestations around citizenship, the academic contestations about the term and out own way of working.

We began – in 2007 in Paris – by trying to find points of commonality about why citizenship mattered to us as a political and academic concept. We proceeded by disputing – disputing others' views and our own. Such an approach to collaboration requires a degree of mutual trust and respect – to frame and contain the disputes and make them productive. It is a way of proceeding that has its risks – and our disputes have sometimes been marked by frustration, misunderstanding and exasperation, as well as the exhaustion that comes from working across different languages. Those of us whose first language is English (JC and KC) have benefited considerably from the commitment and patience of our colleagues. Nevertheless, we have remained attached to the project – and to the way of working – right up to these closing pages. We know that the work is unfinished – and that we, and others, must carry it on. But we think it is worth reflecting on some of the pleasures and problems of working collaboratively in this disputatious way.

In the most basic way, working collaboratively runs against the grain of an academic world that favours an individualised model of scholarly work (the heroic thinker and his – more occasionally, her – great book). This grain has been deepened by changes to the academy in recent decades that have promoted an increasingly competitive, managerialised, individualised and output-oriented model of academic work (Clarke, 2010). We all came to this project with experiences of working collaboratively in other settings – and these in turn had predisposed us towards collective working. We were undoubtedly very privileged to have had three months working together to begin this project. But the habits of intense discussion, reflection and disputation that we established then have become increasingly stretched across time and space while we have tried to write this book. Circulating drafts, offering revisions, accumulating a vast apparatus of marginal notes and comments have been only occasionally interrupted by face-to-face meetings. Long-distance, digitally mediated and disembodied global production still feels like a thin alternative to up-close disputation and reflection. But we have finally limped towards a sort of conclusion.

However, this sense of being disembodied collaborators means that we are still haunted by disputes that remain unresolved or unfinished. This is probably true of most collaborations, but the sense of distance seems to intensify their visibility. So, we have not yet finished arguments about how best to understand the state's place in a wider field of formations of economic, social and political power; how to cope with the geopolitical and cultural differences between North and South, given our different geographical, intellectual and political orientations; how to resolve differences about normative-ethical-political orientations to citizenship and its practices; and how best to deal with the 'perverse confluences' of popular, progressive and dominatory projects to remake citizenship. No doubt, we might have still been talking about them if we had been in the same place, but there is a sense that they have been more intractable because of the distances between us.

Although we are not seeking to excuse ourselves (or the failings of the book), or to claim something revolutionary about our method, we have sought to foreground this interplay of commonality and difference in our thinking and writing. This certainly means that the book reads more strangely than it might, in at least two respects. Each of us is conscious of writing more tentatively than we might be in writing alone, such that the whole book sometimes seems to move in a rather stately, if not cumbersome, fashion. Second, we have approached editing and revising in a similarly tentative fashion: at each point, we have had to ask whether this formulation expresses a point that I disagree with; whether it comes out of a way of writing that is different to mine; or whether it reflects a problem of translation (either academic or linguistic) that should not be suppressed in another moment of anglophone global hegemony. In the processes of thinking and writing (together and apart), we have tried to struggle against a global geopolitics that would have us think of ourselves as either being the same (a globalising universalism) or as located in 'worlds apart'. We have tried to maintain the dynamic tension of being differently but relationally connected. This has meant a sort of hyper-consciousness about the process of producing, as well as worrying about the product. We have been concerned with how to attend responsibly to the partiality of one's own situatedness, without giving it up. That has meant trying to discover what might be common or shared without glossing over real material differences, or intellectual and political disagreements, and without lapsing into the comfortable and comforting claims of false universalisms.

Finally, for all its flaws, difficulties and frustrations, we think that our working ethos and some of our working processes have tried to reflect our view of citizenship as marked by situated, emergent and – at their best – expansively connective practices that seek to bridge difference in making solidarities. Always *imparfaite*, mostly *en travaux*.

References

Abélès, M. (1999) 'Pour une exploration des sémantiques institutionnelles', *Ethnologie française*, vol XXIX, no 4, pp 501–11.

Abélès, M. (2005) 'Itinéraires en anthropologie politique', *Anthropologie et Sociétés*, vol 29, no 1, pp 183–204.

Abram, S. (2002) 'Planning and public-management in municipal government', *Focaal*, no 40, pp 21–34.

Abrams, P. (1988) 'Notes on the difficulty of studying the state', *Journal of Historical Sociology*, vol 1, no 1, pp 58–89.

Aldred, R. (2007) 'Governing "local health economies": the case of NHS Local Improvement Finance Trust (LIFT)', PhD thesis, Goldsmiths College, University of London.

Allen, J. (2003) *Lost geographies of power*, Oxford: Blackwell.

Allen, J. and Cochrane, A. (2007) 'Beyond the territorial fix: regional assemblages, politics and power', *Regional Studies*, vol 41, no 9, pp 1161–75.

Alvarez, S., Dagnino, E. and Escobar, A. (1998) *Cultures of politics, politics of cultures: re-visioning Latin American social movements*, Boulder, CO: Westview Press.

Anderson, B. (1983) *Imagined communities: Reflections on the origin and spread of nationalism*, Londres: Verso.

Anderson, D. (1996) 'Bringing civil society to an uncivilised place: citizenship regimes in Russia's Arctic frontier', in C. Hann and E. Dunn (eds) *Civil society: Challenging Western models*, London: Routledge-EASA, pp 99–120.

Andrijasevic, R., Aradau, C., Huysmans, J. and Squire, V. (2010) 'Unexpected citizens: sex work, mobility, Europe', paper given at a Centre for Citizenship, Identities and Governance Forum, Open University, UK.

Appadurai, A. (1996) *Modernity at large: Cultural dimensions of globalization*. Minneapolis, MN: University of Minnesota Press.

Appadurai, A. (2001) *Globalization*, Durham, NC: Duke University Press.

Aradau, C., Huysmans, J. and Squire, V. (2010) 'Acts of European citizenship: a political sociology of mobility', *Journal of Common Market Studies*, vol 48, no 4, pp 945–65.

Arditi, B. (2011) 'Insurgencies don't have a plan – they are the plan: political performatives and vanishing mediators', roneo, UNAM; Mexico City.

Arendt, H. (1968 [1951]) *The origins of totalitarianism*, New York, NY: Harcourt.

Asad, T. (2004) 'Where are the margins of the state?', in V. Das and D. Poole (eds) *Anthropology in the margins of the state*, Santa Fe/Oxford: School of American Research Press/James Currey, pp 279–88.

Atlani-Duault, L. (2005a) 'Les ONG à l'heure de la "bonne gouvernance"', *Autrepart*, vol 35, pp 3–17.

Atlani-Duault, L. (2005b) *Au bonheur des autres: anthropologie de l'aide humanitaire*, Paris: Société d'ethnologie.

Bache, I. and Flinders, M. (eds) (2004) *Multi-level governance*, Oxford: Oxford University Press.

Balibar, E. (2001) *Nous, citoyens d'Europe? Les frontières, l'État, le peuple*, Paris: La Découverte.

Balibar, E. (2002) *Politics and the other scene*, London: Verso.

Balibar, E. (1994) 'Man and citizen: who's who?', *Journal of Political Philosophy*, vol 2, no 2, pp 99–114.

Banerjee, S. (2010) *Becoming imperial citizens: Indians in the late-Victorian empire*, Durham, NC: Duke University Press.

Barnes, R., Auburn, T. and Lea, S. (2004) 'Citizenship in practice', *British Journal of Social Psychology*, vol 43, pp 187–206.

Basch, L., Schiller, N. and Blanc, C. (1994) *Nations unbound: transnational projects, postcolonial predicaments and de-territorialized nation-states*, London: Routledge.

Bauböck, R. (1999) 'Recombinant citizenship', Working Paper, *IHS Political Science Series* 67 (December).

Bauböck, R. (2003) 'Reinventing urban citizenship', *Citizenship Studies*, vol 7, no 2, pp 139–60.

Bauböck, R. and Guiraudon, V. (2009) 'Introduction: realignments of citizenship: reassessing rights in the age of plural memberships and multiple-level governance', *Citizenship Studies*, vol 13, no 5, pp 439–50.

Baumann, Z. (1999) *Le coût humain de la mondialisation*, Paris: Hachette Littératures.

Bayart, J.-F. (1996) *L'illusion identitaire*, Paris: Fayard.

Bénéï, V. (2005) 'Introduction. Manufacturing citizenship – confronting public spheres and education in contemporary worlds', in V. Bénéï (ed) *Manufacturing citizenship: Education and nationalism in Europe, South Asia and China*, London: Routledge, pp 1–34.

Bennett, T., Grossberg, L. and Morris, M. (eds) (2005) *New keywords*, Oxford: Blackwell.

Benson, P. and Kirsch, S. (2010) 'Capitalism and the politics of resignation', *Current Anthropology*, vol 51, no 4, pp 459–86.

Besserer, F. (2002) *Contesting community: cultural struggles of a Mixtec transnational community*, Stanford, CA: Stanford University Press.

Beveridge, W. (1942) *Social Insurance and Allied Services (Report of the Interdepartmental Committee)*, Cmnd 6404, London: Her Majesty's Stationery Office.

Beveridge, W. (1944) *Full employment in a free society*, London: Allen and Unwin.

Beveridge, W. (1948) *Voluntary action*, London: George Allen and Unwin.

Beyers, C. (2008) 'The cultural politics of "community" and citizenship in the District Six Museum, Cape Town', *Anthropologica, Revue Canadienne d'anthropologie*, vol 50, no 2, pp 359–73.

Biarez, S. (1999) 'Repenser la sphère locale selon l'espace public', in B. François and E. Neveu (eds), *Espaces publics mosaïques. Acteurs, arènes et rhétoriques des débats publics contemporains*, Rennes, Presses Universitaires de Rennes, Collection Res Publica, pp 267–83.

Blackburn, C. (2005) 'Searching for guarantees in the midst of uncertainty: negotiating aboriginal rights and title in British Columbia', *American Anthropologist*, vol 107, no 4, pp 586–96.

Blackburn, C. (2009) 'Differentiating indigenous citizenship: seeking multiplicity in rights, identity and sovereignty in Canada', *American Ethnologist*, vol 36, no 1, pp 66-78.

Blair, T. (1999) Speech given by the Prime Minister to an audience of venture capitalists, 6 July. Available at: http://news.bbc.co.uk/1/hi/uk_politics/3750847.stm

Blair, T. (2004) Speech given by the Prime Minister to the 2004 Labour conference in Brighton, UK. Available at: http://www.guardian.co.uk/politics/2004/sep/28/labourconference.labour6

Blondiaux, L. (2002) 'Où en est la démocratie participative locale en France? Le risque du vide', *Les Cahiers du DSU*, no 35, pp 9–10.

Bosniak, L. (2007) 'Between the domestic and the foreign: centering the nation's edges', *Constitutional Commentary*, vol 24, pp 271–84.

Bosniak, L. (2008) *The citizen and the alien: Dilemmas of contemporary membership*, Princeton, NJ: Princeton University Press.

Bosniak, L. (2009) 'The basic rights of short-term immigrants also need protection', *Boston Review*, May/June.

Boudreau, J., Boucher, N. and Liguori, N. (2009) 'Taking the bus daily and demonstrating on Sunday: reflections on the formation of political subjectivity in an urban world', *City*, vol 13, no 2, pp 336–46.

Boullier, D. (2009) 'Pour une anthropologie des inouïs', in M. Carrel, C. Neveu and J. Ion (eds) *Les intermittences de la démocratie. Formes d'action et visibilités citoyennes dans la ville*, Paris: L'Harmattan, Collection Logiques Politiques, pp 21–38.

Bourdeaux, V. and Flipo, F. (2011) 'Du bon usage de la communauté', *Mouvements*, no 68, pp 85–99.

Bourdieu, P. (1998) *Acts of resistance*, Cambridge: Polity Press.

Brenner, N. (2004) *New state spaces: Urban governance and the rescaling of statehood*, Oxford: Oxford University Press.

Brenner, N., Jessop, B., Jones, M. and MacLeod, G. (eds) (2003) *State/ space*, Oxford: Blackwell Publishing.

Brown, W. (2006) *Regulating aversion: Tolerance in the age of identity*, Princeton, NJ: Princeton University Press.

Burchell, G. (1993) 'Liberal government and techniques of the self', *Economy and Society*, vol 22, no 3, pp 267–82.

Caldeira, T.P.d.R. (2000) *City of walls: crime, segregation, and citizenship in São Paulo*, Berkeley, CA: University of California Press.

Caldwell, K., Ramirez, R., Coll, K., Fisher, T. and Siu, L. (eds) (2009) *Gendered citizenships: Transnational perspectives on knowledge production, political activism and culture*, New York and Basingstoke: Palgrave Macmillan.

Calhoun, C. (1997) *Nationalism*, Minneapolis, MN: University of Minnesota Press.

Cameron, D. (2009) 'The Big Society', Hugo Young Lecture, 10 November. Available at: http://www.conservatives.com?News?Speeches?2009/11/David_Cameron_The_Big_Society (accessed 26 July 2010).

Carrel, M. (2007) 'Pauvreté, citoyenneté et participation. Quatre positions dans le débat sur la "participation des habitants"', in C. Neveu (ed) *Cultures et pratiques participatives. Perspectives comparatives*, Paris: L'Harmattan, pp 95–112.

Carrel, M. and Neveu, C. (eds) (2013) *Citoyennetés ordinaires. Ce que l'enquête empirique fait aux représentations de la citoyenneté*, Paris: Karthala, in press.

Carrel, M., Neveu, C. and Ion, J. (eds) (2009) *Les intermittences de la démocratie. Formes d'action et visibilités citoyennes dans la ville*, Paris: L'Harmattan, Coll. Logiques politiques.

Cartiaux, M. (2008) 'Repères spatiaux au sein d'associations "issues des migrations". Etude de cas autour du GRDR', MA thesis, University of Poitiers.

Carvalho, J. (2001) *Cidadania no Brasil – o longo caminho*, Rio de Janeiro: Editora Civilização Brasileira.

Castells, M. (1994) *The power of identity: The information age: economy, society and culture (Vol 2)*, Malden, MA: Wiley.

Castells, M. (2012) *Networks of outrage and hope: Social movements in the internet age*, Cambridge: Polity Press.

Castles, S. and Miller, M. (2009) *The age of migration: international population movements in the modern world* (4th edn), New York, NY: Guilford Press.

Castoriadis, C. (1998 [1987]) *The imaginary institution of society* (trans. K. Blamey), Cambridge, MA: MIT Press, Cambridge.

Cattelino, J. (2008) *High stakes: Florida seminole gaming and sovereignty*, Durham, NC: Duke University Press.

Centlivres, P., Centlivres-Demont, M., Maillard, N. and Ossipow, L. (1991) *Une seconde nature. Pluralisme, naturalisation et identité en Suisse romande et au Tessin*, Lausanne: L'âge d'homme.

Cerutti, S. (2012) *Etrangers. Etude d'une condition d'incertitude dans une société d'Ancien Régime*, Paris: Bayard.

Chakrabarty, D. (2001) *Provincializing Europe: Postcolonial thought and historical difference*, Princeton, NJ: Princeton University Press.

Chakrabarty, D. (2002) *Habitations of modernity: Essays in the wake of subaltern studies*, Chicago: University of Chicago Press

Chalhoub, S. (1990) *Visões da Liberdade*, São Paulo: Companhia das Letras.

Charlton, J. (2000) *Nothing about us without us: Disability oppression and empowerment*, Berkeley, CA: University of California Press.

Chatterjee, P. (2004) *The politics of the governed*, New York, NY: Columbia University Press.

Clarke, J. (2004) *Changing welfare, changing states: New directions in social policy*, London: Sage.

Clarke, J. (2005) 'New Labour's citizens: activated, empowered, responsibilised, abandoned?', *Critical Social Policy*, vol 25, no 4, pp 447–63.

Clarke, J. (2008a) 'Living with/in and without neo-liberalism', *Focaal*, vol 51, pp 135–47.

Clarke, J. (2008b) 'Reconstructing nation, state and welfare: the transformation of welfare states', in M. Seelieb-Kaiser (ed) *Welfare state transformations: Comparative perspectives*, Basingstoke: Palgrave Macmillan, pp 197–209.

Clarke, J. (2009) 'Culture as the key? Unlocking the politics, policies and practices of education', in W. Melzer and R. Tippelt (eds) *Kulturen der Bildung: Beiträge zum 21. Kongress der Deutschen Gesellschaft für Erziehungswissenschaft*, Leverkusen Opladen: Budrich-Verlag, pp 227–35.

Clarke, J. (2010) 'Enrolling ordinary people: governmental strategies and the avoidance of politics?', *Citizenship Studies*, vol 14, no 6, pp 637–50.

Clarke, J. (2013) 'Contesting the social' in D. Feenan (ed) *Exploring the 'socio' of Socio-Legal Studies*, Basingstoke: Palgrave Macmillan, pp 37-57.

Clarke, J. (forthcoming) 'Community', in D. Nonini (ed) *Companion to urban anthropology*, Oxford: Blackwell Publishing.

Clarke, J. and Fink, J. (2008) 'Unsettled attachments: nationalm identity, citizenship and welfare', in W. van Oorschot, M. Opielka and B. Pfau-Effinger (eds) *Culture and welfare state: Values and social policy in comparative perspective*, Cheltenham: Edward Elgar, pp 225–44.

Clarke, J. and Newman, J. (1997) *The managerial state: Power, politics and ideology in the remaking of social welfare*, London: Sage.

Clarke, J. and Newman, J. (2012) 'Brave new world? Anglo-American challenges to universalism', in A. Anttonen, L. Häikiö and K. Stefánsson (eds) *Welfare, universalism and diversity*, Cheltenham: Edward Elgar, pp 90–105.

Clarke, J., Newman, J. and Westmarland, L. (2007a) 'Creating citizen-consumers? Public service reform and (un)willing selves', in S. Maasen and B. Sutter (eds) *On willing selves: Neoliberal politics vis-à-vis the neuroscientific challenge*, Basingstoke: Palgrave.

Clarke, J., Newman, J., Smith, N., Vidler, E. and Westmarland, L. (2007b) *Creating citizen-consumers: Changing publics and changing public services*, London: Sage.

Coelho de Souza, G. (1997) 'Avaliação Ambiental em Conjuntos Habitacionais', PhD thesis in Social Sciences, University of Campinas.

Coll, K. (2004) 'Necesidades y problemas: immigrant Latina vernaculars of belonging, coalition and citizenship in San Francisco, California', *Latino Studies*, vol 2, no 2, pp 186–209.

Coll, K. (2010) *Remaking citizenship Latina immigrants and new American politics*, Stanford, CA: Stanford University Press.

Coll, K. (2011) 'Citizenship acts and immigrant voting rights movements in the US', *Citizenship Studies*, vol 15, no 8, pp 993–1010.

Collomb, G. (2011) 'Une "citoyenneté" kali'na? Constructions citoyennes, affirmations identitaires, jeux de niveaux en Guyane française', *Citizenship Studies*, vol 15, no 8, pp 981–1010.

Coman, G. (2008) 'Ethnicisation des places publiques en Roumanie. Le cas de la ville de Cluj-Napoca', *Anthropologica, Revue Canadienne d'anthropologie*, vol 50, no 2, pp 323–39.

Cooper, F. and Stoler, A. (eds) (1997) *Tensions of empire: colonial cultures in a bourgeois world*, Berkeley, CA: University of California Press.

Covre, M. (1986) *A cidadania que não temos*, São Paulo: Brasiliense.

Craig, G. (2007) 'Community capacity building: something old, something new?', *Critical Social Policy*, vol 27, no 3, pp 335–51.

Creed, G. (ed) (2007) *The seductions of community: Emancipations, oppressions quandaries*, Santa Fe/Oxford: School of American Research Press/James Currey.

Crenshaw, K. (1991) 'Mapping the margins: intersectionality, identity politics, and violence against women of color', *Stanford Law Review*, vol 43, no 6, pp 1241–99.

Crowley, J. (2003) 'The spaces and scales of citizenship. Some thoughts on "locality"', in R. Leveau, C. Wihtol de Wenden and K. Mohsen-Finan (eds) *De la citoyenneté locale*, Paris: Travaux et recherches de l'IFRI, pp 111–26.

Czarniawska, B. and Sévon, G. (2005) *Global ideas. How ideas, objects and practices travel in the global*, Gothenburg: Göteborg University – School of Economics and Commercial Law and Gothenburg Research Institute.

Dagnino, E. (1994) 'Os Movimentos Sociais e a Emergência de uma Nova Noção de Cidadania', in E. Dagnino (ed) *Os Anos 90: Política e Sociedade no Brasil*, São Paulo: Editora Brasiliense.

Dagnino, E. (1995) 'On becoming a citizen: the story of D. Marlene', in R. Benmayor and A. Skotnes (eds) *International yearbook of oral history and life stories*, Oxford: Oxford University Press.

Dagnino, E. (2002) 'Sociedad Civil, Espacios Públicos y Construcción Democrática en Brasil: Límites y Posibilidades', in E. Dagnino (ed) *Sociedad Civil, Espacios Públicos y Democratización: Brasil*, Mexico: Fondo de Cultura Económica.

Dagnino. E. (2004) 'Sociedade civil, participação e cidadania: de que estamos falando?', in *Políticas de Ciudadanía y Sociedad Civil en tiempos de globalización* (Daniel Mato, ed) Caracas, Venezuela: FaCES, Universidad Central de Venezuela, pp 95–110.

Dagnino, E. (2005a) 'Meanings of citizenship in Latin America', *IDS Working Papers*, 258, University of Sussex, Brighton.

Dagnino, E. (2005b) '"We all have rights but …": contesting conceptions of citizenship in Brazil', in Naila Kabeer (ed) *Inclusive citizenship. Meanings and expressions of citizenship*, London: Zed Books, pp 147–63.

Dagnino, E. (2008a) 'Civic driven change and political projects', in A. Fowler and K. Bierkhart (eds) *Civic driven change. Citizen's imagination in action*, The Hague: Institute of Social Studies, Holland, pp 27–49.

Dagnino, E. (2008b) 'Conceptualizing culture: a perspective from the South', *Cultural Processes (Newsletter of the Research Network Sociology of Culture, European Sociological Association)*, vol 1 (August), pp 18–23.

Dagnino, E. (2011) 'Civil Society in Latin America', in M. Edwards (ed) *Oxford handbook on civil society*, Oxford: Oxford University Press.

Dagnino, E., Olvera, A. and Panfichi, A. (2006) *La disputa por la construcción democrática en América Latina*, Mexico, DF: CIESAS.

Daly, M. (2000) *The gender division of welfare: The impact of the British and German welfare states*, Cambridge: Cambridge University Press.

Das, V. and Poole, D. (eds) (2004) *Anthropology in the margins of the state*, Santa Fe, NM/Oxford: School of American Research Press/James Currey Ltd.

Delanty, G. (2001) *Citizenship in a global age*, Buckingham: Open University Press.

Déloye, Y. (1994) *Ecole et citoyenneté. L'individualisme républicain de Jules Ferry à Vichy: controverses*, Paris: Presses de la FNSP.

Dematteo, L. (2008) 'La 'défense du territoire' en Italie du Nord, ou le détournement des forms de participation locale', *Anthropologica, Revue Canadienne d'anthropologie*, vol 50, no 2, pp 303–21.

Demo, P. (1995) *Cidadania tutelada e cidadania assistida*, São Paulo: Cortez/Editora Autores Associados.

Dench, G., Gavron, K. and Young, M. (2006) *The new East End: Kinship, race and conflict*, London: Profile Books.

Diaz-Barriga, M. (1996) 'Necesidad: Notes on the discourses of urban politics in the Ajusco Foothills of Mexico City', *American Ethnologist*, vol 23, no 2, pp 291–310.

Dobson, A. (2003) *Citizenship and the environment*, Oxford: Oxford University Press.

Dos Santos, W.G. (1979) *Cidadania e Justiça*, Rio de Janeiro: Ed. Campus.

Dunn, E. (1996) 'Money, morality and modes of civil society among American Mormons', in C. Hann and E. Dunn (eds) *Civil society. Challenging Western models*, London: Routledge-EASA.

Durham, E. (1984) 'Cultura e ideologia', *Dados*, vol 27, no 1, pp 71–89.

Edelman, B. (2007) *Quand les Juristes Inventent le Réel*, Paris: Hermann.

Edgar, D. (2008) *Testing the echo*, London: Nick Hern Books.

Edmunds, J. (2012) 'The limits of post-national citizenship: European Muslims, human rights and the hijab', *Ethnic and Racial Studies*, vol 35, no 7, pp 1181–99.

Elyachar, J. (2005) *Markets of dispossession: NGOs, economic development, and the state in Cairo*, Durham, NC: Duke University Press.

Erel, U. (2009) *Migrant women transforming citizenship: Life stories from Britain and Germany*, London: Ashgate.

Erni, J. (ed) (2011) *Cultural studies of rights: Critical articulations*, New York and London: Routledge.

Erni, J. (2012) 'The imagined force of law', Plenary Lecture given at the 9th International Conference Crossroads in Cultural Studies, Paris, France, 2–6 July.

Evergeti, V. and Zontini, E. (2006) 'Introduction: some critical reflections on social capital, migration and transnational families', *Ethnic and Racial Studies*. vol 29, no 6, pp 1025–39.

Ewick, P. and Silbey, S. (1998) *The common place of law: Stories from everyday life*, Chicago, IL: University of Chicago Press.

Fahrmeir, A. (2007) *Citizenship: The rise and fall of a modern concept*, New Haven, CT, and London: Yale University Press.

Fairbanks, R. (2009) *How it works: Recovering citizens in post-welfare Philadelphia*, Chicago, IL: University of Chicago Press.

Fassin, D. (2006) 'Nommer, interpréter. Le sens commun de la question raciale', in D. Fassin and E. Fassin (eds) *De la question sociale à la question raciale? Représenter la société française*, Paris: La Découverte, pp 16–36.

Fassin, D. (2008) 'La politique des anthropologues. Une histoire française', *L'Homme*, no 185/186, pp 165–86.

Fassin, D. and Mazouz, S. (2007) 'Qu'est-ce que devenir français? La naturalisation comme rite d'institution républicain', *Revue française de sociologie*, vol 48, no 4, pp 723–50.

Feenan, D. (ed) (2013) *Exploring the socio of socio-legal*, Basingstoke: Palgrave Macmillan.

Ferguson, J. (1994) *The anti-politics machine: Development, depoliticization and bureaucratic power in Lesotho*, Minneapolis, MA: University of Minnesota Press.

Ferguson, J. (2004) 'Power topographies', in D. Nugent and J. Vincent (eds) *A companion to the anthropology of politics*, London: Blackwell Publishing, pp 383–99.

Ferguson, J. (2013) 'Declarations of dependence: labor, personhood, and welfare in Southern Africa', *Journal of the Royal Anthropological Institute*, vol 19, pp 223–42.

Ferguson, J. and Gupta, A. (2002) 'Spatializing states: towards an enthnography of neo-liberal governmentality', *American Ethnologist*, vol 29, no 4, pp 981–1002.

Flanagan, R. (2008) *The final report of the independent review of policing*, London: Home Office.

Flores, W. and Benmayor, R. (eds) (1997) *Latino cultural citizenship: claiming identity, space, and rights*, Boston, MA: Beacon Press.

Flower, J. and Leonard, P. (1996) 'Community values and state co-optation: civil society in the Sichuan countryside', in C. Hann and E. Dunn (eds) *Civil society: Challenging western models*, London: Routledge, pp 199–221.

François, B. and Neveu, E. (1999) 'Introduction: pour une sociologie politique des espaces publics contemporains', in B. François and E. Neveu (eds) *Espaces publics mosaïques. Acteurs, arènes et rhétoriques des débats publics contemporains*, Rennes: Presses Universitaires de Rennes, Collection Res Publica, pp 13–58.

Frank, D. (2007) 'Ecology and economy', in G. Ritzer (ed) *The Blackwell encyclopedia of sociology*, Malden, MA: Blackwell Publishing, pp 1289–91.

Fraser, N. (2005) 'Reframing justice in a globalising world', *New Left Review*, vol 36, pp 69–88.

Freeman, C. (2001) 'Is local:global as feminine:masculine? Rethinking the gender of globalization', *Signs: Journal of Women, Culture and Society*, vol 26, no 4, pp 1007–37.

Funder, A. (2003) *Stasiland: Stories from behind the Berlin Wall*, London: Granta Books.

Garcia, S. (1994) 'The Spanish experience and its implication for a citizen's Europe', in V.A. Goddard, J.R. Llobera and C. Shore (eds) *The anthropology of Europe, identities and boundaries in conflict*, Oxford: Berg.

Gilroy, P. (2002) *There ain't no black in the Union Jack* (2nd edn), London: Routledge.

Gilroy, P. (2005) *Postcolonial melancholia*, New York, NY: Columbia University Press.

Giraud, M. (2005) 'Revendication identitaire et "cadre national"', *Pouvoirs*, vol 2, no 113, pp 89–100.

Goldsmith, Lord (2007) *Citizenship: our common bond* (The Citizenship Review), London: Her Majesty's Stationery Office.

Godineau, D. (1988) 'Autour du mot citoyenne', *Mots*, no 16, pp 91–110.

Gonin, P. and Kotlok, N. (2013) 'Projets de codéveloppement et citoyenneté des migrants', in M. Carrel and C. Neveu (eds) *Citoyennetés ordinaires. Ce que l'enquête empirique fait aux représentations de la citoyenneté*, Paris: Karthala, in press.

Gonin, P., Lima, S. and Kotlok, N. (2011) 'Entre réseaux et territoires, des mobilités multiscalaires pour le développement. Réseaux migratoires et communes rurales dans la région de Kayes, Mali', *Espace, populations, sociétés*, vol 2, pp 265–78.

Goode, J. and Maskovsky, J. (eds) (2002) *The new poverty studies: The ethnography of power, politics and impoverished people in the United States*, New York, NY: New York University Press.

Gourgouris, S. (1996) *Dream nation: Enlightenment, colonization and the institution of modern Greece*, Stanford, CA: Stanford University Press.

GRAC (Groupe Recherche Action) (2009) 'Resaisir la citoyenneté aux bords du politique. Expériences marginales et experiences instituées de participation politique à l'épreuve des projets de renovation urbaine dans trois pays: Catalogne, France et Québec', Rapport pour le PUCA, Programme Citoyenneté urbaine, Paris.

Gregory, D. (2004) *The colonial present: Afghanistan, Palestine, Iraq*, New York, NY: Wiley-Blackwell.

Guénif-Souilamas, N. (2012) 'What is Paris the name of?' Spotlight Session, Paper presented to Crossroads in Cultural Studies Conference, Paris, June.

Gupta, A. (2006) 'Blurred boundaries: the discourse of corruption, the culture of politics, and the imagined state', in A. Sharma and A. Gupta (eds) *The anthropology of the state: A reader*, Malden, MA: Blackwell, pp 211–42.

Gupta, A. and Ferguson, J. (1992) 'Beyond culture: space , identity and the politics of difference', *Cultural Anthropology*, vol 7, no 1, pp 6–23.

Gupta, A. and Ferguson, J. (1999) [1997] 'Culture, power, place: ethnography at the end of an era', in A. Gupta and J. Ferguson (eds), *Culture, power, place: Explorations in critical anthropology*, Durham, Duke University Press, pp 1–29.

Gupta, A. and Sharma, A. (2006) 'Globalization and postcolonial states', *Current Anthropology*, vol 47, no 2, pp 277–93.

Gutmann, M. (1997) *The meanings of macho: Being a man in Mexico City*, Berkeley, CA: University of California Press.

Guy, D. (2009) *Women build the welfare state: Performing charity and creating rights in Argentina, 1880–1955*, Durham, NC: Duke University Press.

Habermas, J. (1992) 'Citizenship and national identity: some reflections of the future of Europe', *Praxis International*, vol 12, no 1, pp 1–19.

Habermas, J. (2000) *Après l'Etat-nation: une nouvelle constellation politique*, Paris: Fayard.

Hall, C. (2002) *Civilising subjects: Metropole and colony in the English imagination 1830–1867*, Chicago, IL: University of Chicago Press.

Hall, S. (1996) 'The problem of ideology: Marxism without guarantees', in K.-H. Chen and D. Morley (eds) *Stuart Hall: Critical dialogues in cultural studies*, London: Routledge, pp 25–46.

Hall, S., Critcher, C., Jefferson, T., Clarke, J. and Roberts, B. (2013 [1978]) *Policing the crisis: Mugging, the state and law and order* (2nd edn), London: Macmillan.

Hann, C. and Dunn, E. (eds) (1996) *Civil society: Challenging Western models*, London: Routledge.

Hansen, T. and Stepputat, F. (eds) (2001) *States of imagination: Ethnographic explorations of the postcolonial state*, Durham, NC: Duke University Press.

Harper-Ho, V. (2000) 'Noncitizen voting rights: the history, the law and current prospects for change', *Law and Inequality*, vol 18 (Summer), pp 271–322.

Hayduk, R. (2006) *Democracy for all: Restoring immigrant voting rights in the United States*, New York, NY: Routledge.

Heath, D., Rapp, R. and Taussig, K. (2004) 'Genetic citizenship', in J. Vincent (ed) *The anthropology of politics: A reader in ethnography, theory, and critique*, Malden, MA: Blackwell, pp 152–67.

Held, D. (2004) *Global covenant: The social democratic alternative to the Washington Consensus*, Cambridge: Polity Press.

Herzog, T. (2003) *Defining nations: Immigrants and citizens in early modern Spain and Spanish America*, New Haven, CT: Yale University Press.

Hesmondhalgh, D. (2005) *Understanding media: Inside celebrity*, Maidenhead and New York, NY: Open University Press.

Hesse, B. (ed) (2001) *Un/settled multiculturalisms: Diasporas, entanglements, disruptions*, London: Zed Books.

Hevia, F. (2006) 'Participación ciudadana institucionalizada: análisis de los marcos legales de la participación en América Latina', in Dagnino, E., Olvera, A. and Panfichi, A. (eds) *La Disputa por la Construción Democrática en América Latina*, Mexico: Fondo de Cultura Económica, pp 367–95.

Hillyard, P., Pantazis, C., Tombs, S. and Gordon, D. (2004) *Beyond criminology: Taking harm seriously*, London: Pluto Press.

HM Treasury (2002) *The role of the voluntary and community sector in service delivery: A cross-cutting review*, London: The Stationery Office.

HM Treasury (2005) *Exploring the role of the third sector in public service delivery and reform*, London: The Stationery Office.

Hochet, P. (2011) 'Une "citoyenneté paysanne"? Ethnographie comparée parmi les Minyanka et les Bwaba (Mali, Burkina Faso)', *Citizenship Studies*, vol 15, no 8, pp 1031–46.

Hoggett, P. (2005) 'A service to the public: the containment of ethical and moral conflicts by public bureaucracies', in P. du Gay (ed) *The values of bureaucracy*, Oxford: Oxford University Press.

Holston, J. (2008) *Insurgent citizenship: Disjunctions of democracy and modernity in Brazil*, Princeton, NJ: Princeton University Press.

Holston, J. and Appadurai, A. (1996) 'Cities and citizenship', *Public Culture*, vol 8, pp 187–204.

Home Office, The (2008) *The path to citizenship: Next steps in reforming the immigration system*, London: Home Office Border and Immigration Agency.

Hyatt, S.B. (1997) 'Poverty in a "post-welfare" landscape: tenant management policies, self-governance and the democratization of knowledge in Great Britain', in C. Store and S. Wright (eds) *Anthropology of policy: Critical perspectives on governance and power*, London, Routledge, pp 217–38.

Im'Média (1993) *La Saga du Mouvement Beur*, Paris: Im'Média.

Isiksel, T. (2013) 'Citizens of a new Agora: postnational citizenship and international economic institutions', in W. Maas (ed) *Multilevel citizenship*, Philadelphia: University of Pennsylvania Press, pp 184–202.

Isin, E. (2002) *Being political: Genealogies of citizenship*, Minneapolis, MN: University of Minnesota Press.

Isin, E. (2007) 'City.state: critique of scalar thought', *Citizenship Studies*, vol 11, no 2, pp 211–28.

Isin, E. (2009) 'La ville comme lieu du social', *Rue Descartes*, vol 1, no 63, pp 52–62.

Isin, E. (2012) *Citizens without frontiers*, London: Continuum.

Jacob, J.-P. and Le Meur, P.-Y. (2010) *Politique de la terre et de l'appartenance. Droits fonciers et citoyenneté locale dans les sociétés du Sud*, Paris: Karthala.

Jawad, R. (2009) *Religion and social welfare in the Middle East: a Lebanese perspective*, Bristol: The Policy Press.

Jerram, L. (2011) *Streetlife: The untold history of Europe's twentieth century*, Oxford: Oxford University Press.

Jessop, B. (2002) *The future of the capitalist state*, Cambridge: Polity.

Johnson, N. (ed) (2008) *Citizenship,. cohesion and solidarity*, London: The Smith Institute.

Joseph, M. (2002) *Against the romance of community*, Minneapolis, MN: University of Minnesota Press.

Kabeer, N. (2005) 'The search for inclusive citizenship: meanings and expressions in an interconnected world', in N. Kabeer (ed) *Inclusive citizenship: Meanings and expressions*, London: Zed Books, pp 1–30.

Kalb, D. (2005) 'From flows to violence: politics and knowledge in the debates on globalization and empire', *Anthropological Theory*, vol 5, no 2, pp 176–204.

Kaldor, M. (2003) *Global civil society: An answer to war*, Oxford: Polity Press.

Kannabiran, K., Vieten, U. and Yuval-Davis, N. (eds) (2007) *The situated politics of belonging*, London: Sage.

Keane, J. (2003) *Global civil society*, Cambridge: Cambridge University Press.

Kingfisher, C. (ed) (2002) *Western welfare in decline: globalization and women's poverty*, Philadelphia, PA: University of Pennsylvania Press.

Kofman, E., Phizacklea, A., Raghuram, P. and Sales, R. (2000) *Gender and international migration in Europe*, London: Routledge.

Kooiman, J. (ed) (1993) *Modern governance: new government–society interactions*, London: Sage.

Koopmans, R. and Statham, P. (1999) 'Challenging the liberal nation-state? Postnationalism, multiculturalism, and the collective claims making of migrants and ethnic minorities in Britain and Germany', *American Journal of Sociology*, vol 105, no 3, pp 652–96.

Kuper, A. (1999) *Culture: the anthropologist's account*, Cambridge, MA: Harvard University Press.

Larcher, S. (2011) 'L'Autre citoyen. Universalisme civique et exclusion sociale et politique au miroir des colonies post-esclavagistes de la Caraïbe française (Martinique, Guadeloupe, années 1840–années 1890)', Thèse de science politique, EHESS Paris.

Larner, W (2007) 'Expatriate experts and globalising governmentalities: the New Zealand diaspora strategy', *Transactions of the Institute of British Geographers*, vol 32, no 3, pp 331–45.

Latour, B. (2005) *Reassembling the social: An introduction to actor-network-theory*, Oxford: Oxford University Press.

Leca, J. (1991) 'Individualisme et citoyenneté', in P. Birnbaum and J. Leca (eds) *Sur l'individualisme*, Paris: Presses de Sciences Po, pp 159–209.

Leibfried, S. and Zürn, M. (2005) 'Reconfiguring the national constellation', in S. Leibfried and M. Zürn (eds) *Transformations of the state*, Cambridge: Cambridge University Press, pp 1–36.

Lendvai, N. and Stubbs, P. (2007) 'Policies as translation: situating transnational social policies', in S. Hodgson and Z. Irving (eds) *Policy reconsidered: Meanings, politics and practices*, Bristol: The Policy Press, pp 173–90.

Levitt, P. (2001) *The transnational villagers*, Berkeley, CA: University of California Press.

Lewis, G. (ed) (1998) *Forming nation, framing welfare*, London: Routledge.

Lewis, G. (2000) *'Race', gender and social welfare: encounters in a postcolonial society*, Cambridge: Polity Press.

Li, T. (2007b) *The will to improve: governmentality, development, and the practice of politics*, Durham, NC: Duke University Press.

Lima, S. (2006) 'La "fabrique" de territoires politiques au Mali. Quelles articulations entre les espaces de vie des habitants et les mailles fonctionnelles de l'Etat?', in A. Bleton-Ruget, N. Commerçon and P. Gonod (eds) *Territoires institutionnels, territoires fonctionnels*, Mâcon: Institut de Recherche du Val de Saône-Mâconnais, pp 187–97.

Lipsky, M. (1980) *Street level bureaucracy: Dilemmas of the individual in public services*, New York, NY: Russell Sage Foundation.

Lister, R. (2005) 'Young people talking about citizenship in Britain', in N. Kabeer (eds) *Inclusive citizenship: Meanings and expressions*, London: Zed Books, pp 114–31.

Lister, R. (2007) 'Inclusive citizenship: realising the potential', *Citizenship Studies*, vol 11, no 1, pp 49-61.

Lochak, D. (1988) 'Etranger et citoyen au regard du droit', in C. Wihtol de Wenden (ed) *La citoyenneté*, Paris: Edilig-Fondation Diderot, pp 74–85.

Lopez Caballero, P. (2009) *Indiens de la nation. Ethnographier l'État et historiciser l'autochtonie à Milpa Alta, Mexico (17ᵉ–21ᵉ siècle)*, Paris: CERI/Karthala Editions, Col. Recherches internationales.

Loraux, N. (1989) 'Les méandres de l'hellénitude', *Espaces Temps*, no 42, pp 17–22.

Lorcerie, F. (2007) 'Le primordialisme français, ses voies, ses fièvres', in M.-C. Smouts (ed) *La situation postcoloniale. Les Postcolonial Studies dans le débat français*, Paris: Presses de Sciences po, pp 298–343.

Luhtakiallo, E. (2012) *Practising democracy: Local activism and politics in France and Finland*, London: Palgrave and MacMillan.

Lukose, R.A. (2009) *Liberalization's children: Gender, youth, and consumer citizenship in globalizing India*, Durham, NC: Duke University Press.

Maas, W. (2008) 'Migrants, states and EU citizenship's unfulfilled promise', *Citizenship Studies*, vol 12, no 6, pp 583–96.

Maas, W. (ed) (2013) *Multilevel citizenship*, Philadelphia, PA: University of Pennsylvania Press.

Macpherson, C.B. (1967) *Political obligation*, London: Routledge & Kegan Paul.

Maitland, W. (1908) *The constitutional history of England*, Cambridge: Cambridge University Press.

Malkki, L. (1995) *Purity and exile: Violence, memory, and national cosmology among Hutu refugees in Tanzania*, Chicago, IL: University of Chicago Press.

Mamdani, M. (1996) *Citizen and subject: Contemporary Africa and the legacy of late colonialism*, Princeton, NJ: University of Princeton Press.

Mamdani, M. (2004) *Good Muslim, bad Muslim: America, the Cold War, and the roots of terror*, New York, NY: Pantheon Books.

Marshall, T.H. (1950) *Citizenship and social class and other essays*, Cambridge: Cambridge University Press.

Massey, D. (2004) 'Geographies of responsibility', *Geografiska Annaler*, vol 86 B, no 1, pp 5–18.

McDonald, C. and Marston, G. (eds) (2006) *Analysing social policy: A governmental approach*, Cheltenham: Edward Elgar.

Menéndez-Carrión, A. (2002/03) 'Pero donde y para que hay cabida? El lugar de la ciudadanía en los entornos de hoy. Una mirada desde America Latina', *Ecuador Debate*, vol 57 (December)/vol 58 (April), pp 199–230.

Mignolo, W. (2005) *The idea of Latin America*, Oxford: Blackwell Publishing.

Mische, A. (2001) 'Juggling multiple futures: personal and collective project-formation among Brazilian youth leaders', in C. Barker, A. Johnson and M. Lavalette (eds) *Leadership and social movements*, Manchester: Manchester University Press.

Modood, T. (2005) *Multicultural politics: Racism, ethnicity and Muslims in Britain*, Edinburgh: University of Edinburgh Press.

Mooney, G. and Neal, S. (eds) (2008) *Community: Welfare, crime and society*, Maidenhead: Open University Press.

Morley, D. and K.H. Chen (eds) (1996) *Stuart Hall: Critical dialogues in cultural studies*, New York, NY: Routledge.

Morris, M. (2006) *Identity anecdotes: Translation and media culture*, London: Sage.

Morrisens, A. and Sainsbury, D. (2005) 'Migrants' social rights, ethnicity and welfare regimes', *Journal of Social Policy*, vol 34, no 4, pp 637–60.

Muehlebach, A. (2012) *The moral neoliberal: Welfare and citizenship in Italy*, Chicago, IL: University of Chicago Press.

Neveu, C. (1993) *Communauté, nationalité et citoyenneté. De l'autre côté du miroir: les Bangladeshis de Londres*, Paris: Karthala.

Neveu, C. (1994) 'Of a natural belonging to a political nation-state. A French case', Paper presented for the International Symposium no 117 'Transnationalism, Nation-state Building and Culture', Wenner-Gren Foundation for Anthropological Research, 14–22 June.

Neveu, C. (2001a) 'Les comités de quartier de Roubaix aux prises avec la politique de la ville. Un exemple d'associations phagocytées par la municipalité', *Les Annales de la Recherche Urbaine*, vol 89, pp 79–85.

Neveu, C (2001b) 'L'accès à l'espace public entre politiques publiques et "dérive ethnique". L'expérience d'associations "de jeunes" à Roubaix', in A. Vulbeau (ed), *La jeunesse comme ressource. Expérimentations et expérience dans l'espace public*, Saint-Denis: Obvies-Érès, pp 213–27.

Neveu, C. (2003) *Citoyenneté et espace public. Habitants, jeunes et citoyens dans une ville du Nord*, Lille: Editions du Septentrion.

Neveu, C. (2005) *Anthropologie de la citoyenneté*, document de synthèse pour l'Habilitation à Diriger les recherches, Université de Provence.

Neveu, C. (2008a) 'Going public, between being one's own public and constituting "publics"', Paper given to the CRESC Conference 'Culture and citizenship', Oxford, 3–6 September.

Neveu, C. (2008b) 'Deux formes de territorialisation de l'engagement dans l'espace urbain', in H. Bertheleu and F. Bourdarias (eds) *Les constructions locales du politique*, Tours: Presses Universitaires F. Rabelais, pp 69–82.

Neveu, C. (2009) 'Comment faire l'anthropologie d'un objet "rop lourd"? Approche anthropologique de la citoyenneté en France', *Anthropologie et Sociétés*, vol 33, no 2, pp 23–42.

Neveu, C. (2011) 'Habitants, citoyens: interroger les catégories', in M.-H. Bacqué and Y. Sintomer (eds) *La démocratie participative: histoires et généalogies*, Paris: La Découverte.

Neveu, C. (2013a) 'Sites of citizenship, politics of scales', in W. Maas (ed) *Multilevel citizenship*, Philadephia, PA: University of Pennsylvania Press, pp 203–12.

Neveu, C. (2013b) '"E pur si muove", ou comment saisir empiriquement les processus de citoyenneté', *Politix*, no 13, in press.

Neveu, C. and Filippova, E. (2011) 'Citizenship(s) in European contexts', in M. Nic Craith, U. Kockel and J. Frykman (eds) *A companion to the anthropology of Europe*, London: Willey-Blackwell.

Newman, J. (2007) 'Governance as cultural practice: texts, talk and the struggle for meaning', in M. Bevir and F. Trentmann (eds) *Governance, consumers and citizens: Agency and resistance on contemporary politics*, Basingstoke: Palgrave.

Newman, J. (2012) *Working the spaces of power: Activism, neoliberalism and gendered labour*, London: Bloomsbury Academic.

Newman, J. and Clarke, J. (2009) *Publics, politics and power*, London: Sage Publications.

Newman, J. and Tonkens, E. (eds) (2011) *Responsibility, participation and choice: Summoning the active citizen in Western Europe*, Amsterdam: Amsterdam University Press.

Ngai, M. (2004) *Impossible subjects: Illegal aliens and the making of modern America*, Princeton, NJ: Princeton University Press.

Nic Craith, M. (2004) 'Culture and citizenship in Europe: questions for anthropologists', *Social Anthropology*, vol 12, no 4, pp 289–300.

Nugent, D. (1997) *Modernity at the edge of empire: State, individual and nation in the northern Peruvian Andes, 1885–1935*, Stanford, CA: Stanford University Press.

Obi, C. and Rustad, S. (2011) *Oil and insurgency in the Niger Delta: Managing the complex politics of petroviolence*, London: Zed.

Offe, C. (1984) *Contradictions of the welfare state*, Cambridge, MA: MIT Press.

Olsen, E. (2012) *Transnational citizenship in the European Union: Past, present, and future*, London: Continuum.

Ong, A. (1996) 'Cultural citizenship as subject-making: immigrants negotiate racial and cultural boundaries in the United States', *Current Anthropology*, vol 37, no 5, pp 737–62.

Ong, A. (1999a) 'Clash of civilization or Asian liberalism? An anthropology of the state and citizenship', in H.L. Moore (ed) *Anthropological theory today*, London: Polity Press, pp 48–72.

Ong, A. (1999b) *Flexible citizenship: The cultural logics of transnationality*, Durham, NC: Duke University Press.

Ong, A. (ed) (2006) *Neoliberalism as exception: Mutations in citizenship and sovereignty*, Durham, NC: Duke University Press.

Ortiz Leroux, S. (2007) 'Sociedad civil y republicanismo: aproximaciones, problemas y desafíos', in J.M. Sauca and I.M. Wences (eds), *Lecturas de la sociedad civil. Un mapa contemporáneo de sus teorías,* Madrid, Editorial Trotta, pp 163–81.

Ouroussof, A. and Toren, C. (2005) 'Discussion: anthropology and citizenship', *Social Anthropology*, vol 13, no 2, pp 207–9.

Painter, J. (1995) 'Spaces of citizenship: an introduction', *Political Geography*, vol 14, no 2, pp 107–20.

Painter, J. (2006) 'Prosaic geographies of stateness', *Political Geography*, vol 25, no 7, pp 752–774.

Papadopoulos, D. (2002) 'Dialectics of subjectivity. North-Atlantic certainties, neo-liberal rationality, and liberation promises', *International Journal of Critical Psychology*, vol 6, pp 99–122.

Parekh, B. (2000) *The future of multi-ethnic Britain (the report of the Runnymede Trust Commission)*, London: Profile.

Peck, J (2001) *Workfare states*, New York, NY: Guilford.

Peck, J. (2010) *Constructions of neo-liberal reason*, Oxford: Oxford University Press.

Petersen, A., Barns, I., Dudley, J. and Harris, P. (1999) *Post-structuralism, citizenship and social policy*, London: Routledge.

Petric, B. (2008) 'A propos des révolutions de couleur et du soft power américain', *Hérodote*, vol 2, no 129, pp 7–20.

Pezzullo, P. (2012) 'Before the cradle and after the grave: when toxic bodies become ordinary', Plenary Lecture given at the 9th International Conference Crossroads in Cultural Studies, Paris, France, 2–6 July.

Plummer, K. (2003) *Intimate citizenship: Private decisions and public dialogues*, Seattle and London: University of Washington Press.

Poche, B. (1992) 'Citoyenneté et représentation de l'appartenance', *Espaces et Sociétés 2*, no68, pp 15–36.

Pollitt, C. (ed) (forthcoming) *Context in public policy and management – the missing link?*, Cheltenham: Edward Elgar Publishers.

Poole, L. (2001) 'Germany: a conservative regime in crisis?', in A. Cochrane, J. Clarke and S. Gewirtz (eds) *Comparing welfare states* (2nd edn), London: Sage Publications, pp 153–94.

Portantiero, J.C. (1977) *Los Usos de Gramsci*, Mexico: Ediciones Pasado y Presente.

Pozo, L. (2011) 'The essence of "the people": citizenship, class accommodation and the construction of political identities in Britain, c.1640–1850', *Critical Sociology*, vol 37, no 6, pp797–815.

Putnam, R. (1993) 'The prosperous community: social capital and public life', *American Prospect*, vol 4, no 13, pp 65–78.

Putnam, R. (2000) *Bowling alone: The collapse and revival of American community*, New York, NY: Simon and Schuster.

Putnam, R. (2007) 'E Pluribus Unum: diversity and community in the twenty-first century. The 2006 Johan Skytte Prize Lecture', *Scandinavian Political Studies*, vol 30, no 2, pp 137–74.

Pykett, J. (2010) 'Introduction: the pedagogical state: education, citizenship, governing', *Citizenship Studies*, vol 14, no 6, pp 617–19.

Quentin, A. (2005) 'ONG et politiques publiques d'habitat urbain: reflextions a partir de l@Equateur et du Venezuela', *Autrepart*, vol 3, no 35, pp 39-56.

Rabinow, P. (ed) (1984) *The Foucault reader*, New York: Pantheon Books.

Raissiguier, C. (2010) *Reinventing the republic: Gender, migration and citizenship in France*, Stanford, CA: Stanford University Press.

Rajaram, P. (2009) 'Thinking the limits of political space', ENACT Working Paper. Available at: http://www.enacting-citizenship.eu/index.php/sections/deliverables_item/286/

Rancière, J. (1998) *Aux bords du politique*, Paris: Folio-Essais.

Rancière, J. (2000) 'Citoyenneté, culture et politique', in M. Elbaz and D. Helly (eds) *Mondialisation, citoyenneté et multiculturalisme*, Paris: L'Harmattan–Presses Universitaires de Laval, pp 55–68.

Raskin, J. (1993) 'Legal aliens, local citizens: the historical, constitutional and theoretical meanings of alien suffrage', *University of Pennsylvania Law Review* vol 141 (April), pp 1391–470.

Rhodes, R. (1997) *Understanding governance: Policy networks, governance, reflexivity and accountability*, Buckingham: Open University Press.

Richardson, D. (2000) 'Constructing sexual citizenship', *Critical Social Policy*, vol 20, no 1, pp 105–35.

Rodrigues, I. (1997) *Sindicalismo e Política: A Trajetória da CUT*, São Paulo: Scritta/FAPESP.

Root, A. (2007) *Market citizenship: Experiments in democracy and globalisation*, London: Sage Publications.

Rosaldo, R. (1994) 'Cultural citizenship in San José, California', *PoLAR: Political and Legal Anthropology Review*, vol 17, no 2, pp 57–63.

Rosaldo, R. (1999) 'Cultural citizenship, inequality and multiculturalism', in R. Torres, L. Miron and J. Inda (eds) *Race, identity and citizenship: A reader*, Oxford: Blackwell Publishers, pp 253–61.

Rose, N. (1999) *Powers of freedom*, Cambridge: Polity Press.

Rosenfeld, R., Trappe, H. and Gornick, J. (2004) 'Gender and work in Germany: before and after reunification', *Annual Review of Sociology*, vol 30, pp 103–24.

Ross, A. (1998) *Real love: in pursuit of cultural justice*, London and New York, NY: Routledge.

Rouland, N. (1988) 'Anthropologie juridique'. Available at: http://classiques.uqac.ca/contemporains/rouland_norbert/anthropologie_juridique_1988/anthropologie_juridique.html (accessed 14 November 2012).

Ruppert, E. (2007) 'Producing population', ESRC Centre for Research on Socio-Cultural Change (CRESC) Working Paper, Milton Keynes, UK.

Russell, J. (2005) 'Rethinking post-national citizenship: the relationship between state territory and international human rights law', *Space and Polity*, vol 9, no 1, pp 29–39.

Sales, R. (1995) 'The deserving and the undeserving? Refugees, asylum seekers and welfare in Britain', *Critical Social Policy*, vol 22, no 3, pp 456–78.

Sales, T. (1994) 'Raízes da Desigualdade Social na Cultura Brasileira', *Revista Brasileira de Ciências Sociais*, vol 9, no 25, pp 26-37.

Santos, B. (2008) *Another knowledge is possible*, London: Verso.

Santos, B. and Meneses, M.P. (eds) (2009) *Epistemologias do Sul*, Coimbra: Almedina.

Santos, B. and Rodríguez-Garavito, C. (eds) (2005) *Law and globalization from below: towards a cosmopolitan legality*, New York, NY: Cambridge University Press.

Sassen, S. (2005) 'The repositioning of citizenship and alienage: emergent subjects and spaces for politics' *Globalizations,* vol 2, no 1, pp 79–94.

Sassen, S. (2006) *Territory, authority, rights: From medieval to global assemblages*, Cambridge: Cambridge University Press.

Schnapper, D. (1997) 'The European debate on citizenship', *Daedalus*, vol 126, no 3, pp 199–222.

Scott, J.C. (1998) *Seeing like a state: How certain schemes to improve the human condition have failed*, New Haven, CT: Yale University Press.

Secretary of State for Justice and Lord Chancellor (2007) *The governance of Britain*, Cm: 7170, London: The Stationery Office.

Sencébé,Y. (2004) 'Etre ici, être d'ici. Formes d'appartenance dans le Diois (Drôme)', *Ethnologie Française*, vol XXIV, no 1, pp 23–30.

Sharma, A. (2008) 'Crossbreeding institutions, breeding struggle: women's empowerment, neoliberal governmentality, and state (re) formation in India', *Cultural Anthropology*, vol 21, no 1, pp 60–95.

Sharma, A. (2011) 'Specifying citizenship: subaltern politics of rights and justice in contemporary India', *Citizenship Studies*, vol 15, no 8, pp 965–80.

Sharma, A. and Gupta, A. (2006) 'Rethinking theories of the state in an age of globalization', in A. Sharma and A. Gupta (eds) *The anthropology of the state: A reader*, Oxford: Blackwell Publishing.

Shklar, J. (1991) *American citizenship: The quest for inclusion*, Cambridge, MA: Harvard University Press.

Shore, C. and Wright, S. (1997) 'Policy, a new field of anthropology', in C. Shore and S. Wright (eds) *Anthropology of policy: Critical perspectives on governance and power*, London: Routledge-EASA, pp 3–39.

Slaughter, A. (2004) *A new world order*, Princeton, NJ: Princeton University Press.

Smith, D. (2005) *Institutional ethnography: A sociology for people*, Lanham, MD: Altamira Press.

Somers, M. (2008) *Genealogies of citizenship: Markets, statelessness and the right to have rights*, Cambridge: Cambridge University Press.

Soysal, Y (1994) *Limits of citizenship: Migrants and postnational membership in Europe*, Chicago: University of Chicago Press.

Soysal, Y. (2012) 'Post-national citizenship: rights and obligations of individuality' in A. Amenta, K. Nash and A. Scott (eds) *The Wiley-Blackwell handbook of political sociology*, Hoboken, NJ: Wiley-Blackwell.

Souza, J. (2003) *A Construção social da subcidadania*, Belo Horizonte: Ed. UFMG.

Spire, A. (2005) *Etrangers à la carte: l'administration de l'immigration en France, 1945–1975*, Paris: Grasset.

Steinert, H. and Pilgram, A. (eds) (2006) *Welfare from below: Struggles against social exclusion in Europe*, London: Ashgate Publishing.

Stenson, K. (2008) 'Governing the local: sovereignty, social governance and community safety', *Social Work and Society*, vol 6, no 1, pp 2–14.

Stubbs, P. (2005) 'Stretching concepts too far? Multi-level governance, policy transfer and the politics of scale in South East Europe', *Southeast European Politics*, vol VI, no 2, pp 66–87.

Stubbs, P. (2007) 'Civil society or Ubleha?', in H. Rill, T. Šmidling and A. Bitoljanu (eds) *20 pieces of encouragement for awakening and change: Peacebuilding in the region of the former Yugoslavia*, Velgrade: Centre for Nonviolent Action, pp 215–28.

Tambini, D. (2001) 'Post-national citizenship', *Ethnic and Racial Studies*, vol 24, no 2, pp 195–217.

Tarrius, A. (2002) 'Au-delà des états-nations: des sociétés de migrants', *Revue Européenne des Migrations Internationales*, vol 17, no 2, pp 37–61.

Taylor, C. (2003) *Modern social imaginaries*, Durham, NC: Duke University Press.

Taylor, D. (1989) 'Citizenship and social power', *Critical Social Policy*, vol 26, pp 19–31.

Taylor, L. and Wilson, F. (2004) 'The messiness of everyday life: exploring key themes in Latin American citizenship studies introduction', *Bulletin of Latin American Research*, vol 23, no 2, pp 154–64.

Teixeira, A.C. (2003) *Identidades em Construção: Organizações Não-Governamentais no Processo Brasileiro de Democratização*, São Paulo: Annablume/FAPESP.

Teixeira, A.C.C. and Tatagiba, L. (2010) 'Democracia participativa en la ciudad de São Paulo: continuidades y rupturas', in E.I. Vera and A.G. Lavalle (eds) *La innovación democrática en América Latina. Tramas y nudos de la representación, la participación y el control social*, Mexico: CIESAS-Universidad Veracruzana, pp 283–311.

Telles, V.d.S. (1994a) 'A Sociedade Civil e a Construção de um Espaço Público', in E. Dagnino (ed) *Os Anos 90: Política e Sociedade no Brasil*, São Paulo: Brasiliense, pp 91–102.

Telles, V.d.S. (1994b) 'Sociedade civil, direitos e espaços públicos', *Polis*, vol 14, pp 43–53.

Telles, V.d.S. (2001) *Pobreza e Cidadania*, São Paulo: Editora, p 34.

Terray, E. (1986) 'L'Etat, le hasard et la nécessité. Réflexions sur une histoire', *L'Homme*, vol 26, no 97–8, pp 213–24.

Texture (1987) *De l'antiracisme à la revendication de citoyenneté. Contribution au débat*, Lille: Ronéo.

Thompson, E.P. (1963) *The making of the English working class*, London: Penguin Books.

Thompson, E.P. (1978) *The poverty of theory*, London: Merlin.

Trouillot, M.-R. (2001) 'The anthropology of the state in the age of globalisation: close encounters of a deceptive kind', *Current Anthropology*, vol 42, no 1, pp 125–38.

Turner, B. (2009) 'T.H. Marshall, social rights and English national identity', *Citizenship Studies*, vol 13, no 1, pp 65–73.

Tzanelli, R. (2006) '"Not my flag!" Citizenship and nationhood in the margins of Europe (Greece, October 2000/2003)', *Ethnic and Racial Studies*, vol 29, no 1, pp 27–49.

Varsanyi, M. (2006) 'Interrogating "urban citizenship" vis-à-vis undocumented migration', *Citizenship Studies*, vol 10, no 2, pp 229–49.

Wahnich, S. (1997) *L'impossible citoyen, l'étranger dans le discours de la Révolution française*, Paris: Albin Michel.

Walters, W. (2004a) 'Secure borders, safe haven, domopolitics', *Citizenship Studies*, vol 8, no 3, pp 237–60.

Wappenstein, S. (2004) 'Citizenship "from below": public contestation and democratic practice in neoliberal Argentina', Paper presented at the 'New Scholars' Conference in Citizenship Studies', Center for the Study of Citizenship, Wayne State University, 27 February.

Watt, C.A. (2004) *Serving the nation: Cultures of service, association and citizenship*, Oxford: Oxford University Press.

Watts, M. (2007) 'The sinister political life of community: economies of violence and governable spaces in the Niger Delta, Nigeria', in G. Creed (ed) *The seductions of community: Emancipations, oppressions, quandaries*, Santa Fe/Oxford: School of American Research Press/ James Currey.

Wemyss, G. (2006) 'The power to tolerate: contests over Britishness and belonging in East London', *Patterns of Prejudice*, vol 40, no 3, pp 215–36.

Wemyss, G. (2009) *The invisible Empire: White discourse, tolerance and belonging*, London: Ashgate.

Wetherell, M., Lafleche, M. and Berkeley, R. (eds) (2007) *Identity, ethnic diversity and community cohesion*, London: Sage.

Williams, R. (1977) *Marxism and literature*, Oxford: Oxford University Press.

Williams, R. (1983 [1976]) *Keywords: A vocabulary of culture and society*, New York, NY: Oxford University Press.

Wilson, E. (1977) *Women and the welfare state*, London: Routledge.

Wimmer A. and Glick-Schiller, N. (2003) 'Methodological nationalism, the social sciences, and the study of migration: an essay in historical epistemology', *International Migration Review*, vol 37, no 3, pp 576–610.

Wind, M. (2009) 'Post-national citizenship in Europe: The EU as a "welfare rights generator"?', *Columbia Journal of European Law*, vol 15, no 2, pp 239–64.

Yuval-Davis, N. (1997) *Gender and nation*, London: Sage.

Zander, U. (2010) 'Conscience nationale et identité en Martinique', doctorat EHESS, Paris.

Zhang, L. (2002) 'Spatiality and urban citizenship in late socialist China', *Public Culture*, vol 14, no 2, pp 311–34.

Zivi, K. (2012) *Making rights claims: A practice of democratic citizenship*, Oxford: Oxford University Press.

Index

Note: The following abbreviation has been used – *t* = table